Electoral Politics in Po

Stan Hok-Wui Wong

Electoral Politics in Post-1997 Hong Kong

Protest, Patronage, and the Media

 Springer

Stan Hok-Wui Wong
Department of Government
    and Public Administration
Chinese University of Hong Kong
Shatin, Hong Kong SAR

ISBN 978-981-287-386-6   ISBN 978-981-287-387-3   (eBook)
DOI 10.1007/978-981-287-387-3

Library of Congress Control Number: 2015932425

Springer Singapore Heidelberg New York Dordrecht London

Printed on acid-free paper

Springer Science+Business Media Singapore Pte Ltd. is part of Springer Science+Business Media (www.
springer.com)

Acknowledgments

The conception of this book began over a casual lunch conversation with my colleague Ngok Ma, who made a thought-provoking claim, "One does not understand Hong Kong politics without knowing the political significance of the District Councils." It is thought-provoking because as the lowest elected tier of Hong Kong's political structure, the District Councils have long been perceived as powerless and hence politically inconsequential. Paradoxically, the resources that Beijing-sponsored parties have invested in the District Councils are enormous. How can this happen? There are only two possibilities – either because these parties are hopelessly irrational or because the popular belief is fallacious. I tended to believe in the latter, although at that time I had no evidence to substantiate my conjecture. And so the journey of my research began.

For this reason, my thanks first go to Ngok Ma, not only for the inspiration for this book but also for the countless stimulating lunch conversations we had over the past years.

I am indebted to Barbara Geddes and Hiroki Takeuchi for their thoughtful and detailed comments on the previous drafts, not to mention their encouragement from the very beginning. I also received a lot of constructive comments from Kuan Hsin-chi. Their input has significantly improved this book's quality. Over the years, I benefited tremendously from interactions with my colleague Ivan Choy, whose insights into Hong Kong politics helped me avoid many intellectual detours. I am particularly grateful to my friend, Joy DeVera, for her important suggestions on writing, and Jayanthie Krishnan, the editor, for her interests in this project. Special thanks go to my father, whose deep knowledge of Chinese history provides me a constant source of inspiration.

This book contains a large amount of original data. The collection of these data would not have been possible had I not met two exceptionally capable research assistants, Kelvin Chan and Tim Tang. Tim helped me lead a team of students to collect the geo-coordinates of Hong Kong's residential buildings, so that I could analyze the intricacies of electoral redistricting. Kelvin led another team of students to compile data on the media coverage of political parties during election campaigns. Their tasks involved a great deal of coding, checking, double-checking, and coordination among students. I am incredibly thankful for their assistance.

In addition to Kelvin and Tim, many student helpers contributed their time to the data collection. They included Ngai-Keung Chan, Sze-Hang Chan, Hon-Lam Cheung, Lorant Ching, Kwan-Yu Chung, Yue Guan, Yalin Hung, Po-Chun Kan, Lap-Hang Li, Yan-Yan Lo, Chun-Fai Tsang, Anna Tso, Ho-Yu Wong, Kiu-Yan Wong, Ying-Hin Wong, Nicole Wu, Amina Yam, and Ting Ting Yu.

I gratefully acknowledge the financial support of the Hong Kong RGC-GRF grant (490112), the Courseware Development Grant, and the Direct Allocation Grant at the CUHK for funding part of the collection of the data used in this book.

I would also like to thank all my interviewees. Their surprising candor helped answer many long-standing puzzles I had had in mind. Unfortunately, for the sake of protecting their privacy, I cannot identify them individually here.

Finally, I am grateful to my wife, who got pregnant while I was writing this book. Her tolerance of my busy schedule is crucial to the timely completion of this project.

Shatin, Hong Kong   Stan Hok-Wui Wong
October 2014

Contents

Abbreviations

ADPL	Association for Democracy and People's Livelihood
ASPDMC	Alliance in Support of the Patriotic Democracy Movement in China
CCP	Chinese Communist Party
CHRF	Civil Human Rights Front
CP	Civic Party
CTU	Hong Kong Confederation of Trade Unions
DAB	Democratic Alliance for the Betterment and Progress of Hong Kong
DCC	District Council Constituency
DP	Democratic Party
FTU	Hong Kong Federation of Trade Unions
HKPA	Hong Kong Progressive Alliance
HKSAR	Hong Kong Special Administrative Region
KMT	Kuomintang
LP	Liberal Party
LSD	League of Social Democrats
ND	Neo Democrats
NPC	National People's Congress
NPCSC	Standing Committee of the National People's Congress
NPP	New People's Party
NWSC	Neighborhood and Workers Service Centre
PP	People Power
PRC	People's Republic of China
PTU	Hong Kong Professional Teachers' Union

Chapter 1
Introduction

"Organization is the road to power, but it is also the foundation of political stability and thus the precondition of political liberty." Samuel Huntington, *Political Order in Changing Societies*

Political repression is pervasive in China. Direct elections do not exist beyond the village level. There is no opposition party in sight. In fact, it is not just the opposition party, as one would neither find any non-state-sanctioned civil society organization with a national presence. The absence of such an organization is the result of the state's stringent regulations on civil society. This heavy-handed control reflects the Chinese authorities' fear of subversive mass mobilization organized at the national level. An effective way to reduce such kind of collective political actions is to segregate social groups from each other. When social groups cannot freely communicate with each other, the authorities can effectively nip subversive elements in the bud. This is why Chinese authorities also dictate the media with an iron fist. Many foreign Web sites, including *Facebook* and *YouTube*, are blocked in China. Sensitive words – that is, words that are censored from online search engines – number in the hundreds. Hundreds of thousands of undercover online commentators, known as the "fifty-cent party," are also reportedly hired to manufacture public opinions.

The manifestations of political repression discussed above, namely, the low degree of media freedom, the absence of a robust civil society, the paucity of electoral competition, and the lack of a resilient opposition force, form a popular impression of the Chinese authoritarian state. But an interesting question to ask is, will democracy arrive in China when these unfavorable factors recede? Or to put it in another way, can authoritarianism survive in China without such political repression?

The best way to find an answer to these questions is to conduct a political experiment: introduce direct elections of government officials, permit the existence of opposition parties, remove regulations on civil society, and tear down the controls of the media. Then, after implementing all these changes, observe whether or not

© Springer Science+Business Media Singapore 2015
S.H.-W. Wong, *Electoral Politics in Post-1997 Hong Kong*,
DOI 10.1007/978-981-287-387-3_1

the single-party dictatorship can maintain its dominant position. Such an experiment would no doubt sound like a sheer fantasy to many. But few are aware that a similar political experiment has actually been running for more than 15 years somewhere in China. That experiment is called Hong Kong.

It was in 1997 when the British transferred sovereignty of Hong Kong back to China, and since then, Chinese authorities have demonstrated a high degree of self-restraint in their management of Hong Kong affairs. They have also shown willingness to preserve and adapt to the political order left by the colonial administration. Remarkably, the "one country, two systems" principle allows Hong Kong to retain its own political institutions that are distinct from those in the PRC. Hong Kong people have continued to more or less enjoy the same level of civil liberties that they had in the last decade of British colonial rule. For instance, opposition media have been permitted to exist, so, too, with prodemocracy opposition parties whose political ascendancy was largely built upon an anti-Communist sentiment pervasive in Hong Kong prior to the sovereignty transfer. They can contest half of the legislative seats in competitive elections that are generally considered free and uncorrupted. However, tolerance does not mean endorsement. While Beijing allows these opposition parties to exist, it has cultivated political parties to represent its own interests and, above all, to counter the political influences of the opposition force.

This book is about this ongoing political experiment that Beijing has run since 1997. It studies how a relatively liberal media environment, competitive elections, and the interaction of these factors have shaped the balance of power between the opposition force and the Beijing-sponsored elite in the democratic enclave of China that is Hong Kong.[1] Paradoxically, it is the latter who consistently benefits from the mixture of these seemingly prodemocracy factors. In this book, I provide an explanation for why Hong Kong's prodemocracy elite ends up failing to turn these factors to their own advantage.

The book centers on the politics of Hong Kong, which is only one city in China. The lessons drawn from a single city may have limited bearings on other parts of this vast country. However, what makes Hong Kong a valuable analytical case is precisely its uniqueness. There is no other place in China where people can enjoy such a high degree of media freedom. The heavy-handed state repression that is commonplace in China is also absent in Hong Kong. However unique Hong Kong is, the strategies Beijing has deployed to rule the city should not look wholly unfamiliar to students of Chinese politics. As I will show in the subsequent chapters, there are actually striking similarities between Beijing's Hong Kong policies and the strategic maneuvers of the early Chinese Communist Party (CCP). For this reason, by studying how Beijing manages Hong Kong and succeeds in sidelining the prodemocracy opposition, we are able to see that repression is not the only factor underpinning the long-running resilience of its authoritarian rule.

---

[1] By calling Hong Kong a "democratic enclave," I do not mean that the political system of Hong Kong is fully democratic. I use the term in the same sense as Gilley (2010) does; a democratic enclave is defined as a well-defined geographical region "where the authoritarian regime's writ is substantively limited and is replaced by an adherence to recognizably democratic norms and procedures (p. 390)."

Of course, this book is also intended to engage the literature on Hong Kong politics. Many extant studies in this field focus predominantly on events and changes that occur in Hong Kong, paying surprisingly little attention to Beijing's overarching strategy, which has cast a long shadow on the political development of postcolonial Hong Kong. This glaring omission is unwarranted. As I will show in this book, one cannot fully understand contemporary Hong Kong politics without considering the Beijing factor.

1.1 Media Environment and Civil Society in Hong Kong

Although the government of Hong Kong has never been democratically elected, Hong Kong citizens have retained a high degree of civil liberties, including media freedom, despite the city's sovereignty transfer to the People's Republic of China in 1997. According to the 2013 World Press Freedom Index, published by Reporters Without Borders, Hong Kong ranked the world's 58th, a notch below Italy.

The high level of freedom of expression can be attested by the presence of a relentless opposition media company, Next Media. Its flagship newspaper, the *Apple Daily*, habitually produces cartoons, opinion pieces, political commentaries, and even online videos which openly mock or lambast government leaders. Thanks to its diligent paparazzi, this tabloid-style newspaper also regularly features exposés of the wrongdoings of political figures and government officials. More remarkably, Next Media dares to challenge not only local leaders but even the Chinese authorities. Its editorials frequently complain against the Chinese authorities for mishandling Hong Kong affairs, including their lack of commitment to the implementation of universal suffrage in the city. Because Hong Kong citizens generally support democratization, the *Apple Daily*'s daring approach and unambiguous prodemocracy stance help earn it huge readership, making it one of the most widely circulated newspapers in Hong Kong for the past two decades.[2]

In addition to a high degree of freedom of its press, residents of Hong Kong continue to enjoy unbridled access to the Internet. Political Web sites are not blocked from public access, nor does there exist a list of sensitive keywords which are made invisible from online search engines. No one has also been sued for posting negative comments about political leaders on the Internet.[3]

---

[2]This is not to say that political interference in the media is completely absent in Hong Kong. Ma (2007b) points out that media companies and frontline reporters do face subtle political and economic pressures from the authorities, and self-censorship is not uncommon among some media workers. In recent years, there have also been a few incidents in which the government sued or arbitrarily detained reporters.

[3]Mainland citizens are blocked from seeing many Hong Kong newspapers and Web sites. Although in some regions of China citizens are able to watch Hong Kong's live television broadcasts, there exists a real-time monitoring system that replaces politically sensitive contents with TV commercials.

If citizens perceive no fear of political persecution, they would not restrain their contempt for the people in power. Indeed, many Hong Kong people feel comfortable using the Internet to express their discontent with the government. *Facebook* and *Weibo*, the Chinese version of *Twitter*, are the most common tools, as they allow users to leave and share quick comments on current affairs. There is also a panoply of online discussion forums where users can find a specific page dedicated to the discussion of political events. Apparently, not every citizen can afford the time of writing political commentaries or engaging in lengthy political discussion. Yet even busy citizens are able to benefit from these online media because, for example, they can easily subscribe to the *Facebook* fan pages of online opinion leaders and thereby constantly get updates on the latest political talking points.

The high degree of media freedom that Hong Kong enjoys is remarkable, considering that nondemocratic governments generally dislike free media. This is not only because autocrats, like ordinary people, are averse to criticisms, but also because free media undermine their political power. When media are controlled, citizens hear mostly the glorification of the regime. News about policy failures goes unreported and citizens can hardly receive information about the regime's unpopularity.[4] This lack of access to true political information and criticisms of rulers prevents any effective mass mobilization against the regime for one obvious reason: deposing an autocrat is an extremely risky endeavor. Citizens are generally reluctant to participate in anti-regime activities unless they are certain that a large number of people are also willing to get involved (Chwe 2003). No one would be willing to take the risk of being the only person protesting on the streets against an autocrat.

When media are free, citizens have easy access and read both good and bad reports about the autocracy. They can also initiate public discourse on policies, exchange views on the regime, and, perhaps more importantly, communicate among themselves about possible collective actions. When the unpopularity of the ruling elite becomes common knowledge, every disgruntled citizen is aware that he is not alone in his dissatisfaction. Their disincentive for participating in anti-regime protests therefore decreases as a result.

For fear of such collective political actions, many autocracies are willing to spend a considerable amount of state resources limiting media freedom as a way of suppressing the communication of subversive ideas. Common tactics include silencing critics using legal or illegal means, blocking the free flow of information with media censorship and online surveillance,[5] and manufacturing public opinions though the use of propaganda or undercover commentators.

---

[4]Many studies have shown that media freedom is conducive to good governance. See, for example, Adsera et al. (2003), Brunetti and Weder (2003), and Treisman (2007)

[5]Some media are easier to control than others because the technologies involved are more centralized. Edmond (2013) provides a formal model to show that more decentralized sources of information, epitomized by social media, make overthrowing a dictator easier.

Given the high level of media freedom in Hong Kong, it is not surprising to see that the city's media have played an important role in facilitating political activities. The prime example that illustrates the mobilization power of media is the July 1, 2003 protest, where half a million people took to the streets to vent their anger at the Chief Executive. Although at that time, social media had yet to gain its current popularity, the Internet itself already showed its great potential as an effective mobilization tool; prior to the protest, many people voluntarily sent mass emails and instant messages to urge their friends and relatives to take part in the rally. The high turnout was in part due to the unprecedented emergence of a huge volume of these online messages. One indicator of this word-of-mouth effect according to one study (Chan and Chung 2003) is that 93 % of the demonstrators joined the protest in the company of their acquaintances. More interestingly, more than half of the respondents could not remember whether the idea of joining the demonstration was first raised by themselves or their friends. Taking to the streets became not only common knowledge but also a common calling.

Some traditional media also took an active role in mobilizing the political rally. In the month leading up to the protest, popular phone-in radio programs were swamped with calls of angry citizens who made harsh comments about the administration. As expected, Next Media also published numerous news articles and reports that faulted the government for mishandling the economy and for other policy failures. On the day of the protest, the *Apple Daily* even featured a full-page, colored protest poster that read "No Tung Chee-hwa," in reference to the former Chief Executive. During the procession, countless demonstrators were waving this poster while chanting "Down with Tung."

The July 1, 2003 protest is arguably a highly unusual political event such that its effective use of information technology for popular mobilization has not been exploited in other collective political actions. For one thing, no public demonstration after 2003 has achieved the same level of turnout, despite the increasing prevalence of social media and smart phones. However, Hong Kong observers generally agree that collective political actions have shown no sign of abatement in Hong Kong since 2003, as evidenced by the proliferation of politically active concern groups focusing on different social issues, ranging from the conservation of historic buildings and the right to local self-government to a movement against politically indoctrinated education. All of these groups have tried, in one way or another, to take advantage of the mobilization power of the Internet. Their basic tool kits include Web sites, *Facebook*, and *Twitter*. Activists with technology savvy would also produce eye-catching multimedia objects such as infographics and videos to attract followers and promote their movements.

There are also cases where a movement itself was born from the Internet. A notable example was the 2012 Anti-Patriotic Education Movement, which culminated in an occupation of the government headquarters by tens of thousands of citizens. The movement was directed against the government's plan of implementing a national education curriculum, which was viewed by many as political indoctrination. The causes of such a large-scale social movement were complex, but suffice it to say that the movement did not gain traction – or go viral – until several concerned parents created a *Facebook* page entitled "National Education Parents Concern Group" just two months prior to the occupation. That page provided a focal point for concerned citizens to share information and connect with each other.

1.2 Elections in Hong Kong

As already discussed, a free media creates opportunities for undermining authoritarian regimes. Given the high degree of freedom of expression and an increasingly vocal civil society in Hong Kong, one would expect that opposition parties would have an easy time building their political clout. Surprisingly, the reality is quite the opposite.

A useful indicator of parties' political influences is their seat shares in the parliament. In Hong Kong, although the Chief Executive is not democratically elected, half of the seats of the city's legislature, known as the Legislative Council (or the LegCo), are decided by universal suffrage every four years. These elected seats, also known as the geographical constituencies, are the major battlefield between two political camps: (a) the pro-establishment camp consisting of Beijing-sponsored parties and (b) the pan-democratic camp constituted by prodemocracy opposition parties.[6] These two political camps are archrivals. While the latter actively promotes the cause of democratization, the former advocates a Chinese-style patriotism, namely, supporting the single-party regime.

In the final years before the city's sovereignty transfer, the opposition elite had gained a dominant position in the colonial legislature, owing to its prodemocracy political stance, which held a strong appeal for the former colony that had been gripped by a fear of Communist rule. After 1997, Beijing wielded the power to rewrite the rules of the game in the city. It kept a limit on the number of directly elected seats for fear that the opposition elite would ride on the wave of its popularity to control the legislature of the newly established Hong Kong Special Administrative Region (HKSAR). The non-directly elected seats, known as the functional constituencies, have been overrepresented by pro-Beijing interests and have been widely perceived to be a stumbling block to the city's democratization.

While the existence of the functional constituencies has significantly limited the influence of the pan-democrats in the legislature, the geographical constituencies provide a relatively level playing field for the pan-democratic camp to demonstrate its popular support and hence political power vis-à-vis the pro-establishment camp. The vote and seat shares of the two political camps in the geographical constituencies are displayed in Fig. 1.1.

As seen clearly from the graphs, the pan-democratic camp has consistently obtained more than 50 % of the vote in all elections. Nevertheless, what is striking

---

[6]In this book, the terms "pan-democratic camp" and "prodemocracy elite" are used interchangeably.

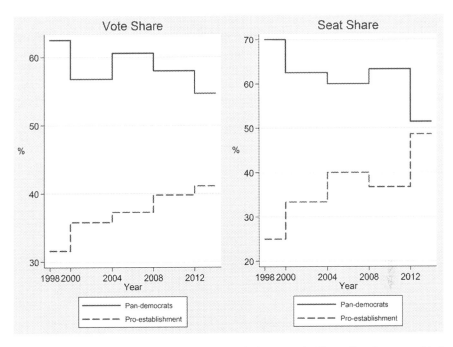

Fig. 1.1 Vote and seat shares of the two political camps in Hong Kong's geographical constituencies since 1997

about Fig. 1.1 does not lie in the levels, but in the changes. The gap between the two camps with respect to either their vote share or their seat share has been narrowing over time. In particular, the vote share of the pro-establishment camp (dashed line) has steadily increased at the expense of the pan-democratic camp. More strikingly, the difference between their seat shares has shrunk more rapidly than that of their vote share. Within 12 years, their seat share difference had been reduced from about 40 % to less than 4 %. If the vote share received by a party in a direct election is a valid measure of its popularity among voters, Fig. 1.1 would no doubt indicate an unambiguous rising trend of the pro-establishment camp's popularity.

1.3   The Puzzle

Juxtaposing the electoral performance of the pro-establishment camp with our early discussion of Hong Kong's media environment, one sees a puzzling picture. On the one hand, because of the existence of a high degree of freedom of expression and freedom of association, there are Hong Kong media outlets that are highly critical of the government, and such media are popular among the people. Also, the city possesses an increasingly vocal civil society that has demonstrated in various occasions its readiness for and its capability of mass mobilization (most notably, the July 1, 2003 protest and the 2014 Umbrella Movement). On the other hand, Hong Kong is witnessing an uninterrupted rising trend in the electoral popularity of some Beijing-sponsored pro-establishment parties, who are well known for their lack of support for the promotion of democratization. Compared with mass mobilization, the participation cost of voting is significantly lower. When more people are willing to take part in costly mass mobilization to defend their interests, why would fewer and fewer people use a relatively low-cost means – that is, their votes – to punish the parties that stand in the way of universal suffrage, their fundamental political right?

On the surface, one possible explanation is that those who participate in mass mobilization are not a representative sample of the population. That is, while mass mobilization has increased in number and scale, the majority of citizens remain inactive in these social movements, and the silent majority actually favors the political status quo or could be indifferent to democratization.

However, upon closer examination, this explanation is factually problematic. While it is true that frontline social activists are always in the minority, the demand for democratization in Hong Kong is by no means feeble. The Basic Law of Hong Kong, the city's mini-constitution, stipulates that the selection of the Chief Executive will be ultimately conducted by universal suffrage. How to reform the current political system in order to achieve that ultimate aim has been an ongoing and highly charged public issue in Hong Kong since the sovereignty transfer. At each round of the negotiations between the government and the pan-democratic camp over political reforms, polls conducted at different points in time found overwhelming public support for implementing universal suffrage at the soonest possible time. For instance, in 2007, the Public Opinion Program of the University of Hong Kong showed that almost 60 % of the respondents opined that Hong Kong should be ripe for universal suffrage by 2012, the time when the next Chief Executive is selected. The Chinese University of Hong Kong conducted a similar survey in 2011 and found that 79 % of the respondents supported the immediate implementation of universal suffrage in both the Chief Executive and the LegCo elections. These surveys present essentially the same picture: the majority of the Hong Kong population has deemed political democratization long overdue. The fact that most people remain inactive in social movements does not imply that they are complacent about the political status quo.

Nor can electoral frauds explain away the puzzle. Most authoritarian regimes that hold elections adopt a secret ballot (Geddes 2005), as in the case of Hong Kong. In other words, for ordinary voters, the cost of voting against the pro-establishment camp is actually very low. Furthermore, electoral violence is virtually nonexistent in Hong Kong, and there have never been reports of voters being coerced to vote (or not to vote) for a certain party. Although several incidents of "ghost votes" were discovered in the 2011 District Council election, no evidence shows that these votes, which were too sporadic, had ever decided any election outcome. In the absence of other electoral frauds such as ballot stuffing and postelection vote rigging, elections of the geographical constituencies in Hong Kong are generally viewed as free and uncorrupted.

Economic factors also have limited explanatory power. Since 1997, the small open economy of Hong Kong has weathered the 1997 Asian Financial Crisis, the 2000 Dot-Com Bubble Burst, and the Global Financial Crisis between 2007 and 2008. Despite the occurrence of these economic shocks, the pro-establishment camp, as Fig. 1.1 shows, has managed to maintain an uninterrupted rising trend with respect to its vote share received in legislative elections. Their resilient electoral performance, however, does not imply that the government has done a great job managing the economy, such that voters would show their approval of the government by voting for the pro-establishment parties. In fact, the first Chief Executive, Tung Chee-hwa, stepped down in the midst of a protracted economic downturn. His successor, Donald Tsang, was widely viewed as incapable of containing the soaring housing price and eradicating the perceived "collusion between government and business." Tsang's term ended in 2012, with his popularity rating plummeting to 39 %, only slightly higher than Tung's record low. Remarkably, in the same year, the pro-establishment camp achieved its best electoral performance in history.

Part of the reason why the pro-establishment camp could stay unaffected by unpopular Chief Executives is that the executive branch has been made insulated from party politics; the law stipulates that the Chief Executive cannot be a member of any political party. As a result, despite the brazen image of the pro-establishment parties as staunch supporters of the government, they can at times distance themselves from policy failures committed by the Chief Executive. This shows why economic factors have only limited explanatory power over the increasing popularity of the pro-establishment camp.

This book aims to provide a more nuanced explanation for why voters who support democracy nevertheless vote for pro-Communist policy makers. This puzzle cannot be solved without a thorough understanding of the strategic interaction between the ruling elite and the opposition parties in the presence of a high degree of media freedom and diverse voter preferences. The coexistence of the increasingly popular ruling elite and an increasingly assertive civil society and relatively liberal media environment is, as I discuss later, not a coincidence. It is precisely the presence of this liberal media environment that sets a limit on the electoral appeal of the opposition force among voters, which in turn helps the ruling elite strengthen its own electoral support. In other words, quite contrary to the conventional wisdom, the analysis in this book provides a different perspective on the effects of media freedom in authoritarian regimes. Media freedom is a double-edged sword; it can limit the opposition's popularity in the same way that it can undermine political support for the authoritarian incumbent.

1.4 My Argument

In democracies, an important function of elections is to allow voters to choose desirable policies. When the incumbent's policy fails to deliver results, voters can oust him by voting for the opposition that advocates an alternative policy. Even if the policies of the incumbent and the opposition sometimes look very much alike, this does not imply politicians ignore what voters want. On the contrary, their similarity in policy may suggest that voter preference has affected both the incumbent and the opposition such that they both adopt voters' most preferred policy in order to maximize their respective chances of getting elected. Scholars who study voting behaviors (Black 1958; Downs 1957) have long observed that such policy convergence occurs most often in a majoritarian election system.

Elections in authoritarian regimes are quite different. Although many consider elections as a defining feature of democracies, a large number of autocracies actually hold regular, and somewhat competitive, elections, especially after the end of the Cold War (Levitsky and Way 2010). Some view such elections as no more than a facade of democracy. However, a fast-growing literature in comparative politics shows that elections in authoritarian regimes do have significant political effects such as enhancing regime survival (Cheibub et al. 2010; Gandhi 2008; Magaloni 2006). This is not to say that by holding elections, an autocracy can become forever immune to political instability. Some studies show the possibility of "democratization by election," in which the authoritarian incumbent is voted out of office, resulting in a transition to democracy (Lindberg 2006; Schedler 2002; Bratton and Van de Walle 1997). Such a possibility notwithstanding, few would dispute that a level playing field is nonexistent in autocratic elections, and the opposition elite has to fight an uphill battle against the incumbent (Levitsky and Way 2010). In most cases, the chance of defeating the incumbent is vanishingly small.

When removing an incumbent through elections is very unlikely, elections lose their function of providing a mechanism for voters to select policies.[7] Voters cannot simply replace the incumbent who carries out the policy, no matter how unpopular an existing policy is, with an opposition party that advocates an alternative. Under such circumstances, voters in authoritarian regimes should have little incentive to vote for the opposition (or to vote at all). Nevertheless, we do observe that opposition parties in many authoritarian elections receive a considerable amount of voter support. Why is it possible?

I argue that voters in authoritarian regimes, even fully aware of the flimsy chance of replacing the incumbent with the opposition through elections, would still vote for the latter for two reasons. First, they vote for the opposition in order to demonstrate their dissatisfaction with the incumbent. Even if they know that the opposition has a low chance of getting elected due to the lack of a level playing field, they may enjoy supporting the opposition because doing so can suppress the margin of victory of the incumbent party. A low margin of victory not only makes the incumbent party lose face but may also undermine the political stability of the regime. Magaloni (2008) observes that autocratic leaders have an incentive to run an expensive election campaign, even though the opposition is too weak to pose any serious challenge.

---

[7]This does not imply that citizens in autocracies have no way of affecting policies. Many studies show that even in authoritarian regimes, citizens still have some room to effect policy changes through channels other than elections such as public demonstration (O'Brien and Li 2006).

This is because by securing a high margin of victory through intensive campaigning, autocratic leaders can demonstrate their invincibility and hence prevent defection within the ruling elite, which is a major source of political instability in autocracies.[8]

In addition to the expression of dissatisfaction with the incumbent, voters in autocracies may vote for the opposition because of a personal connection. By personal connection, I refer to all kinds of personal relationships that connect a voter with an opposition candidate. For instance, they may come from the same clan, neighborhood, school, or religious sect. Apart from this primordial bonding, another common form of relationship comes from the distribution of patronage; the voter has received from the opposition candidate some personal favors, ranging from perks and privileges to constituency services such as grievance redress and legal consultation.[9] Motivated by a sense of kinship, reciprocity, or moral obligation, voters may throw their support behind an opposition candidate, regardless of the candidate's chance of getting elected.

Assuming voters have heterogeneous preferences for protest and relationship with respect to voting, some cast the vote with an intention to punish the incumbent, while others are driven more by the personal relationship with the opposition candidate. Let us further assume that protest voters are more critical of the incumbent than relationship voters.[10] From the opposition's point of view, attracting the protest vote and attracting the relationship vote both require different strategies and resource inputs. Given the significant resource constraint faced by the opposition in autocracies, an opposition candidate needs to solve a maximization problem: how to distribute his limited resources between the protest vote and the relationship vote in order to maximize his overall chance of getting elected.

This is where media freedom comes into play. When the media[11] environment is relatively liberal, which implies that the opposition is able to publicly question, challenge, or even condemn the ruling elite, the cost of attracting the protest vote would decrease relative to the cost of attracting the relationship vote. The opposition elite would be incentivized to take a more radical position against the incumbent.

---

[8] This is not to say that voters who vote for the opposition are necessarily conscious of this indirect effect of their vote; that is, the probability of defection within the ruling elite is increased by suppressing the incumbent's margin of victory. For most who vote for the opposition, they simply vote to protest against the incumbent.

[9] Many have written about the distribution of patronage in authoritarian regimes (e.g., Lust-Okar 2009; Diaz-Cayeros et al. 2003). But the extant literature focuses primarily on the political machine of the incumbent. In this book, I argue that even the opposition parties, once they get elected, can gain access to some form of resources that can help them provide constituency services or other patronage activities. Nevertheless, there is no doubt that the incumbent enjoys far more resource advantages over any opposition party because the former has monopoly of access to state resources.

[10] One interpretation of this assumption is that because these voters hold the incumbent in low regard, they are more inclined to cast a protest vote.

[11] In this book, I define the media as all kinds of channels through which ordinary citizens can acquire political information. By my definition, the media include newspapers, radio broadcasts, television stations, online forums, social media, and the like.

For example, members of the opposition elite may become more critical of the ruling elite, refuse to negotiate with the government, decry major government policies, organize more street protests, or simply try to "act tough" in the media. These moves are likely to please the protest voters, but not without cost. First, focusing on the protest vote inevitably reduces resources for the relationship vote. For instance, when members of the opposition elite devote more time on organizing street protests or appearing in radio talk shows to lambast the incumbent, their time spent on strengthening grassroots organization, including the provision of constituency services, is likely to decrease. Consequently, they may lose support from some voters who value such services. Second, pandering to the protest vote stimulates political radicalism, which is likely to move the ideological position of the opposition elite farther away from that of moderate voters. The electoral implication of this is that when moderate voters find the opposition's virulent attack on the ruling elite deviate too much from what they have seen and personally experienced, they may start to question the opposition's credibility or find the opposition unable to represent their interests, thereby reducing the opposition's electoral support.

Moderate voters most likely exceed radical voters in number. Any rational opposition party, of course, would not court the protest vote at the expense of the relationship vote. However, a prodemocracy movement may consist of other stakeholders than a single opposition party. This is especially the case when the authoritarian state permits a certain degree of civil liberties. For example, civil society organizations may exist and actively participate in a prodemocracy movement. It is also possible to have multiple opposition parties, with some more radical than the others.[12] In short, not all stakeholders within a prodemocracy movement may share the same objective and face the same constituency as a "rational" opposition party that has an eye on moderate voters. Different political objectives lead to different kinds of opposition tactics. If the media are free to cover the opposition movement, civil society organizations or radical parties are likely to crowd out moderate opposition parties in the news due to the formers' willingness to adopt unconventional, if not controversial, tactics. When radical views dominate the media's coverage of the prodemocracy movement, moderate voters are alienated. This explains why we may observe a decline in electoral support of the entire opposition camp even in the presence of opposition parties that build political support on the relationship vote.

From the ruling elite's point of view, undermining the opposition's electoral support is not a sufficient guarantee of its political survival. Holding an election would entail political uncertainties, however small they are, because voter preference is never perfectly predictable. Dictators do not want to hold elections unless they find that the risk of being ousted is vanishingly small. For all dictators,

---

[12]I use "moderate" and "radical" only in a relative sense. A "radical" party is defined as one that is more receptive to the use of extreme methods to achieve its political goals and less willing to make compromise. Extreme methods do not necessarily imply political violence.

they have to face a quintessential question: How can they calculate the electoral uncertainty *ex ante*?[13] Investing in the relationship vote is an effective way to reduce such an electoral uncertainty. Attracting the relationship vote requires a large-scale distribution of patronage, which cannot be accomplished without a well-functioning political machine. It is this political machine that assists the ruling elite to collect detailed information on voter preference (Blaydes 2010). Such information is useful not only for calculating its electoral risk but also for efficiently allocating resources to buy political support.

My theory highlights a strategic dilemma confronting the opposition elite. As Schedler (2002) observes, the prodemocracy opposition has two political objectives when participating in an authoritarian election. On the one hand, it attempts to capture elected offices in the formal political institution. On the other hand, it struggles to change the same political institution that is the source of the fundamental political inequality. While some scholars view that these two objectives are mutually reinforcing – that is, gaining a seat in a dictator-controlled legislature is conducive to the overall democratization prospect – my theory suggests that the relationship between the two is more complicated. For one thing, courting the protest vote may increase the probability of getting elected by shoring up the support of the protest voters, but it runs the risk of alienating the moderate voters and thereby limiting the popular appeal of the opposition as a credible leading force behind a prodemocracy movement.

My theory can be applied to understand the political development of Hong Kong after 1997 and explain the puzzle discussed above. Thanks to the existence of a relatively liberal media environment, the media have been playing an important role in monitoring the government. Media companies, most notably Next Media, frequently expose not only the wrongdoings of the government but also the undemocratic nature of the political system. In the 1990s and early years after the sovereignty transfer, opposition parties were major beneficiaries of this liberal media environment. As the prodemocracy media openly criticized the undemocratic political institutions, the opposition force, just by virtue of being an opposition to the regime, could automatically establish credentials as a defender of political rights for ordinary people. Such credentials paid off handsomely during early post-transfer elections.

Beijing-sponsored parties, as part of the ruling elite, knew that they could hardly compete with their opposition counterparts over the protest vote. However, they could encroach on the opposition's relationship vote. Since 1997, major pro-establishment parties such as the Democratic Alliance for the Betterment and Progress of Hong Kong (DAB) have stepped up their effort in the provision

---

[13]The incumbent, when defeated, always has an option of rigging the vote after the election. But vote rigging involves additional political uncertainties. Blatant electoral fraud would provide a focal point for mass mobilization of voters to protest "stolen elections" (Bunce and Wolchik 2006). In other words, *ex post* vote rigging is not necessarily a solution to the incumbent's *ex ante* risk of being deposed in an election.

of patronage activities and the development of grassroots support networks and organizations. This has posed a serious challenge to the pan-democrats, who needed to spend significantly more for resources over constituency services, if they wanted to compete with Beijing-sponsored parties. In other words, the grassroots efforts of the Beijing-sponsored parties have substantially increased their rivals' cost of attracting the relationship vote. This also implies that for the pan-democrats, the relative cost of attracting the protest vote has been lowered. A practical consequence of this is that political radicalism has been on the rise in the past decade, and many opposition parties find it more cost-effective to shore up political support by acting tough on the government, which can often get media attention, rather than to commit more resources on mundane constituency services. The gradual change in the ideological position of the opposition camp has weakened its electoral support as a whole for two reasons. First, it has alienated some of the moderate supporters of the prodemocracy movement. Second, as the opposition parties provide fewer constituency services, they have lost relationship voters and have been crowded out by pro-establishment parties in local districts. A shrinking grassroots network poses a serious threat to the long-term development of these opposition parties.

A caveat is in order. Although my argument suggests that free media may limit the opposition's electoral strength under a given condition, this is not to suggest that a liberal media environment is necessarily an obstacle to democratization. Media freedom certainly helps citizens monitor the ruling elite and communicate with each other, reducing the information cost of mass mobilization. Nor do I argue that elections are the only possible means of democratic transition. Indeed, the majority of authoritarian leaders in history were toppled through revolutions and coups d'etat. The ouster of Hosni Mubarak, the former dictator of Egypt, is a case in point. He was overthrown by hundreds of thousands of ordinary Egyptians who gathered in Cairo's Tahrir Square in protest of his autocracy. Although the media environment of Egypt under Mubarak was far from liberal, protesters did use social media to organize among themselves at least in the early stage of the protest. Some Western media even characterize Egypt's uprising as a Facebook Revolution (Huffington Post 2011; Washington Post 2011).

Perhaps one day Hong Kong's civil society will be able to produce similar mass mobilization as in Egypt which demolished the authoritarian edifice. But this will not downplay the political significance of opposition parties in the struggle for democracy, which is the focus of this book. The reason is that the current opposition parties will not vanish after a successful democratic transition. Rather, they will play a decidedly more important role in a democratic system. If these parties are ineffectual, the nascent democratic system may not be able to take root, as with the case of post-Mubarak Egypt.

This underlines the importance of studying elections if one wants to understand Hong Kong politics. Hong Kong is in the midst of a protracted democratic transition. The tug-of-war between Beijing and the prodemocracy elite over whether, when, and how universal suffrage should be implemented has eclipsed all other issues in the realm of politics. But successful democratization does not end in the moment when universal suffrage is adopted. The political survival of a democratic system depends on whether the ruling and opposition coalitions both accept that democratic elections are the "only game in town." For this reason, studying how authoritarian elections have benefited or undermined opposition parties is central to our ability to understand Hong Kong's democratization in the past and future and hence Hong Kong politics in general. This is also the reason why this book focuses on electoral politics.

1.5 Why Hong Kong?

In this book, I have developed a theory about the competition between the ruling elite and the opposition force in authoritarian regimes that run regular elections (also known as competitive authoritarianism). My theory, which centers on the effects of two domestic factors – media environment and patronage activities – on electoral competitions, is broadly comparative because these factors exist to varying degrees in contemporary authoritarian regimes. Consider patronage activities. The scope and scale of patronage activities vary from autocracy to autocracy. While personalist regimes tend to deliver huge patronage benefits to a coterie of supporters, more institutionalized autocracies can mobilize their political machine to dole out privileges to more individual citizens.[14] As for media environment, although many may equate autocracies with media controls, some authoritarian regimes actually have a relatively high tolerance of media freedom. Figure 1.2 displays the relationship between press freedom[15] and political regimes.[16] As may be seen from the figure, although press freedom is positively correlated with democracy in general, substantial variations exist within regime types. In fact, autocratic regimes such as Burkina Faso, Haiti, and Mauritania rank significantly higher in press freedom than many democracies including India, Mexico, and Turkey.[17]

The empirical evidence supporting my theory is drawn from the experience of Hong Kong after the sovereignty transition. I select post-1997 Hong Kong as my case for two reasons.

The first reason is that the unique experience of Hong Kong helps identify the causal effect of the variables of interest. On the surface, Hong Kong does not make

---

[14]Scholars of authoritarian politics have long noted that party institutionalization varies from autocracy to autocracy (Cheibub et al. 2010; Geddes 1999).

[15]The 2013 Press Freedom Index in Fig. 1.2 is published by Reporters Without Borders. It has been rescaled such that a high value indicates a high ranking of press freedom.

[16]The measure of political regime in Fig. 1.2 is taken from the Polity IV Project's variable Polity2, which runs from -10 (full autocracy) to $+10$ (full democracy).

[17]Egorov et al. (2009) provide one explanation for why some autocracies tolerate relatively free media. They argue that free media help the incumbent in checking the performance of the bureaucrats. Even in China, criticisms of political leaders are not strictly prohibited. King et al. (2013) provide an interesting empirical analysis of millions of social media posts, which shows that online censorship is mostly aimed at forestalling social mobilization.

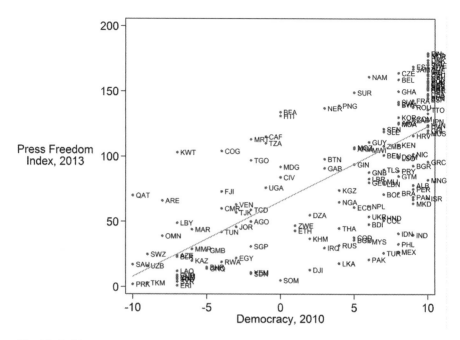

Fig. 1.2 Political regimes and media freedom across countries

a good comparative case for various reasons. For example, it is not a sovereign state but merely a city of the PRC. It also has a small open economy, whose dependence on trade is exceptionally high by world standards. Perhaps more importantly, it experienced an unusual political event in 1997, the transfer of its sovereignty. One can hardly find a historical replication in other countries.

However, I argue that it is precisely this unique historical experience of the city that allows us to tackle a nontrivial methodological problem that plagues research on competitive authoritarianism. When studying how a certain factor affects the electoral competition between the incumbent and the opposition in the context of autocracies, one cannot omit from the analysis the effect of the opposition's weakness. For instance, if one wants to examine whether media freedom can help the opposition defeat the incumbent, one may not be able to detect any significant effect of the media, when the opposition party under study is inherently too weak to take advantage of media freedom (e.g., lacking resources to place any campaign ad or lacking candidates to participate in elections). The absence of a significant effect in this case, however, reflects the opposition's inherent weakness, rather than the media's lack of any causal force on elections.

Worse still, the spurious effect of the opposition weakness is further complicated by another methodological problem known as reciprocal causality. Even if one can find a case in which the opposition is strong enough to benefit from the media influences, one still needs to worry whether the identified effect truly belongs to media freedom because the strength of the opposition is often predetermined by the strength of the incumbent, which is precisely the outcome that one wants to study in the first place. As Gandhi and Lust-Okar (2009) correctly point out, two possibilities exist as to why opposition parties manage to oust the incumbents through elections in some authoritarian regimes:

> It may be that electoral coalitions among opposition parties lead to their victory and control over the chief executive office, but it is equally plausible that already-weakened incumbents both allow opposition coalitions and desist from using fraud and manipulation as part of a predetermined 'step out' of power (p. 416).

Their observation suggests that unless we researchers can intervene in the data-generating process – that is, imposing a (strong) opposition force on an authoritarian regime that runs elections – we cannot measure to what extent the media empower or undermine the opposition, as the identified media effect by itself may merely signal the underlying strength of the incumbent, which is seldom observable.

Hong Kong serves as a valuable analytical case because it experienced an exogenous event in 1997. The sovereignty of Hong Kong was transferred to a resilient single-party dictatorship. In the decade before its handover, the city had witnessed the emergence of a strong prodemocracy opposition force, arguably fostered by the former colonial government. In other words, the nondemocratic government established in Hong Kong in 1997 was forced to inherit an opposition force, whose political power had been cultivated in the previous sovereign state. The strength of the opposition force at the time of the sovereignty transfer was therefore independent of the strength of the newly established government backed by the single-party dictatorship of the PRC. This helps eliminate the above methodological problems; that pro-Beijing parties can win seats in elections is not because the opposition parties are inherently weak, unpopular, or unknown to voters in the first place. Nor does the opposition's strength originate from an innate regime weakness. That is, it is not that the ruling elite, who came to govern Hong Kong after 1997, is lacking in organizational capacity or in resources that has led to the empowerment of the opposition.

In other words, Hong Kong's sovereignty transfer, unique as it is, provides a useful quasi-experimental setup, in which a strong incumbent is made to confront a strong opposition. It is useful because it helps deal with important confounding factors, so that we can single out the causal effect of the variables of interest. Concretely, when we can identify a certain effect of the causal variable on the election outcome, we are confident that the effect comes from the causal force of the variable of interest, rather than from other spurious relationships.

The analytical advantage of the Hong Kong case is also relevant to the studies of the Chinese authoritarian rule for the same reason. Political repression has been given much attention when analyzing the resilient performance of the regime such that one may wonder what else the single-party dictatorship can count on to sustain its rule in the absence of its iron fist. It is difficult to uncover other important factors because repression has already become an inseparable part of Chinese politics. In this regard, Hong Kong, with its political system largely unmolested by the Chinese government's repressive rule, presents an instructive analytical perspective to this question.

1.6   The Methodology

Because my argument is concerned with not only electoral competitions between the ruling elite and the opposition but also with civil society – in particular the role of the media – there is no single research methodology that is able to deal with so many issues all at once. I have to rely on a combination of methods to tackle various research challenges. For instance, when analyzing how opposition parties use the media as a mobilizing agent, I conduct a content analysis of thousands of news articles published during elections. When studying the causal effect of controlling District Councils on the election outcomes of the Legislative Council, I have to employ "large-N" statistical analyses. To verify the existence of "gerrymandering," I need to make use of techniques related to geographic information systems (see Chap. 5 for details). The most daunting challenge is to assess Beijing's strategic considerations for governing postcolonial Hong Kong. Authoritarian regimes are opaque, and the PRC is no exception. Beijing would not announce how it plans to marginalize Hong Kong's prodemocracy parties.

One way to overcome this challenge is to plow through political leaders' speeches, memoirs, and biographies to look for clues. Speeches by top leaders such as Deng Xiaoping and Jiang Zemin are easy to come by, but they usually contain only general guidelines. Fortunately, more and more senior Chinese officials in charge of Hong Kong affairs during the 1980s and 1990s have retired and published memoirs.[18] Their works reveal more details about their political operations and the logic behind them. Biographies of important figures such as Liao Chengzhi and Deng Xiaoping provide an ample source in order to corroborate the data.

However, what is told in those publications may not accurately reflect the reality. Even if these senior leaders speak their mind, their plans can go seriously awry when it came to implementation due to the lack of cooperation from local officials. For this reason, in addition to written publications of senior leaders, I also conduct extensive interviews with many grassroots members of pro-Beijing parties in Hong Kong to gain insight into their perception of grassroots politics and the inner workings of the political machine that they run. I would not discount the possibility that the interviewees give biased comments or incomplete answers. Yet my experience suggests that these politicians, even those coming from the pro-Beijing camp, turn out to be more candid than I expected. Part of the reason is perhaps that many of them occupy a relatively low position in their party structure. As "foot soldiers" of a large political machine, they feel less pressured to guard the party's political

---

[18]They include Chen Zuoer, Li Hou, Lu Ping, Qian Qichen, Xu Jiatun, Zhang Junsheng, and Zhou Nan.

strategies (or are less sensitive to such a need). Despite their willingness to share their experiences, I remain cautious on what they tell me and take advantage of the multiple interviews to cross-examine the validity of the interviewees' answers whenever possible.

All my pro-establishment interviewees occupy an elected office known as the District Councils. Altogether I interviewed about thirty current and former District Councillors between the mid-2012 and the mid-2014. While some of them identified themselves as politically independent, most District Councillors I interviewed come from either the pro-establishment camp or the prodemocracy one. Each interview lasted for at least an hour, and most of them took place in the District Councillors' office. In addition to District Councillors, I also interviewed some leading social activists and ordinary voters. For a list of my interviews conducted, see the Appendix.

1.7 Plan of the Book

This book is organized as follows. Chapter 2 presents my theory. In particular, I provide a simple game-theoretic model to explain how media freedom and patronage activities have shaped the electoral strategies of both the opposition and the pro-establishment elite. The game-theoretic model is not a mere formality. It allows me to derive testable hypotheses, which will be examined in the subsequent chapters.

Chapter 3 presents an overview of Hong Kong's political system and the development of the city's civil society. How did Hong Kong become China's democratic enclave? Why would the Chinese authoritarian state, which is notoriously draconian, permit the city to keep a relatively liberal political and media environment? How did the Chinese authoritarian state design the political institutions of Hong Kong in order to defend its political interests? I address these questions based on an analysis of the formal political institutions of postcolonial Hong Kong and the city's political developments in the 1980s and 1990s.

What pan-democratic parties did to overcome the obstacles to democratization, including the rising electoral challenges of the pro-establishment camp, is the focus of Chap. 4. I discuss the changing strategies of different pan-democratic parties and their causes. In particular, I highlight an underappreciated long-term electoral effect of the July 1, 2003 protest, the largest mass mobilization since the sovereignty transfer; it has diverted many pan-democrats' attention from the relationship vote to the protest vote.

Chapter 5 deals with a puzzle: why would some pro-establishment parties devote an enormous amount of resources to capturing the District Councils, the lowest elected tier of the government that has been generally viewed as politically insignificant? To answer this question, I first define pro-establishment parties in Hong Kong and touch on the changes and continuities of their relationship with the regime in China. Then I discuss how Beijing-sponsored parties have endeavored to uproot the relationship vote as well as the grassroots network previously developed by the pan-democratic parties. The seemingly insignificant District Council offices turned out to carry far-reaching political influences, as they have become the political tool of the pro-establishment camp to undermine its rival. The reason for focusing on the District Councils is that as part of the formal government structure, the District Council office provides access to government resources, not to mention grassroots networks. Drawing on my interviews with the pro-establishment elite, I would discuss the inner workings of its grassroots political machine, and how this machine contributes to the electoral success of some Beijing-sponsored parties.

Chapter 6 examines the actual electoral effect of the relationship vote-oriented grassroots strategy of Beijing-sponsored parties and the pandering of the pan-democrats to the protest vote. Did the Beijing-sponsored parties' grassroots strategy really achieve their intended effect? In this chapter, I demonstrate not only how their grassroots strategy led to their electoral successes in the District Councils but also how occupying the District Councils allowed them to marginalize the pan-democrats in the major battlefield, the Legislative Council. The empirical evidence again challenges the conventional wisdom that the District Councils are politically insignificant.

In Chap. 7, I conclude with a discussion on possible lessons we can derive from the experience of postcolonial Hong Kong with respect to electoral competitions between the incumbent and the opposition in the setting of competitive authoritarian regimes.

Chapter 2
Protest and Patronage: A Theory of Electoral Contest in Competitive Authoritarianism

Civil liberties remain largely intact in postcolonial Hong Kong. Opposition media continue to exist, and Hong Kong people have unbridled access to alternative information through old and new media. The degree of media freedom that Hong Kong people enjoy may seem like a nightmare to many dictators, for it allows antigovernment information to propagate and restive citizens to coordinate. Indeed, since 1997, Hong Kong society has experienced incessant waves of social movement which have been aimed to challenge the political status quo. Paradoxically, pro-establishment parties, namely, those supporting the status quo, have been receiving ever-increasing public support in popular elections. In the introduction to this book, I outline an explanation to this puzzle. In this chapter, I formalize the discussion by providing an analytical model, which involves the interaction between four major stakeholders pertaining to authoritarian elections: the incumbent, the opposition, the media, and the voters. The model focuses on the scenario when the cost of imposing media controls is too high for an authoritarian government. What can the government do to minimize its political risk? How would that affect the opposition parties? The key insight of the model is that media freedom tends to promote political radicalism, which may end up undermining the overall electoral support for the opposition elite.

This chapter unfolds as follows. In the first section, I examine the characteristics of these four stakeholders and devise a number of behavioral assumptions about them. These behavioral assumptions provide the basis for me to model their strategic interactions, which are discussed in the second section.

2.1 The Stakeholders

The first stakeholder is the ruling elite. Recent political science studies emphasize that authoritarian institutions, including the size of the ruling coalition, vary significantly from one dictatorship to another (Geddes 1999; Bueno de Mesquita

© Springer Science+Business Media Singapore 2015
S.H.-W. Wong, *Electoral Politics in Post-1997 Hong Kong*,
DOI 10.1007/978-981-287-387-3_2

et al. 2003). Some dictatorships are led by a military junta that consists of no more than a dozen of high-ranking military officers. Others are ruled by an oversized party with an elaborate organizational structure and a gigantic membership. Because the model is a stylized representation of authoritarian politics, I treat the ruling elite as a unitary player in the model and define it as a group of individuals who control both the national government and legislature of the authoritarian regime. This is not to deny that members of any ruling coalition may have a wide diversity of opinion or policy preferences. But regardless of what preferences they want to pursue, they have to stay in power first (Bueno de Mesquita et al. 2003; Boix and Svolik 2013, The foundations of limited authoritarian government: Institutions and power-sharing in dictatorships, unpublished manuscript). Hence, we have the first assumption:

Assumption 1 *The goal of the ruling elite is to stay in power.*

The incumbent elite[1] use various tools to enhance their political survival. One of the most widely studied political tools available to authoritarian regimes is elections. As Geddes (2005) notes, although elections are a defining feature of democracies, many authoritarian regimes in the postwar period also hold somewhat competitive elections on a regular basis. Although opposition parties are often allowed to participate in such elections, these nominally democratic elections, albeit somewhat competitive, are notorious for their lack of a level playing field. Admittedly, a perfectly level playing field is arguably nonexistent even in democracies. But the incumbency advantage in democracies only pales in comparison with that of autocracies. As Levitsky and Way (2010) point out, a notable feature of competitive authoritarian regimes is that the incumbents widely abuse state institutions to develop unfair electoral advantages over challengers (p. 10). Experiences from various dictatorships show that by controlling the regulatory bodies of elections, the incumbents can easily marginalize opposition parties through gerrymandering (Gandhi and Lust-Okar 2009), malapportionment (Lust-Okar 2006), short notice of election (Brownlee 2007; Ortmann 2011), restricted media access (Levitsky and Way 2002; Gandhi and Lust-Okar 2009), and limiting the number of seats for electoral contest, as in the case of Hong Kong. In addition, authoritarian governments usually control, if not monopolize, important economic sectors such as energy and banking, which confer upon them enormous resources for rewarding their supporters in times of elections. With such privileged political and economic positions, authoritarian incumbents may not even need to resort to electoral irregularities such as ballot stuffing and vote rigging to guarantee electoral victories (Gandhi and Lust-Okar 2009, p. 412). Of course, when electoral fraud indeed occurs, the incumbents are unlikely held accountable as the court system is usually under the state's firm control (Ginsburg and Moustafa 2008).

Simply put, in most authoritarian regimes, the existence of elections would not alter the basic political reality that the incumbent government is the "only game in town." In fact, in their famous study of democracy and development, Przeworski

---

[1]Throughout the book, I would use the terms "incumbent elite" and "ruling elite" interchangeably.

(2000) defines dictatorships as regimes that have not experienced power alternation. By this definition, citizens of any authoritarian regime would never have seen their current government fall from power.[2] In other words, few voters would form the *ex ante* expectation that the incumbents can be easily toppled in any single election.

Taken these factors together, we have the following assumption:

Assumption 2 *The playing field of authoritarian elections is so uneven that the chance of voting out the ruling elite is always small.*

It is important to note that Assumption 2 does not preclude the possibility that the incumbent leaders can be ousted through non-electoral means, such as revolutions or coups d'etat.

Disadvantaged as they are, opposition candidates, the second stakeholder of our analytical model, may still choose to participate in authoritarian elections because the elections offer them an opportunity to promote their cause, make themselves more widely known, and receive donations. In many authoritarian regimes, it is not uncommon for opposition parties to manage gaining a few seats in a dictator-controlled legislature. To most political parties, occupying a public office is a crucial step to expand their political influences. As a result, opposition parties usually find it difficult to resist the temptation to participate in authoritarian elections, however unfair they are.

Note, however, that not all opposition groups are able to participate in authoritarian elections. Authoritarian governments may have an incentive to exclude some opposition groups. Drawing on the experience of the Arab world, Lust-Okar (2005) points out that the incumbents are able to undermine the unity of the opposition elite by selective co-optation. In particular, these excluded groups, in order to justify their exclusion, are likely to identify those who are allowed to stand for elections as running dogs of the regime, since their participation legitimizes an unfair political system.[3] Because my analytical model is concerned with the electoral contest between the incumbents and the opposition, the second stakeholder refers to these opposition members who can participate in authoritarian elections. From now on, when mentioning opposition parties, unless specified otherwise, I refer to those who are not excluded from elections.

The next assumption is concerned with the incentive of opposition parties:

Assumption 3 *The goal of opposition parties is to defeat the ruling elite in elections.*

Assumption 3 is intended to distinguish between true opposition parties and auxiliary parties that form part of the authoritarian establishment. Examples of the latter include the eight "democratic parties" of the PRC. These parties have

---

[2]Once they have witnessed it, they would no longer be citizens of this authoritarian regime.

[3]Or at least, they are investing their political career in the existing authoritarian political order (Magaloni 2008). This provides another reason why authoritarian regimes are willing to hold regular elections, as they can trap the opposition forces (Gandhi and Przeworski 2007).

no substantive political power, and their existence is mainly ornamental, creating a multiparty image for a single-party dictatorship. In the context of authoritarian elections, having no intention to defeat the ruling elite is tantamount to having no intention to change the political status quo. Such parties pose no political threat to the authoritarian incumbent and, hence, would not be considered in my model.

The third stakeholder is the media. As discussed in the previous chapter, contrary to the popular impression, some authoritarian regimes allow a relatively high degree of media freedom. One reason for their tolerance is that the media help in monitoring lower officials (Egorov et al. 2009). But even in countries where the media are under stringent government controls, media agencies produce more than political propaganda. This is because comprehensive media controls are costly, and there is no need for the incumbents to regulate every single aspect of news content, especially when the underlying news is remotely political (e.g., sports, entertainment, etc.). In addition, sometimes media companies in authoritarian regimes also have to face market competition. They have an incentive to produce quality journalism to vie for readership. Media companies in China are a case in point. Since 1978, the state has drastically reduced its financial support for state-owned media, which has led to a significant transformation of the media environment (Zhao 2000). In order to survive, these media companies have to produce content that interest readers. In other words, market competition has brought the Chinese media closer to consumers' preferences. One example is *Southern Weekly*, a state-owned weekly newspaper famous for its liberal orientation and courage to deviate from the official stance on many issues. Its outspoken reputation has earned it a huge readership; as of 2013, its circulation has exceeded 1.7 million copies and is growing at an annual rate of 15 %.[4]

Based on these observations, we have the following assumption:

Assumption 4 *After observing the acceptable political limits, media companies in authoritarian regimes strive to enlarge their audience size.*

The last stakeholder of our analytical model is voters. In democracies, voters are able to punish political leaders by voting them out of office. In authoritarian regimes, voters, for reasons discussed above, can seldom oust the incumbents through elections. Because the election outcomes are predetermined almost surely,[5] voters should be aware that whether they vote for the incumbents – or whether they vote at all – would not make any difference. In this regard, it is crucial to explain why voters would bother going to the voting booth to support someone who will win regardless.

Ideological affinity is a common reason why people support a political party. The ruling party of a dictatorship is no exception. One may argue that such an affinity

---

[4]*Southern Weekly* Web site: http://www.infzm.com/aboutus.shtml [Accessed on November 29, 2013].

[5]In their famous paper, Alvarez et al. (1996) define democracy as a political system in which electoral contestation involves "*ex ante* uncertainty (p. 5)."

is manufactured, as authoritarian regimes typically invest a fair amount of resources in propaganda. Indeed, Geddes and Zaller (1989) show that citizens who have a moderate level of education tend to be the most loyal to an authoritarian regime. They explain that this is because at this education level, people are knowledgeable enough to be exposed to the regime's propaganda, but not sufficiently sophisticated to differentiate propaganda from the political reality. That said, one cannot rule out the possibility that some citizens may genuinely support the ruling party even in the absence of propaganda; they may simply approve of its leadership and economic programs. This leads to the next assumption:

Assumption 5 *Voters in authoritarian regimes can have different ideological affinities.*

In addition to ideology, Magaloni (2006) provides a supply-side explanation. Drawing on the experience of Mexico under the dictatorship of the Institutional Revolutionary Party (PRI), she observes that even if opposition candidates are too weak to pose any political threat, authoritarian incumbents would still run an expensive election campaign and dole out an enormous amount of one-off material benefits to constituencies. She argues that this is because such a campaign, together with the ruling party's largess, can signal the incumbents' invincibility. When the incumbents appear invincible, its members are less likely to split from the ruling coalition, which is a common cause of authoritarian breakdown (Svolik 2012). Magaloni's account reveals the logic behind voters' support for the incumbents; they are able to obtain tangible rewards by voting for the ruling elite.[6]

The foregoing discussion suggests that voters in authoritarian regimes are backward-looking; they vote for the incumbents because they approve of what the incumbents have done for them, ranging from state economic policies to tiny giveaways (retrospective voting). This is not to say that voters in authoritarian regimes are not forward-looking such that they vote for the incumbents, hoping that they can bring about a better future (prospective voting). But in any mature authoritarian regime, voters must have at least a modicum of familiarity, if not disillusionment, with the ruling party and its policy stance. As a result, empty campaign promises that make no reference to the past can hardly impress voters. We, therefore, have the next assumption:

Assumption 6 *Voters in authoritarian elections vote retrospectively.*

---

[6]Voters are not always motivated by positive reinforcement, however. The PRI dictatorship of Mexico is again a case in point. Diaz-Cayeros et al. (2003) and Fox and Hernández (1995) show that the ruling party punished disloyal constituencies by cutting government funding. Although fear of the ruling elite's retaliation may also explain why voters bother voting at all, using punishment to guarantee electoral victory is arguably an authoritarian government's last resort. There are many less obtrusive and less costly tricks to prevent constituencies from defecting to the opposition such as redrawing the constituency boundaries to merge disloyal constituencies into loyal ones. Moreover, an important function of holding elections is to legitimize the authoritarian rule. If the ruling elite's electoral success is solely based on voter intimidation, they would be better off by not holding elections at all.

Thus far, the discussion focuses on why voters would support the authoritarian incumbents. A closely related question is as follows: why would citizens vote for the opposition? As already discussed, the playing field of authoritarian elections is so skewed that the opposition would have only a slim chance of defeating the ruling elite and controlling the government. Why would citizens bother voting for someone who stands to lose? I argue that they share a motivation akin to those who support the incumbents. First, non-programmatic benefits matter.[7] The opposition, by definition, does not control the government. As a result, there is no way for opposition parties to offer any programmatic benefit that has an across-the-board social effect. However, they may be able to capture seats in an election. These public offices provide the opposition access to at least some state resources. They can use such resources to deliver non-programmatic benefits to their constituencies in much the same way as the incumbents would do. Although the perks and privileges that opposition parties can deliver pale in comparison with those provided by the ruling elite, the opposition's ability to dole out non-programmatic benefits breaks the ruling elite's monopoly as a provider of such benefits. Opposition parties generally find this beneficial to their long-term political development.

Assumption 7 *In authoritarian elections, voters are more likely to vote for candidates who have offered them non-programmatic benefits.*

It is important to emphasize that Assumption 7 does not presume that non-programmatic benefits are necessarily tangible, such as free meals and liquor. An elderly citizen may vote for a candidate because the candidate gave her a call on her birthday. A jobless man may support a candidate because the candidate pounded on the door of the social welfare department to get his unemployment benefits, even unsuccessfully. The services these candidates offer are not something tangible, but are nevertheless valuable to the affected constituents. In other words, the interaction between political parties and voters involves a lot of human touch, and non-programmatic benefits comprise a complex system of reward that voters can derive from the exchanges with political parties. Two political implications follow from this. First, it should not be surprising that people who have savored the ruling party's sumptuous feast could still vote for an opposition candidate who fails to offer any free meal. These people may have received some other less tangible non-programmatic benefits from the opposition candidate. I call these votes, which are driven by non-programmatic benefits, the *relationship votes*.

---

[7]By non-programmatic benefits, I refer to benefits followed from distributive policies, which, according to Aldrich (1995), are defined as policies that concentrate benefits in one or a few districts, but distribute costs broadly across all districts. Various types of distributions can be subsumed under this label, including pork barrel funds, patronage, constituency services, and vote buying. The study of Stokes et al. (2013) contains a detailed discussion of the nature of these non-programmatic benefits. The analytical model presented in this chapter does not make further distinction between these different types of non-programmatic benefits, which may vary by their target recipients (Stokes et al. 2013) and scope and timing of distribution (Schaffer 2007).

The second political implication is that while the opposition faces tight budget constraints, it is still able to offer non-programmatic benefits that are not necessarily capital intensive. As in the above examples, calling local residents on their birthdays and helping them deal with the bureaucracy are constituency services[8] that do not involve significant monetary input. All they require is the candidate's time. In short, the resource-poor opposition is still able to gain political support by delivering labor-intensive constituency services.

The use of non-programmatic benefits to drum up political support is not confined to opposition groups engaging in authoritarian elections. DeNardo (1985, p. 45) notes that opposition elites who participate in high-intensity political struggles such as revolutions also exploit organizational resources to recruit followers, who join the movement that offer them "bonds of friendship, a means to support one's family, threats and coercion, or the call to adventure." In other words, their participation has little connection to the larger political goal of the movement itself. Most notably, the majority of Mao Zedong's early followers, as DeNardo (1985, p. 26) points out, became revolutionary only after they had been recruited into the Red Army.[9] If non-programmatic benefits are sufficient for motivating people to participate in high-intensity political struggles, they should no doubt be able to provide crucial incentives for low-intensity political actions such as voting.

Ideological discontent with the ruling elite is another crucial factor for voters to support the opposition. There is a host of reasons why citizens should despise an authoritarian regime. First and foremost, the exclusionary nature of the political order of authoritarianism is ideologically unappealing in today's world. It is at odds with political rights and civil liberties. In addition, many dictatorships are riddled with rampant corruption. Public officials abuse their political power to allocate economic resources based on favoritism. Citizens have little recourse to hold the ruling elite accountable for malfeasance and misdeeds. Of course, as with all other governments, democratic or not, dictatorships may mismanage the economy or fail to deliver programmatic benefits, which fuel public discontent. When citizens are dissatisfied with, or feel enraged at, the incumbents, they are likely to support the opposition, not necessarily because they endorse the opposition's political platforms or have not received the incumbents' largess, but because they want to cast a *protest vote*. Hence, we have the following assumption:

Assumption 8 *In authoritarian elections, voters are more likely to vote for opposition candidates when they are dissatisfied with the ruling elite based on ideological grounds.*

Having set out the relationship between voters and political parties, we next consider the interaction between voters and the media. A great variety of news is

---

[8]Constituency services refer to problem-solving services that elected officials offer, often indiscriminately, to local residents. Fenno (1978) provides a detailed account of the logic and practice of constituency services in the United States.

[9]DeNardo (1985) refers these followers as "organizational recruits."

accessible to ordinary citizens, including news on sports, business, and education. For the purpose of our analytical model, we are concerned only with political news here. By political news, I refer to information that deals with elections and government policies.

Citizens can acquire information about politics, political parties, and election candidates through personal experiences. For example, one gets to know candidates by chatting with them during an election rally held in one's community. A street vendor feels indebted to an opposition party, who exposes the illegal protection fees the police extorts from her. A government employee comes to know the government's policy orientation after losing his job as a result of public spending cuts. In some grassroots elections, such as village elections in China, voters may be acquainted with the candidates since their elementary school days (Takeuchi 2013, p. 74). Apart from these personal encounters, the mass media are an important channel for citizens to obtain political information. This does not imply that citizens in authoritarian regimes necessarily find the mass media credible. They are probably aware of the bias of the state-controlled media, but they have no alternative source to acquire information pertaining to their country or locality. Even if alternative information exists, it may be too costly for ordinary citizens to access due to the state's information controls.[10] By this reasoning, we derive the following assumption:

Assumption 9 *Voters evaluate the performance of the ruling elite based on their personal experience and the information provided by the media.*

Although few citizens are willing to go to great lengths to seek alternative political information, this does not necessarily imply that the majority of the population would always accept what state-controlled media present to them. For instance, when people are dying from famine everywhere, no matter how much the state media extol the economic achievement of the ruling elite, people will not believe the propaganda. In her study of the media in China, Stockmann (2012) shows that ordinary Chinese are actually more resistant to political messages conveyed by official state-run media than by nonofficial newspapers because the latter's "perceived apolitical nature and closeness to society enhances their credibility (p. 12)." Therefore, we can make the following assumption:

Assumption 10 *Voters would discount the credibility of the information provided by the media if it deviates too much from their personal experience.*

---

[10]For instance, China has invested a tremendous amount of resources to maintain a tight Internet censorship system infamously known as the Great Firewall (Deibert 2010, pp. 449–487). But even with such an expensive and comprehensive monitoring system, circumvention is possible and, arguably, not difficult. Solutions such as using a proxy server or a virtual private network (VPN) have been known for years. For the majority of Chinese netizens, however, they have no strong incentive to explore these alternatives for the sake of getting uncensored political information, especially when knowing the political truth does not make them any more likely to bring about political changes.

In his seminal work on democratic politics, Downs (1957) argues that voters are too busy to become well informed of politics. For any individual voter, the probability that his vote is decisive in an election is vanishingly small, which implies that whether he votes or not would probably have no effect on the election outcome. It, therefore, makes little sense for him to invest a significant amount of time and energy in acquiring political information. In short, as Downs (1957) contends, it is rational on the part of individual voters to stay ignorant about politics. Zaller (1999) extends Downs' insight to argue that given voters' precious time, they would be very selective of the political news they read. In particular, as Zaller reasons, voters are not interested in political consensus, because when there is no disagreement among members of the political elite, the underlying policy is still likely to be accepted no matter who is in office. It is only when politicians fail to reach consensus that voters have an incentive to find out which side is better and which party endorses what, so that they know whom to vote for in an election.

Although the works by Downs and Zaller are concerned with democracies, their observations can be applied to competitive authoritarian regimes. The reason is that voters in nondemocracies are no less busy than their democratic counterparts, but the chance that their votes can effect political changes is even smaller. For this reason, we should expect to find in autocracies the same type of rationally ignorant citizens, who avoid spending time acquiring political information.

Given that their time is scarce, voters in authoritarian regimes would also consume political news selectively. What kind of political news would appeal to voters in authoritarian regimes? I argue that they would also be intrigued more by political conflicts than by political consensus. By political conflicts, I refer to any disagreement between political parties or within them. The rationale behind is not entirely the same as what Zaller explains that voters want to find out an appropriate candidate to vote for. After all, their choice of candidate, in all likelihood, will not matter in an authoritarian election anyway. Rather, I argue that the reason is threefold. First, conflicts are inherently more colorful, for they often produce winners and losers, let alone dramas. Even if the outcomes are beyond ordinary citizens' control, they would still find political conflicts amusing, as if they were spectators of an exciting horse race. Second, authoritarian politics is opaque. In some autocracies, citizens will only be able to see a standing ovation of the parliament at the end of a dictator's speech. Rarely can the public observe open confrontations between members of the political elite. In other words, political conflicts can pique ordinary citizens' curiosity about the inner workings of the mysterious authoritarian state, even if they support neither side of the conflicts. Finally, conflicts that involve an open challenge against the ruling elite (e.g., watching an opposition legislator disparaging high-ranking government officials in parliamentary proceedings) are particularly engaging because ordinary people have neither the chance nor the courage to do likewise in their everyday life. Thus, we have the next assumption:

Assumption 11 *High-intensity political conflicts are more likely to capture voters' attention than low-intensity ones.*

It is important to note that Assumption 11 does not presume that voters will identify with people who initiate high-intensity political conflicts. Parliamentary brawls can arrest voters' attention, but it does not imply that voters would be more likely to vote for legislators who start the fight.

2.2   The Analytical Model

In this section, I discuss the analytical model based on the behavioral assumptions presented in the previous section. The formal details of the derived results are presented in the appendix to this chapter. The model consists of a sequence of moves by the four stakeholders, namely the ruling elite, the opposition, the media, and a representative voter. The representative voter refers to an individual from whom the opposition (and the ruling elite) courts political support. She may be a regular prodemocracy voter or a voter in a local constituency where the opposition has fielded a candidate. She may not be the "median voter," whose vote would decide an election. Even if she is the median voter, of course, her vote may not be decisive as is commonly assumed in studies of democratic elections. This is because the playing field of authoritarian elections is skewed heavily in favor of the ruling elite (Assumption 2). For example, in Hong Kong, only a limited number of legislative seats are open for direct election. As a result, even if the opposition obtains a majority vote in a popular election, it still cannot become the parliamentary majority.

The ruling elite moves first by making two political decisions. The first is to decide the level of media freedom, α. For simplicity, I assume that media freedom takes two possible values: α_H and α_L, with $\alpha_H > \alpha_L$. As with most political decisions, restricting media freedom comes at a cost, as the state may need to set up a bureaucracy to constantly monitor printed material and broadcasted content and hire IT experts to develop a comprehensive Internet censorship system. More importantly, tight information controls are associated with a serious economic side effect. Market capitalism depends on the free flow of information (Friedman 2009; Hayek 1945). When information is suppressed for political reasons (e.g., financial reporters are not allowed to expose the corruption of state-owned banks), resources cannot be allocated efficiently, and economic agents would fail to get the prices right. To characterize the costliness of limiting media freedom, denote the ruling elite's cost of imposing α by μ, where $\mu(\alpha_H) = 0$ and $\mu(\alpha_L) > 0$.

The second decision is to set the amount of resources invested in non-programmatic politics ("patronage"),[11] $\beta \in (0, 1)$, with a high value indicating more patronage. Presumably, distributing private benefits is costly. The cost lies not

---

[11]Patronage in some extant studies refers to a specific kind of non-programmatic politics that involves intraparty transfers of benefits (e.g., Stokes et al. 2013). For simplicity, I use the terms patronage and non-programmatic politics interchangeably in this chapter.

only in the spoils themselves but also in the establishment and management of a pervasive and operative distribution network. Wang and Kurzman (2007) provide a vivid account of how expensive such a system was in Taiwan. Based on their fieldwork during an election period in 1993, they found that in order to construct a political machine in a country with no established local factions, the ruling party Kuomintang had to recruit more than 600 local brokers, which amounted to 3 % of the county's voting population. For many dictatorships, however, setting such a high β is not financially feasible because their economy is underdeveloped. Comparatively, the cost of imposing media controls ($\mu(\alpha_L)$) to them is lower, precisely because they lack a vibrant market economy that would require free flows of information.

There are, of course, authoritarian regimes where the state intervenes heavily in the economy, while achieving impressive economic growth. Examples include some famous developmental states, such as Taiwan under the Kuomintang dictatorship and the current PRC. Because the state sector of these regimes profits directly and handsomely from the economic development, the ruling elite have substantial resources at their disposal. As a result, they can afford maintaining an expansive patronage system down to the neighborhood level (i.e., a high β), together with tight media controls. As shown in Eq. 2.4, α_L and a high β would severely constrain the opposition's ability to attract electoral support. However, compared with all dictatorships that have existed in human history, this kind of developmental authoritarian regimes is more the exception than the rule. Most authoritarian regimes have enduring economic underperformance, which limits the ruling elite's ability to distribute spoils. Their state capacity may permit them only to exercise media controls, but not to simultaneously maintain a nationwide spoil system to marginalize the opposition.

The ruling elite would select α and β as long as the respective marginal benefit is greater than or equal to the marginal cost.[12] Because we are interested in knowing

---

[12]Formally, let η denote the cost of patronage, which increases in β (or mathematically, $d\eta/d\beta > 0$). Define the ruling elite's objective function as

$$B(\alpha, \beta) - \mu - \eta$$

where $B(\alpha, \beta)$ denotes the political benefit derived from manipulating α and β, with $B(\alpha_L) > B(\alpha_H)$ and $\partial B/\partial \beta > 0$. The benefit of manipulating α and β, namely, B, stems from lowering the probability that the representative voter would vote for the opposition, although minimizing the opposition's vote share is possibly not the only factor that the ruling elite would consider when deciding α and β. The ruling elite would opt for media freedom if

$$B(\alpha_L) - \mu(\alpha_L) \geq B(\alpha_H)$$

and raise patronage inputs to the point where

$$\frac{\partial B}{\partial \beta} \geq \frac{d\eta}{d\beta}.$$

how media freedom may affect authoritarian elections, the following analysis focuses primarily on a case in which the ruling elite finds the cost of media controls too high to pay, such that the authoritarian government permits media freedom, namely, α_H.

After observing the ruling elite's decisions, the opposition responds by making two political decisions. The first is to decide the amount of resources invested in local constituencies, denoted by a nonnegative number y. By Assumption 7, voters value non-programmatic benefits offered by political parties. As a result, the opposition has an incentive to cater to the voters' demands in this respect. It is also important to note that non-programmatic benefits, as was discussed, are not confined to tangible items such as money, meals, and public construction works.

Non-programmatic benefits are not the only tool that the opposition would utilize to gain political support. By Assumption 8, voters in authoritarian regimes would be more likely to support the opposition when they are dissatisfied with the ruling elite on ideological grounds. Therefore, another effective way for the opposition to drum up support is to "educate" voters by exposing the shortcomings and wrongdoings of the authoritarian establishment. The more people notice the regime's problems, the higher the public dissatisfaction is with the ruling elite. The opposition can achieve this by signaling voters about the demerits of the ruling elite, denoted by a nonnegative number x. However, since the opposition is unable to communicate directly with voters, its signal has to be transmitted through the media. The media are certainly not the opposition's mouthpiece such that the opposition elite can dictate to them what to report. What the opposition can do, though, is to engage in noisy political actions, in hopes of getting the media's attention. By noisy political actions, I refer to all kinds of lawful resistance actions against the authoritarian regime, including, but not limited to, public demonstrations, sit-in movements, hunger strikes, public speeches, online and offline petitions, writing an op-ed in newspapers, tweeting satirical comic strips, and posting scandalous videos of government officials on YouTube.[13] These actions aim to (a) expose the ills of the ruling elite and (b) create noise to attract the public's attention. For the sake of simplicity, I call all these actions "protests."

From this perspective, one can interpret the opposition's signal, x, as the amount of protests it stages, which is essentially the second decision the opposition must make. Suppose that the opposition faces a resource constraint such that $x + y \leq n$. One simple way to interpret n is to suppose that offering constituency services (material benefits) and organizing protests require only labor inputs. Then, n is the total amount of labor available to the opposition.

After the opposition makes its choices, the media have to decide how to handle news which tarnish the reputation of the ruling elite or threaten the authoritarian political order. Two factors condition the media's decision. The first is the media controls by the government. Suppose that when media freedom is low, α_L, the

---

[13]I exclude illegal activities such as terrorism from the list because when an opposition party commits such offenses, it would be banned by the state and hence be disqualified from elections.

media can carry only positive comments about the ruling elite. In other words, social protests, including the opposition's resistance actions, which may expose the ills of the government, are censored.[14] Alternatively, when media freedom is high, α_H, the media are free to carry whatever news they deem fit. In this case, the second factor, market consideration, comes into play. By Assumption 4, media companies in authoritarian regimes also have an incentive to enlarge their market share, which implies that they would report news that interests their audience. In the realm of political news reporting, what kind of news can appeal to the consumers (namely, voters)? By Assumption 11, voters are drawn by political conflicts. Therefore, in the absence of government controls, the media have an incentive to carry news featuring political conflicts.

By this reasoning, we can characterize the media's decision in a simple mathematical structure. Denote the media's political news reporting by θ_A. We have the **media decision function**:

$$\theta_A = \begin{cases} x & \text{if } \alpha_H \\ x_0 & \text{if } \alpha_L, \end{cases} \tag{2.1}$$

where x_0 is the lowest possible level of protest activities that can be observed in a society.

The representative voter is the last one to move. In particular, she has to decide whether to vote for the opposition or not.[15] By Assumption 6, her vote choice depends on what the opposition has done in the past. In particular, as discussed throughout this chapter, voters consider casting their vote for the opposition based on two factors: (1) the amount of non-programmatic benefits received and (2) the extent of their ideological discontent with the ruling elite. It is worth elaborating on the second factor in greater detail.

Voters' belief about the ruling elite's performance comes from their own personal experience and the media (Assumption 9). Voters in authoritarian regimes, however, may not always take media reports at face value. When the information provided by the media deviates too much from their personal experience, as suggested by Assumption 11, voters would discount the credibility of the information. Denote the representative voter's dissatisfaction with the ruling elite by θ. We have the **voter decision function**:

$$\theta = \begin{cases} \theta_A & \text{if } (\theta_A - \theta_P)^2 \le c \\ \theta_P & \text{if } (\theta_A - \theta_P)^2 > c, \end{cases} \tag{2.2}$$

---

[14]The censorship can be carried out by government agencies or by the media themselves. Self-censorship in authoritarian regimes is common due to the existence of severe punishment.

[15]From the ruling elite's perspective, they may be concerned about not only the amount of vote the opposition receives but also their own vote share. As Magaloni (2006) points out, the ruling coalition has an incentive to achieve an overwhelming electoral victory as a way to discourage its own members from defecting. Because our model here deals with the interaction among the ruling elite, the opposition, and the media, we focus on the representative voter's decision of whether or not to vote for the opposition.

where θ_P is a nonnegative number denoting the voter's opinion about the ruling elite based on personal encounters, with higher values indicating greater resentment, and c is a positive constant. One can interpret c as the extent to which voters are willing to trust the media. When the trust is high, voters would believe the media even if their reports significantly deviate from the voters' personal experience.

The vote share the opposition receives is denoted by v, which is a function of θ, y, and β.

To summarize, the timeline of the analytical model is as follows:

1. The ruling elite decides media freedom and patronage, denoted by α and β, respectively.
2. The opposition decides its own patronage inputs and protests, denoted by y and x, respectively.
3. The media decide the kind of political news to report, denoted by $\theta_A(x, \alpha)$.
4. Voters vote for the opposition, who ends up receiving a vote share $v(y, \beta, \theta)$.

The model contains multiple possible equilibria. For the purpose of our discussion of the effect of free media on authoritarian elections, I would focus on the equilibrium in which the ruling elite, for various reasons, opt for low media controls. I will first present the baseline model, in which there exists only a single source of political protests, namely, an opposition party.

2.2.1 Baseline Model: Single Source of Protests

We can solve the model using backward induction. In particular, knowing that voters' support is a function denoted by $v(y, \beta, \theta)$ and that the media report news in accordance with Eq. 2.1, the opposition party needs to solve the following constrained maximization problem:

$$\underset{x,y}{\text{maximize}} \quad v(y, \beta, \theta(\theta_A(x, \alpha), \theta_P))$$

$$\text{subject to} \quad x + y = n \tag{2.3}$$

$$(\theta_A(x, \alpha) - \theta_P)^2 = c,$$

where $\theta_A(.)$ is equal to the media decision function defined in Eq. 2.1 and $\theta(.)$ the voter decision function defined in Eq. 2.2. Note also that the first equality is the opposition's resource constraint, while the second one is the representative voter's belief constraint in connection with Eq. 2.2. Both constraints hold with equality because the opposition party is assumed to have a desire of defeating the ruling elite in elections (Assumption 3), which implies that it will exhaust all possible means to increase its vote share.

In order to maximize its vote share v, the opposition party needs to court the representative voter. Suppose there exists a function f such that $f : g \rightarrow v$, where g is a function of θ, y, and β which the representative voter uses to evaluate the opposition party. Then we can replace the objective function in Eq. 2.3 with $g(\theta, y, \beta)$. Without loss of generality, assume that $g(.)$ takes the following additively separable functional form:

$$g = \theta(\theta_A(x, \alpha), \theta_P) + (1 - \beta)y$$

This functional form captures the idea that the extent to which voters would support the opposition party hinges on the opposition's protests (x), patronage (y), and media outputs. Note that patronage is associated with a weight, $1-\beta$, suggesting that the effectiveness of the opposition's patronage is inversely related to the ruling elite's own patronage inputs. Admittedly, when the ruling elite is able to launch a massive patronage blitz in local constituencies, the resource-poor opposition would have a hard time impressing voters with their own constituency services. The opposition can signal the ruling elite's shortcomings by staging protests, but its signal is nested inside the media and voter decision functions, suggesting that whether their protests can eventually appear in the media (θ_A) would depend on media freedom (α) and whether the reported protests can influence the voter's belief depends on their distance from the voter's personal experience (θ_P).

We can then simplify Eq. 2.3 as

$$\text{maximize}_{x,y} \quad \theta(\theta_A(x, \alpha), \theta_P) + (1 - \beta)y$$

$$\text{subject to} \quad x + y = n \tag{2.4}$$

$$(\theta_A(x, \alpha) - \theta_P)^2 = c$$

If the ruling elite opts for α_L and under such circumstances, $\theta_A(x, \alpha_L) = x_0$. In other words, the media under tight government control would suppress the reporting of any protest activity. Because media outputs no longer depend on x, the voter belief constraint in Eq. 2.4 becomes irrelevant. Nor does the objective function rely on x anymore. The optimal level of protests in this case would be $x^* = 0$, while the optimal patronage level would be $y^* = n$. This would mean that the opposition would invest all the resources in the distribution of patronage, as its protests can never reach voters.

A more interesting case is that the members of the ruling elite are hamstrung by a high cost of media controls such that they have to choose α_H. Under such circumstances, the opposition can signal the ruling elite's demerits by staging protests, and the ruling elite can only count on β to undermine the electoral appeal of the opposition. How can the opposition take advantage of this case? We can find out the opposition's optimal response by solving Eq. 2.4, using the Lagrange multiplier method.

Result 1 The optimal level of protests with a single source of protests is

$$x_S^* = \theta_P + \frac{\beta}{2\lambda}$$

where λ is the Lagrange multiplier with respect to the voter belief constraint. With x_S^*, the optimal patronage inputs are simply $y_S^* = n - x_S^*$.

The subscript S indicates that there exists a single source of protests. One can see that x_S^* is a function of two parameters: β and λ; in particular, the greater the incumbent's investment in β, the more restive the opposition is. As mentioned, x_S^* is the opposition's signal about the ruling elite's shortcomings. At a high level of media freedom, the opposition would always characterize the regime as something worse than the public perception (θ_P), and their signal is deviated by the term $\frac{\beta}{2\lambda}$. Because the deviation[16] also depends on λ, it is instructive to give this parameter a political interpretation. Note that mathematically, λ measures the change of the objective function at the optimal values of x and y with respect to the changes in the constraint term c. In the context of this model, λ captures the increase in the probability of the representative voter supporting the opposition when her trust in the media also increases. If the vote choice of the representative voter is not sensitive to how much she trusts the media (i.e., a small λ), the optimal level of x would then be higher, indicating that the opposition's portrayal of the ruling elite would deviate more from the public perception, as only an extreme characterization of the ruling elite can excite the representative voter.

Some argue that authoritarian elections are able to reduce political confrontations by enticing the opposition away from regime-threatening activities in exchange for public offices (Gandhi and Przeworski 2006). The result here shows that opposition parties who participate in authoritarian elections may still have an incentive to rely on protests and political confrontations to draw political support, especially when they are unable to compete with the ruling elite over the distribution of patronage. However, this strategy has its limits, as the voter belief constraint discourages the opposition from deviating too much from the social norm.

To summarize, at a high level of media freedom, the ruling elite have an incentive to raise their patronage inputs to marginalize the opposition, and the best response for the opposition is to escalate its protests and criticisms against the ruling elite. The representative voter is able to acquire information about the opposition's protests and criticisms from the media. Whether her likelihood of voting for the opposition would increase depends on the actual values of β and x.

---

[16]I choose not to use "bias" to describe the deviation to avoid a misconception that the representative voter's own belief θ_P is unbiased. As discussed, authoritarian politics is generally opaque, and the information about the ruling elite accessible to voters is necessarily limited. It is therefore improbable to assume that voters' belief about the ruling elite is any more accurate than the opposition's.

2.2.2 Multiple Sources of Protests

The baseline model assumes that no one but an opposition party would stage protests in an authoritarian regime. In this section, I relax this assumption and examine its consequences.

Social protests in authoritarian regimes can arise from multiple sources. First, the opposition is not necessarily a monolithic entity. In their struggle for democracy, opposition parties may pursue different strategies because they face different constituencies, leading to a variation in their protest activities. In Malaysia, for instance, the Pan-Malaysian Islamic Party (PAS) and the Democratic Action Party (DAP) are two major opposition parties. While the DAP's followers are predominantly ethnic Chinese, the PAS draws support from Muslims. Rivalry among opposition parties is commonplace, as evidenced by the early relationship between the PAS and the DAP (Ufen 2009). Similar tensions within the opposition camp can be found elsewhere. In her study of authoritarian politics in Egypt, Jordan, and Morocco, (Lust-Okar 2005) points out that for fear of being replaced by radical parties and losing privileges doled out by the regimes, moderate parties are reluctant to seriously challenge the incumbents.

The second reason for the existence of multiple sources of social protests is that authoritarian regimes usually lack an effective and fair institutional mechanism to resolve social disputes, in part because of widespread official corruption and in part because of the lack of judicial independence. Individuals often have no means to voice out their problems other than protests. For example, the annual number of collective resistance incidents in China had reached 180,000 in 2010 (Fewsmith 2013). Behind this staggering number is hundreds of thousands of aggrieved individuals who were forced to learn how to negotiate their rights through resistance, as the court system has failed to redress their grievances (O'Brien and Li 2006).

Finally, nonpartisan social activists can also organize protests in authoritarian regimes. Although authoritarian regimes are generally associated with a low level of civil liberties, civil society organizations nevertheless exist in many authoritarian regimes. The experience of countries such as the Philippines, South Korea, and Taiwan suggests that labor unions and religious groups can play an active role in the democratization through protests and dissenting publications.

When dealing with different kinds of social protests, how would the media prioritize their reporting? According to Assumption 4, the media endeavor to enlarge their audience size, so they have an incentive for delivering news that appeals to news consumers, provided that their news reports are within acceptable political limits. Going by Assumption 11, news consumers, or voters in general, are engaged more by high-intensity political conflicts than by low-intensity ones. Consequently, if the media behave rationally, they would give priority to extraordinary protests, rather than garden-variety political gestures. An important implication from this is that extreme political events would be overrepresented in the news under a relatively free media environment. This observation is in line with the experience in the United

States, where media freedom is high. Paletz and Entman (1981) have long observed that "drama is a defining characteristics of news...[a]n event is particularly newsworthy if it has some elements of a dramatic narrative (p. 17)." Bennett (2012) points out that the predilection for dramatized news has led the American media to "look for the most extreme cases rather than the most representative examples of a subject (p. 57)."

To characterize the media's reporting preference over competing sources of protest activities, we can rewrite the media decision function (Eq. 2.1) as

$$\theta_A = \begin{cases} \max\{x_1, x_2, \dots\} & \text{if } \alpha_H \\ x_0 & \text{if } \alpha_L, \end{cases} \tag{2.5}$$

where x_0 is the lowest possible level of protest activities that can be observed in society and $\{x_1, x_2, \dots\}$ is a list of actual protest activities organized by different parties and groups.

Again, we are interested in knowing what would happen to the opposition when media freedom is high. Consider a simple case, in which there are multiple protesting civil society groups, plus one opposition party.

Result 2 As β approaches 1, the electoral support of the opposition party would decrease if a civil society group that is more radical than the opposition party exists.

This result suggests that media freedom may not always serve the opposition party's interests. When political news is overwhelmingly dominated by a radical civil society group, voters would find the media uninformative about the true performance of the ruling elite. They will discount the media's credibility and evaluate the ruling elite based on their own personal experience. This implies that the opposition would no longer be able to take advantage of media freedom to influence the public perception of the ruling elite. Combined with the ruling elite's aggressive distribution of patronage ($\beta \to 1$), the resulting probability of voting for the opposition is lower than that found in the baseline model.

In reality, how common is it to find civil society groups that are more radical than the opposition party? That is, is it common to have civil society groups willing to engage in more radical protests than the opposition party? I argue that this is highly plausible. Although I do not model the behavior of civil society organizations in the analytical model, one can imagine that their behavior would be somewhat akin to that of the opposition party. In particular, civil society organizations also have their own constituents (McCarthy and Zald 1977). While they have to take action (such as protests) to advance their constituents' interests, their action is simultaneously constrained by the norms of their constituents. Norms, or acceptable limits of action, vary from one organization to another. Because for most civil society organizations, the constituents they represent are substantially smaller than the constituents of an elected official, one would observe an enormous variation with regard to their norms. It is not surprising that some organizations tolerate political actions that are deemed improper in society.

In many authoritarian regimes, civil society is not developed enough as to produce sufficient protest-prone organizations that crowd out the voice of the opposition in the media. But the foregoing "curse" of media freedom is still relevant to them, as long as their opposition force is in disunity. Opposition parties in authoritarian regimes may have a common enemy, but their political ideologies can be poles apart. Some parties take a radical stance and base their support in a narrower constituency. For example, Malaysia's PAS endorses Islamic fundamentalism, which has limited its electoral appeal vis-á-vis more centrist opposition parties. Because their sources of political support are different, opposition parties' incentives to protest would also vary. This variation leads to an unequal distribution of media attention, which would in turn affect the electoral chances of the opposition camp as a whole.

We can characterize their interaction by modifying the baseline model to include two opposition parties: the moderate (M) and the radical (R).[17] To focus on intra-opposition competition, I assume that only the opposition parties are able to mount protests, implying that civil society organizations are excluded.

The moderate and radical opposition parties draw political support from different constituencies, which is a result that follows from Assumption 5 that voters have heterogeneous ideologies such that some individuals are more receptive to political radicalism than others. Because of voters' heterogeneous ideologies, the voting decision of the model no longer belongs to one representative voter. Instead, suppose that there exist two groups of voters, moderate and radical, who separately make a voting decision.

Denote the share of moderate voters, who constitute at least half of the population, by $\tau \geq \frac{1}{2}$. The share of radical voters is, thus, $1 - \tau$. The opposition parties would conceivably target different constituencies; the moderate opposition courts the support of moderate voters, while the radical opposition the support of radical voters.

As in the baseline model, these parties need to solve a constrained maximization problem similar to Eq. 2.3. However, because they base their support on different constituencies, they face a different voter belief constraint in their respective constrained maximization problems. Without loss of generality, assume the moderate opposition's voter belief constraint is the same as the baseline model, $(\theta_A(x_M, x_R, \alpha) - \theta_P)^2 = c$. But the radical opposition's version is $(\theta_A(x_M, x_R, \alpha) - \theta_P)^2 = \frac{c}{\omega}$, for some $\omega \in (0, 1)$. The parameter ω suggests that the voter belief constraint of the radical opposition is more lax than that of its moderate counterpart. The rationale behind this laxity is that radical voters, namely, the target constituency of the radical opposition, tend to have greater tolerance of, if not desire for, political radicalism. Assuming that ω is negatively related to τ, this implies that fewer voters endorse extreme political values. Further, assume that ω is common knowledge

---

[17] I use the terms "moderate" and "radical" in the relative sense. The definition of radical varies from society to society. In some countries, throwing eggs at officials is considered radical, while in others, this is a mild expression of discontent.

in the model, so that the opposition parties are aware of each other's ideology (moderate or radical). We can then derive the following result:

Result 3 *The electoral support of the opposition camp as a whole would decrease, as the radical opposition party becomes more radical.*

The derivation of this result, which is presented in the appendix to this chapter, is similar to that of Result 2. The main idea is that the radical opposition party would crowd out the moderate opposition party in the media, thereby alienating the latter's supporters. A notable feature of Result 3 is that it holds true regardless of the electoral rule. It is easy to see why this is the case when the electoral rule is a single-member district system. The radical opposition party, given its narrow constituency, has no chance of capturing a seat in a single-member district. Because only the moderate party may be able to win, crowding it out in the media would undermine the electoral support of the entire opposition camp. On the other hand, when the electoral rule is proportional representation, one may expect to see a certain "division of labor" among the opposition elite – the moderate party attracting moderate voters and the radical party attracting radical voters – such that the aggregate vote share of the opposition camp would increase. This is not the case. As shown in the appendix, political messages of the moderate party would not be able to reach its intended audience due to the overrepresentation of the radical party's messages in the media. Consequently, the opposition camp would lose the support of moderate voters.

Result 3 suggests that the opposition camp would be worse off if the radical opposition party becomes more extreme. An important follow-up question is would the opposition camp be worse off by having a radical opposition party at all? In other words, we would like to know if having a diverse group of opposition parties, instead of a single one, is always bad for the opposition camp.

Result 4 *As β approaches 1, the electoral support received by a diverse group of opposition parties would be lower than that received by a single opposition party unless $1 - \tau \geq \omega$.*

To put Result 4 into perspective, recall that $1 - \tau \leq \frac{1}{2}$ is the share of radical voters and ω is a parameter that determines radical voters' tolerance of deviating protest signals. Suppose that radical voters constitute exactly half of the population $(1 - \tau = \frac{1}{2})$. The result here then suggests that ω is smaller than or equal to $\frac{1}{2}$ at least. This implies that, by inspecting the voter belief constraint of radical voters, radical voters' tolerance is double than that of moderate voters'. In other words, the polity needs to have half of the population who are a hundred percent more radical than the remaining half. This is a stringent condition in all likelihood. If this stringent condition fails to hold, the electoral support received by a diverse group of opposition parties would be lower than that received by a single opposition party. Result 4, thus, suggests that even in the presence of media freedom, the ruling elite is still able to undermine the opposition camp by using patronage, as long as there are multiple parties within the opposition camp.

The foregoing result suggests a rather counterintuitive result. In isolation, media freedom, a vibrant civil society, and a pluralistic coalition of opposition parties are each considered good for democratic transitions. When taken together, however, their positive effects may somehow cancel out each other. It is important to emphasize that the result does not suggest that media freedom is harmful to democratization. In fact, it can be shown that even if multiple opposition parties exist, having media freedom is always better than otherwise, all else held constant:

$$g_{M.R|\alpha_H} > g_{M.R|\alpha_L},$$

where $g_{M.R|\alpha}$ is the probability of voters casting votes for the opposition parties given α.

2.3 Conclusion

The analytical model presented in this chapter, albeit stylized, captures some key aspects pertaining to the electoral contestation between the ruling elite of an authoritarian regime and the opposition parties in the presence of a free media. Authoritarian regimes dislike media freedom for various reasons. My model illustrates that to the members of the opposition elite who participate in authoritarian elections, having media freedom is always better than not having it at all, as the media help the opposition promote its cause among voters. But my model also shows that the positive effect of media freedom should not be overrated; it may not be a vital threat to the ruling elite because of the following reasons:

1. *The benefits of media freedom tend to accrue to radical political players (parties or social activists) rather than to moderate ones.*
2. *The benefits of media freedom that the opposition camp as a whole can reap in elections would decrease in the radicalness of its radical members.*
3. *The ruling elite can further marginalize the moderate members of the opposition elite by distributing patronage.*

The analytical model has laid important foundations for understanding the politics of Hong Kong after 1997. In particular, it provides an answer to the puzzle that I discussed in the introductory chapter, namely, why the electoral support of prodemocracy opposition parties keeps shrinking, when the social demand for democratization remains high, if not higher than before. The reason is that Beijing-sponsored parties, constrained by a liberal media environment inherited from the colonial government, have found it necessary to develop an extensive grassroots network from scratch to counter the electoral threats of the opposition elite. This strategy has turned out to be a great success, as attested by these major parties' ever-increasing vote and seat shares in the legislature since the retrocession. Meanwhile, the opposition elite has been splintered into smaller political parties. Facing Beijing-sponsored parties' increasing effort in patronage distribution, these smaller parties deprioritize constituency services. Instead, they resort to more radical actions to drum up political support, a strategy that sets them apart from older opposition parties. This "division of labor," however, is accelerating the decline in the opposition camp's overall electoral support. Paradoxically, all this is happening in a period that has witnessed a flourishing civil society and media freedom largely unscathed by political repression.

The rest of the book will discuss how the electoral politics between the pro-establishment elite and the opposition has been playing out according to the model's predictions as follows:

- Chapter 3 will present background information on Hong Kong's political institutions after 1997 and discuss how postcolonial Hong Kong has inherited a high degree of media freedom from the former colonial administration.
- Chapter 4 will examine how media freedom tends to favor the radical members of the opposition elite by lowering the cost of reaching out to the target constituency. While benefiting these radical members, the media end up marginalizing the voices of the moderate members of the opposition elite, thereby alienating the moderate prodemocracy voters. Consequently, the electoral support for the opposition camp as a whole declines.
- Chapter 5 will explain why Beijing-sponsored parties in Hong Kong are keen on developing grassroots political networks, although they are widely perceived to be politically insignificant, so as to further marginalize the moderate members of the opposition elite.
- Chapter 6 will present empirical evidence that shows how the grassroots strategy of Beijing-sponsored parties has contributed to undermining the opposition in legislative elections.

Appendix: Proofs

This appendix provides the formal details of the results in this chapter.

Result 2 As β approaches 1, the electoral support of the opposition party would decrease if a civil society group that is more radical than the opposition party exists.

Suppose the opposition party solves its constrained maximization problem given in Eq. 2.4 and sets $x = x_S^*$. Unlike in the baseline model, the media, given the media's reporting preference in Eq. 2.5, they would not report x_S^* if there exists some $x_G > x_S^*$, where x_G is a protest staged by civil society group G. Suppose $\theta_A = x_G$. This would change θ, the representative voter's assessment of the ruling elite. According to Eq. 2.2, when $\theta_A = x_G$, $\theta = \theta_P$ because x_G no longer satisfies the voter belief constraint. Knowing that its choice of x_S^* would not affect θ, the opposition party, by backward induction, would not protest at all. Instead, it would put all its resources into distributing patronage. Hence, we have $x_{CS}^* = 0$ and $y_{CS}^* = n$, where the subscript CS denotes the situation when a radical civil society group exists. Substituting θ_P for θ in $v(.)$, which is the representative voter's probability of voting for the opposition, and then expressing v in terms of $g(.)$, we have

$$g_{CS} = \theta_P + (1 - \beta)n < x_S^* + (1 - \beta)y_S^* = g_S.$$

The above inequality holds true because $\beta \to 1$ and $\theta_P < x_S^*$.

Result 3 *The electoral support of the opposition camp as a whole would decrease, as the radical opposition party becomes more radical.*

First, note that the constrained maximization problems for the moderate and radical opposition parties are, respectively,

$$\begin{aligned}\underset{x_M,y_M}{\text{maximize}} \quad & v(y_M, \beta, \theta(\theta_A(x_M, x_R, \alpha), \theta_P)) \\ \text{subject to} \quad & x_M + y_M = n_M \\ & (\theta_A(x_M, x_R, \alpha) - \theta_P)^2 = c\end{aligned} \tag{2.6}$$

and

$$\begin{aligned}\underset{x_R,y_R}{\text{maximize}} \quad & v(y_R, \beta, \theta(\theta_A(x_M, x_R, \alpha), \theta_P)) \\ \text{subject to} \quad & x_R + y_R = n_R \\ & (\theta_A(x_M, x_R, \alpha) - \theta_P)^2 = \frac{c}{\omega}\end{aligned} \tag{2.7}$$

To find out the optimal protest level for these opposition parties, we first check how they solve the constrained maximization problems independently (i.e., without considering the protest level of the other side). Substituting the function $g(.)$ for v and using the Lagrange multiplier method, the optimal protests level for the radical opposition is

$$x_R^* = \theta_P + \frac{\beta}{2\lambda\omega}$$

For the moderate opposition, because its constrained maximization problem independent of x_R is essentially shown in Eq. 2.4, the solution for x_M would be identical to that of Eq. 2.4. Call this value $x_M^{\text{Baseline}} = \theta_P + \frac{\beta}{2\lambda}$. Note that x_M^{Baseline} is not the optimal protest level for the moderate opposition because θ_A is nevertheless dependent on both x_M and x_R. In particular, because $0 < \omega < 1$, $x_R^* > x_M^{\text{Baseline}}$, this suggests that at a high level of media freedom, political news would be swamped by the radical opposition's actions, namely, $\theta_A = x_R^*$. As the radical opposition crowds out the moderate opposition in the media, only the former's protest signal can reach voters.

This has two implications for the moderate opposition party. First, its voter belief constraint no longer depends on its signal x_M, which means that this constraint becomes irrelevant. Nor does its objective function rely on x_M. This is because moderate voters are exposed to the radical party's protests in the news, which deviates too much from their personal experience. Consequently, moderate voters will disregard the radical's signals and evaluate the ruling elite based solely on their personal experience, θ_P. Aware that its signal would be overwhelmed by the radical opposition, using backward induction, the moderate party would find the best protest level simply $x_M^* = 0$. This may violate its voter belief constraint, but as mentioned, this constraint is no longer active due to the domination of the radical opposition's signal in the media. When $x_M^* = 0$, according to the resource constraint, $y_M^* = n_M$. In other words, the moderate opposition party would focus all its resources in the distribution of patronage, rather than protests.

The extent to which voters would support the opposition as a whole, given media freedom, is

$$g_{M.R} = \tau(\theta_P + (1 - \beta)n_M) + (1 - \tau)(x_R^* + (1 - \beta)y_R^*) \tag{2.8}$$

The first term on the right is the probability of moderate voters casting votes for the opposition times their population share, while the second term is the radical voters' probability times their respective population share. By assumption, τ is negatively related to ω. Thus, if the radical party tries to woo extreme voters (with small ω), $g_{M.R}$ would decrease because τ increases.

Result 4 As β approaches 1, the electoral support received by a diverse group of opposition parties would be lower than that received by a single opposition party unless $1 - \tau \geq \omega$.

We need to find out the condition for the following:

$$g_{M.R} \geq g_S = x_S^* + (1 - \beta)y_S^* \tag{2.9}$$

where g_S is the evaluation of the opposition by the representative voter when only a single opposition party exists.

When $\beta \rightarrow 1$, Eq. 2.9 can be reduced to

$$\tau\theta_P + (1 - \tau)x_R^* \geq x_S^*$$

$$\frac{x_R^* - x^*}{x_R^* - \theta_P} \geq \tau$$

$$1 - \tau \geq \omega,$$

using the fact that $x_R^* = \theta_P + \frac{\beta}{2\lambda\omega}$ and $x_S^* = \theta_P + \frac{\beta}{2\lambda}$.

Chapter 3
Birds in a Cage: Political Institutions and Civil Society in Hong Kong

All political systems have some kinds of institutions, under which political agents interact with each other and learn how to play by the rules over time. Although institutions are not immutable, changing them is often difficult due to the resistance of vested interests, who have benefited from the existing institutions after spending years learning how to exploit the system (Olson 2008). Given the importance and stickiness of institutions, when there is a chance to change them, rational political agents have a strong incentive to design the rules to maximize their long-run interests.

When Great Britain ended its colonization of Hong Kong in 1997, all political rules of the city had to be rewritten. Not surprisingly, the formal political institutions of postcolonial Hong Kong are a piece of political craftsmanship of Beijing. The Basic Law, the mini-constitution of the Hong Kong Special Administrative Region, which provides the foundation of all political institutions established after 1997, offers plenty of examples that illustrate how Beijing maximized its interests under various constraints in the 1980s when the Basic Law was drafted and adopted. In particular, Beijing's main interest was to entrench the colonial political order characterized by executive dominance and low democratic accountability, while preserving the city's prosperity grounded in a robust free market economy (Scott 2000; Lee 1999; Xu 1993).

The rest of this chapter consists of three parts. First, I will discuss the historical background of Hong Kong's sovereignty transfer and the challenges Beijing faced while negotiating Hong Kong's handover with the Great Britain. Then, I will provide an overview of major political institutions in postcolonial Hong Kong. Finally, I examine how Hong Kong's civil society developed under the postcolonial political system.

© Springer Science+Business Media Singapore 2015
S.H.-W. Wong, *Electoral Politics in Post-1997 Hong Kong*,
DOI 10.1007/978-981-287-387-3_3

3.1   Historical Background

Hong Kong's reunification issue emerged in the 1970s, when the lease of a certain part of the territory (the New Territories) was due to expire. While the British government was eager to keep Hong Kong, the PRC at that point showed little interest in extending what was considered "unequal treaties" which the Qing court signed at gunpoint in the mid-nineteenth century.[1] In fact, in his New Year's message of 1979, Deng made national reunification one of the three top political agendas for China (Vogel 2011, p. 479). Beijing was therefore pleased to discuss Hong Kong's sovereignty issue with Great Britain.

From Beijing's perspective, Hong Kong's retrocession had at least two important values to the PRC. First, successful reunification with Hong Kong would establish a precedent, or at least suggest a solution, to deal with reunification with Taiwan. Second, Hong Kong by that time had already achieved great economic success and became one of the major sources of foreign direct investment to China.[2] Some even compared Hong Kong to "the goose that laid the golden eggs" (Lieberthal 1992, p. 671). Getting Hong Kong back would certainly help the PRC pursue another of its top political agenda: Four Modernizations.[3]

However, the retrocession of Hong Kong had been a challenging task to Beijing from the outset for several reasons. First, politically, the city had been separated from the mainland for over a century. The population had developed its unique way of life in the postwar era, largely unscathed from the political turbulence that engulfed the Communist China. This is not to say that the influences of communism had never reached the city. In fact, as early as 1938, the Central Committee of the Chinese Communist Party set up an office of the Eighth Route Army in Hong Kong. After the Second World War, the CCP further established various agencies, including the Hong Kong Federation of Trade Unions (FTU) and the Xinhua News Agency, as part of its united front work. In addition, some pro-Communist groups have attempted a few times to subvert the colonial administration (e.g., the 1967 Leftist Riots). Despite all these covert infiltration and overt subversion attempts, the political influences of pro-Communist leftists were severely limited by the colonial government's heavy-handed controls and a lack of support from Beijing.[4]

---

[1] Before Deng took the helm, Beijing had declined Portugal's requests to return Macao in 1967 and 1974. Mao Zedong also indicated to a former British Prime Minister in 1975 that the time for resolving the Hong Kong issue was not ripe (Vogel 2011, p. 488).

[2] In 1985, Hong Kong's investment in China accounted for 49 % of the country's total FDI (State Statistical Bureau, the People's Republic of China 1987, p. 221).

[3] The goal of Four Modernizations was to promote the country's agriculture, industry, science and technology, and national defense.

[4] After the CCP took over China, it decided to adopt a pragmatic policy, known as "long-term planning and full utilization" (*changqi dasuan, chongfen liyong*)," to deal with Hong Kong (Yep 2009, p. 86). This is because the CCP saw Hong Kong as a British colony had certain strategic value to Beijing. For instance, during the Korean War, when the PRC faced Western trade embargoes,

Hong Kong had a highly developed and globally integrated economy, touted by many, economist Milton Friedman included, as an exemplar of free market capitalism. In particular, it had already transformed itself into a modern business metropolis and an emerging world financial center by the 1980s. Two decades of spectacular growth, with a per capita GDP that leapfrogged from HK$2,300 in 1961 to HK$23,000 in 1979 (Census and Statistics Department, 2013), made the city internationally known as one of the "Four Little Dragons" in Asia. By contrast, until the mid-1970s, the socialist economy of mainland China had mired in long-term economic stagnation.

Socially, Hong Kong has long been known as a "refugee society" (Miners 1995; Hughes 1968), as a significant portion of the population were mainland Chinese who came to Hong Kong to seek refuge from political unrest. Of the Chinese immigrants, many were former victims of the CCP's suppression or supporters of the Kuomintang. With their deep-seated suspicion of and antagonism toward the CCP, they constituted a potent social force in opposition to the authoritarian state of the PRC.

That said, there were also people critical of British colonialism as well as Western-style capitalism. To these people, the Communist China had once presented an attractive ideological alternative. However, it had lost much of its appeal by the 1970s, in part because political turmoil at home and in the mainland triggered widespread disillusionment with the CCP (Mathews et al. 2007; Scott 1989) and also because the colonial administration began to engage in community development to meet rising local demands (Lui et al. 2005). Most notably, the government started implementing a nine-year compulsory education in 1978. The expansion of education opportunities helped spread the ideas of Western democracy and human rights that gradually took root in Hong Kong society.

In short, when the PRC and Great Britain negotiated Hong Kong's sovereignty in the early 1980s, the city had already achieved a high degree of affluence, developed a mature free market economy, and had fostered an increasingly assertive civil society. None of these factors seemed favorable to Hong Kong's reunification with an economically backward mainland China that was still under the authoritarian rule of the CCP. Indeed, within a year after then British Prime Minister Margaret Thatcher's visit to Beijing to discuss Hong Kong's future, the colony's currency lost one-third of its original value, as the local people began to dump the Hong Kong dollar in exchange for foreign currencies that they felt to be safe. To contain the financial crisis, the colonial government announced in 1983 the implementation of a fixed exchange rate by pegging the city's currency to US dollar.

Although the new exchange rate system helped stabilize the financial market, it failed to solve the confidence crisis that struck the former colony. Most notably, in 1984, Jardine Matheson, a huge British business conglomerate based in Hong

---

Hong Kong served as an important back door for Beijing to acquire foreign resources (Carroll 2007, p. 142).

Kong for more than a hundred years, announced the change of its legal domicile to Bermuda. The confidence crisis was not confined to the British business community. Prominent local families such as the Hotungs and the Cheung Yuk-leungs also gradually sold off their Hong Kong assets (Feng 1997).

It was not only the business elite that lacked confidence in their city's future. As mentioned, a sizable population of Hong Kong had been former mainland refugees, and they were gripped by the fear that their refuge would soon become part of the state from which they fled. In one public opinion survey conducted in 1982, only 2 % of the respondents preferred the mainland to Hong Kong as their place of residence, while 86 % preferred otherwise (Cheng 1984). For this reason, starting from the mid-1980s, more and more people began to vote with their feet in response to the uncertain future of their city. A massive wave of emigration emerged. Conceivably, those who had the financial means to acquire a foreign nationality were also economically productive. Their departure meant not only a brain drain but also a great loss of capital, as these people had brought their assets abroad. According to one estimate, each outgoing family took HK$1.5 million away from Hong Kong (Lam 1989), resulting in a total capital outflow of HK$160 billion between 1982 and 1992.

These negative developments deeply troubled Beijing (Xu 1998). Deng Xiaoping was fully aware of the challenges of taking back Hong Kong. He saw that the Hong Kong problem was not only about gaining its sovereignty from Great Britain[5] but also about securing a smooth transition, in order to avoid jeopardizing the city's prosperity (Deng 2004). A smooth transition required restoring the city's confidence in its future. Deng opined that the greatest chasm between the PRC and Hong Kong lay in their economic systems. The following comment Deng made to Thatcher in 1984 succinctly summarized his view:

> If we had wanted to achieve reunification by imposing socialism on Hong Kong, not all three parties would have accepted it. And reluctant acquiescence by some parties would have led to turmoil. Even if there had been no armed conflict, Hong Kong would have become a bleak city with a host of problems, and that is not something that we would have wanted (cited in Ghai (1999, p. 140)).

Unusual as it was, Deng's candor was understandable. The target audience of his speech was probably not only Thatcher but also the citizens of Hong Kong themselves. He wanted to convey a clear message that Beijing had no intention of tampering with the way of life Hong Kong people had enjoyed. Meanwhile, Beijing accelerated its united front work to mobilize support from Hong Kong society. In particular, thanks to the colonial administration's initiation of limited political liberalization, the early 1980s witnessed the emergence of a new generation of political leaders, who entered politics through grassroots elections. Although they

---

[5]The British government was reluctant to return Hong Kong to the PRC. Margaret Thatcher once made a proposal that separated sovereignty from administration: while the mainland resumed Hong Kong's sovereignty, Great Britain would continue to keep the city's administration. Deng firmly rejected her proposal.

represented only a narrow constituency in Hong Kong, some of these grassroots leaders were invited to visit Beijing to meet top leaders such as Deng and to review the National Day military parade (Ma 2012, p. 12). Another example was that some Hong Kong student activists wrote a letter to Zhao Ziyang, then the Premier of the PRC, calling for "reunification with democratization" (*minzhu huigui*), i.e., allowing Hong Kong to have democracy at the time of reunification. Zhao not only gave them a reply but also affirmed that democratic governance of Hong Kong was beyond doubt (*lisuo dangran de*) (Ma 2012, p. 56). All these moves demonstrated how anxious Beijing was in courting the Hong Kong people's political support.

These political gestures were nothing but cheap talk, however. Deng knew that there was no way to convince Hong Kong people unless the CCP tied its own hands. Against this background, Deng proposed an unprecedented idea: one country, two systems.[6] The "one country, two systems" principle guarantees that Hong Kong can preserve its own capitalist system, which would be separate from the socialist system of the PRC. As will be discussed, this principle actually goes beyond the economic realm, as Hong Kong after the transition was also allowed to keep political institutions distinct from the rest of China. Deng further pledged to apply the "one country, two systems" principle in Hong Kong for 50 years.[7] But most remarkably, Hong Kong as a Chinese city was permitted to have its own mini-constitution, namely, the Basic Law, which contains the aforementioned pledges made by Deng. Because the Basic Law provides a contractual basis that delimits the power relationship between the central authorities and Hong Kong, it can be considered as a good example to illustrate how an authoritarian ruler uses political institutions to establish a credible commitment not to abuse his subjects (Gehlbach and Keefer 2011; Magaloni 2008).

While seeing the necessity of making concessions, Beijing was conscious of the importance to defend its own political interests. It carefully designed the Basic Law in order to reconcile these conflicting objectives. Beijing's political craftsmanship manifests itself in postcolonial Hong Kong's institutional arrangements, which I will examine in detail in the following section.

3.2 Major Institutional Arrangements Under the Basic Law

As discussed, Hong Kong experienced a massive outflow of both capital and talent in the 1980s due to a widespread confidence crisis. The most important task for Beijing was to convince the runaway economic elite that Hong Kong was safe to stay even

---

[6]The "one country, two systems" principle was originally designed for the reunification with Taiwan.

[7]What would happen after 50 years? Deng suggested that there was no need to worry, as the two systems would gradually converge after 50 years (Deng 2004, pp. 18, 38, and 64).

after the sovereignty transition. For this reason, many provisions of the Basic Law were intended to preserve the economic system that existed in colonial Hong Kong.

The colonial economic system was worth preserving because Hong Kong achieved its prosperity under this very system. Many touted the colonial government for its adherence to free market capitalism, characterized by a balanced budget, low taxation, and a small and noninterventionist government, which, as some believe, underpinned the city's miraculous growth in the postwar period. Nevertheless, more and more academic studies point out that Hong Kong's laissez-faire capitalism is a myth at best. In particular, some argue that "laissez-faire" is simply an euphemism for the colonial government's lack of commitment in the long-term development of the colony (Goodstadt 2005; Ngo 2002), while others point out that government intervention was very much alive in major factor markets such as housing (Schiffer 1991; Fong and Yeh 1987; Youngson 1982).

Even if the colonial government did intervene in the market more frequently than some thought, no one can dispute that its intervention still paled in comparison with that of the PRC. To Hong Kong's economic elite, therefore, they strictly preferred entrenching the existing economic order to experimenting with some unknown arrangement imposed by the PRC. In addition, the laissez-faire model, however inaccurate a description of the colonial economic system it may be, is inherently pro-capitalist. If the members of Hong Kong's economic elite were to select one economic system to protect their business interests after 1997, apparently the laissez-faire model would be their safest bet.

3.2.1 Relationship Between the Central Government and the HKSAR

First and foremost, Article 5 of the Basic Law spells out the separateness between the system in Hong Kong and in the PRC:

> The socialist system and policies shall not be practised in the Hong Kong Special Administrative Region, and the previous capitalist system and way of life shall remain unchanged for 50 years.

Capitalism, of course, is a malleable concept, as its practice varies from country to country. To further allay worries, Article 6 states explicitly that the HKSAR government needs to protect private ownership. And what about public ownership? Article 7 stipulates that the land and natural resources of Hong Kong are exclusively at the disposal of the HKSAR, rather than the Beijing government.

Levi (1989) points out that the extent to which a ruler can tax his subjects depends on their relative bargaining powers. Hong Kong's remarkable bargaining power – at least during the time when the Basic Law was being drafted – is evident in the taxation arrangements between Hong Kong and the Central Government. Unlike other Chinese subnational governments that need to submit part of their incomes to the Central Government, the HKSAR government can keep all the revenues for its own use (Article 106). Nor can Beijing levy any tax in the HKSAR. Departments of the Central Government and other subnational Chinese governments are not allowed to interfere in the HKSAR's affairs (Article 22). More remarkably, the HKSAR is allowed to keep its own currency (Article 111), set its own monetary policies (Article 110), sign international trade agreements, and maintain a customs territory separate from that of the PRC (Article 116).

Because Hong Kong people can continue to enjoy a capitalist system distinctive from the PRC's socialist system, it is important to define who the Hong Kong people are. Article 24 provides a detailed definition of "Hong Kong residents," while Article 22 stipulates that Chinese nationals who are not Hong Kong residents must apply for approval prior to their entry to the HKSAR.[8]

The desire to embrace free market capitalism had been so strong that some provisions of the Basic Law may appear a bit too rigid, if not dogmatic. For instance, Article 114 stipulates that Hong Kong should not impose any tariff unless prescribed by law. Similarly, Article 115 states that Hong Kong should pursue free trade and safeguard the free movement of capital and goods.

3.2.2 Judiciary

Free market capitalism requires an independent judiciary capable of enforcing contracts, protecting private property rights, ensuring unfettered market competition, and observing the rule of law (Hayek 1960). Although the colonial government was undemocratic, the principle of the rule of law was largely upheld, thanks to the colonial administration's respect for judicial independence (Tsang 2001, p. 1). So what is the "rule of law?" One can find an official definition on the Web page of the HKSAR's Department of Justice:

> Its principal meaning is that the power of the government and all of its servants shall be derived from law as expressed in legislation and the judicial decisions made by independent courts. At the heart of Hong Kong's system of government lies the principle that no one, including the Chief Executive, can do an act which would otherwise constitute a legal wrong or affect a person's liberty unless he can point to a legal justification for that action. If he cannot do so, the affected person can resort to a court which may rule that the act is invalid and of no legal effect.

In other words, the rule of law prevents the exercise of arbitrary power by the state, which was precisely what Hong Kong people wanted written into the Basic Law. For this reason, to convince Hong Kong people that capitalism can truly survive after 1997, Beijing also provides in the Basic Law the institutional arrangements that safeguard the rule of law. Most notably, while the legal system of the PRC comes from civil law tradition, Article 8 prescribes that the HKSAR can maintain its common-law system inherited from Britain. Trial by jury, a notable

---

[8]Right of abode in Hong Kong has continued to be a contentious issue since the handover, as a number of court cases challenged the constitutionality of the government's immigration policies.

common-law feature, which is considered an important judicial mechanism to return power from the state to the people (Hamilton et al. 2008), is preserved under Article 86. Article 84 expressly provides that all courts can refer to precedents of foreign common-law jurisdictions. In addition, the HKSAR can continue to enjoy independent judicial power, including the power to make final adjudication (Article 19). Article 18 further states that laws in force in the HKSAR come from domestic legislation, and national laws of the PRC would not be applied to the HKSAR, except for a few laws such as those concerning national flag and national anthem.

The job security of judges is central to judicial independence. A fair number of provisions in the Basic Law are concerned with the security of tenure of members of the judiciary. For example, according to Article 88 and 89, the appointment and removal of judges require the recommendation of an independent commission composed of judges. For senior judges, their appointment and removal have to fulfill an additional requirement: the endorsement of the Legislative Council (Article 90 and 73(7)). All these articles help reduce the government's interference in the judicial process. Also, Article 85 prescribes that judges can enjoy judicial immunity.

3.2.3 Civil Liberties

Free market capitalism also requires the free flow of information, which would allow economic agents to receive accurate price signals and make judicious decisions. Freedom of speech and freedom of the press are both essential to safeguard the freedom of information. It is difficult to convince Hong Kong people that freedom of speech or freedom of the press can survive when other civil liberties are left unprotected. Therefore, the Basic Law also includes a whole gamut of articles in its Chapter III that aims to protect the general human rights of Hong Kong people against the powers of the government. In particular, Article 27 prescribes that

> Hong Kong residents shall have freedom of speech, of the press and of publication; freedom of association, of assembly, of procession and of demonstration; and the right and freedom to form and join trade unions, and to strike.

Article 32 provides that Hong Kong people enjoy freedom of conscience as well as religious freedom. Freedom of choice of occupation and academic freedom are also guaranteed by Article 33 and 34, respectively. Article 39 stipulates that international human rights instruments including the International Covenant on Civil and Political Rights and the International Covenant on Economic, Social and Cultural Rights are still applied to the HKSAR. These provisions, together with a few additional ones, establish the fundamental rights of Hong Kong residents, who are able to enjoy no fewer civil liberties than what the colonial government provided in the last decades of its rule. As Ghai (1999, p. 156) observes, not all of these rights exist in Western democracies where capitalism is in place.

The discussion thus far indicates that Beijing yielded substantial concessions to Hong Kong people, as the Basic Law has preserved not only the former colony's economic system based on free market capitalism but also a high degree of policy-making and judicial autonomy. Indeed, leaders in Beijing took pride in their institutional creation, which has given Hong Kong far greater autonomy than any Western democracy has provided for its subnational unit (Vogel 2011, p. 508).

While one may marvel at the extensive concessions Beijing made to Hong Kong, it is important to note that the Basic Law is also designed to ensure that Beijing has the ultimate control over the HKSAR's political system. The Basic Law, for instance, promises that both the Chief Executive and the legislature will eventually be elected by universal suffrage, and it has provided the prodemocracy opposition a focal point as well as a constitutional basis to fight for political liberalization. Yet, the Basic Law offers neither a specific time frame nor a clear road map for achieving this ultimate aim. Such ambiguity has given Beijing room to delay Hong Kong's political liberalization. In the succeeding section, I will discuss the major constraints the Basic Law has imposed on Hong Kong's political system.

3.2.4 Chief Executive

A good starting point to understand Beijing's subtle controls over Hong Kong's political system is Article 45, which deals with the selection procedure of the Chief Executive:

> The Chief Executive of the Hong Kong Special Administrative Region shall be selected by election or through consultations held locally and be appointed by the Central People's Government.
> The method for selecting the Chief Executive shall be specified in the light of the actual situation in the Hong Kong Special Administrative Region and in accordance with the principle of gradual and orderly progress. The ultimate aim is the selection of the Chief Executive by universal suffrage upon nomination by a broadly representative nominating committee in accordance with democratic procedures.
> The specific method for selecting the Chief Executive is prescribed in Annex I: "Method for the Selection of the Chief Executive of the Hong Kong Special Administrative Region."

This article states clearly that the Chief Executive has to be elected and that eventually universal suffrage would be adopted as the election method. However, however, the article is also fraught with obscurely worded terms that permit flexible interpretations. For one thing, the meaning of "gradual and orderly progress" is unspecified. Any political liberalization reform, no matter how insignificant, should be consistent with the principle of "gradual and orderly progress." The meaning of "democratic procedures" is also open to interpretation. Without clearly defining "democratic procedures," it is possible that the nominating committee would lapse into becoming Beijing's gatekeeper to screen out unwanted candidates. In addition, since the Chief Executive has to be appointed by Beijing, it possesses the ultimate veto power over leadership selection.

Before reaching the ultimate aim of universal suffrage, the Chief Executive has to be elected in accordance with the method specified in Annex I of the Basic Law.

According to Annex I and its amendments, the Chief Executive is selected every five years by a constitutional body known as the Election Committee, which consists of 1,200 members[9] representing four major social sectors: (a) industrial, commercial, and financial sectors; (2) the professions; (3) labor, social services, religious, and other sectors; and (4) the political sector, including Legislative Councillors, District Councillors, Hong Kong deputies to the National People's Congress, and Hong Kong representatives to the Chinese People's Political Consultative Conference. It has been widely observed that these members are predominantly pro-Beijing figures, many of whom are members of the local business elite (Cheung 2000, p. 303).

The election of the Chief Executive is also governed by the Chief Executive Election Ordinance, which contains more detailed provisions than what is covered in Annex I. A noteworthy provision of the Ordinance is that the Chief Executive cannot be a member of a political party (Section 31). Although candidates can always quit their parties before standing for the election, this particular provision reflects Beijing's aversion to party politics or the potential threat of opposition parties (Ta Kung Pao 2013; Hong Kong Economic Journal 2012).

Beijing's vigilance is understandable, considering that the Chief Executive is vested with substantial political powers. The Chief Executive has powers to make policies and issue executive orders (Article 48(4)); nominate principal officials including, but not limited to, the Commissioner Against Corruption, the Director of Immigration, and the Director of Audit (Article 48(5)); and dissolve the Legislative Council in times of legislative impasse (Article 50).

3.2.5   Legislature

The powers of the Legislative Council are modest compared with those of the Chief Executive. For one thing, Article 74 stipulates that the LegCo is not permitted to introduce any bill related to (a) public expenditure, (b) political structure, and (c) the operation of the government. Bills concerning government policies can be raised – but only upon the approval of the Chief Executive. The institutional weakness of the legislature again reflects Beijing's political preference; the legislature had never been intended to check the executive branch. Deng mentioned more than once that the concept of the separation of powers does not apply to Hong Kong (Deng 2004, p. 56). Those who drafted the Basic Law also believed that colonial Hong Kong's economic success stemmed from a dominant and efficient bureaucracy (Lee 1999, p. 943), rather than from a representative government.

The LegCo is not completely toothless, however. It does possess powers to authorize government expenditure and budgets, to endorse the appointment and removal of senior judges, to question government policies, and to impeach the Chief

---

[9]The membership size has expanded twice, from 400 to 800 and then from 800 to 1,200.

Executive (Article 73). In other words, given that the opposition can gain control of the LegCo, it would have opportunity to constrain the executive branch. Perhaps for this reason, Beijing has installed additional "safety valves" in the Basic Law to prevent opposition parties from controlling the legislature. In particular, Article 68, which deals with elections of the LegCo, is a parallel version of Article 45:

> The Legislative Council of the Hong Kong Special Administrative Region shall be constituted by election.
> The method for forming the Legislative Council shall be specified in the light of the actual situation in the Hong Kong Special Administrative Region and in accordance with the principle of gradual and orderly progress. The ultimate aim is the election of all the members of the Legislative Council by universal suffrage.
> The specific method for forming the Legislative Council and its procedures for voting on bills and motions are prescribed in Annex II: "Method for the Formation of the Legislative Council of the Hong Kong Special Administrative Region and Its Voting Procedures".

Universal suffrage is again the ultimate aim for electing all LegCo members. But before reaching this lofty aim in a "gradual and orderly" fashion at some point in the future, elections are conducted using a method outlined in Annex II. According to Annex II, the Legislative Council is composed of two distinct groups of members. One group is elected from functional constituencies, while the other group from geographical constituencies. Since the third term, both groups have had the same number of seats.

Functional constituencies represent a variety of professions, economic sectors, and social groups. By contrast, geographical constituencies are popularly elected. For this reason, LegCo members elected from functional constituencies tend to serve a narrower constituency than those elected from geographical constituencies. The total number of eligible voters for functional constituencies before the 2010 political reform was 240,735[10] or about 7 % of the voting-age population.[11] As for the electoral formula, right after the retrocession, the HKSAR government replaced the plurality rule, which had been introduced by the last colonial governor Christopher Patten, with proportional representation (PR). The PR electoral formula has significantly benefited pro-Beijing parties, because these less popular parties would be hard put to compete in a winner-take-all system created by the plurality rule (Ma and Choy 1999).

In his study of local people's congresses in China, Cho (2010) points out that local Chinese legislatures perform four functions: legislation, supervision, representation, and regime support. The first three functions have attracted increasing scholarly attention (Manion 2014; Cho 2010; Xia 2007), as local people's congresses became more institutionalized and professional. Interestingly, in Hong Kong, the "regime support" function, which is performed essentially by functional

---

[10]The figure comes from the HKSAR Electoral Affairs Commission. http://www.elections.gov.hk/legco2012/chi/facts.html. Accessed May 26, 2014.

[11]The 2010 political reform produced five new functional constituencies representing the District Councils. Unlike the remaining 30 seats for functional constituencies, these 5 seats have an electorate that encompasses about 93 % of the total voting-age population.

constituencies, seems to be an outstanding feature of the postcolonial legislature. Functional constituencies help protect Beijing's interests because they have been controlled predominantly by pro-Beijing politicians. No matter how popular opposition parties are among the general public, they have great difficulty cracking into these sector-based constituencies. Their stronghold remains in geographical constituencies, which account for only half of the LegCo seats. Functional constituencies, therefore, act as the gatekeeper for Beijing. Their existence effectively relegates opposition parties to a minority position in the LegCo. Annex II of the Basic Law further strengthens the gatekeeping function of functional constituencies by requiring all motions, bills, or amendments raised by Legislative Councillors (or private bills) to be voted separately in the two groups of constituencies. The passage of a private bill requires the support of both functional and geographical constituencies. On the other hand, Annex II also provides that bills proposed by the government require only a simple majority vote of the entire legislature. This mixed voting system favors the government but disadvantages minority interests, including the prodemocracy opposition.

Thanks to these functional constituencies, many bills that would embarrass Beijing or attempt to accelerate political liberalization are defeated. For instance, every year prodemocracy politicians propose a motion to call for a vindication of the 1989 prodemocracy movement in Beijing. This motion has never gotten passed in the postcolonial legislature. Functional constituencies are gradually seen as a stumbling block to political liberalization. Not only is their raison d'être questioned. Some functional constituencies, such as the labor constituency, exclude individual electors, and their electorate is based entirely on corporate bodies. The reason why only certain economic sectors or social groups are recognized as a constituency remains unclear. For example, there is no functional constituency for college professors, although "higher education" is recognized as a sector in the Election Committee for the Chief Executive.[12] In addition, malapportionment is not only a problem that sets geographical and functional constituencies apart from each other but is also a problem of functional constituencies themselves. The functional constituency for "financial services," for instance, has only one seat, the same as another constituency for "agriculture and fisheries," although the former profession outweighs the latter in terms of employment size and economic outputs by orders of magnitude. However odd these arrangements appear, it is arguably the combination of these irregularities,[13] namely, malapportionment, arbitrary functional representation, and uneven electoral bases, that ensures the overrepresentation of pro-Beijing politicians in functional constituencies.

---

[12]Prior to the retrocession, Beijing and the British government had a heated discussion about the scope and franchise of functional constituencies. See, for example, Lo (1994).

[13]For a detailed discussion of the problems of functional constituencies, see Young et al. (2004) and Ma and Choy (2003).

3.2.6   Interpretation and Amendment of the Basic Law

Confusion sometimes arises when a constitution is put into practice. Under such circumstances, constitutional interpretation or even an amendment is necessary. The issues of interpretation and amendment are particularly relevant to the Basic Law because many of its provisions contain obscurely worded terms (Ghai 1999, p. 185), as attested by Articles 45 and 68 concerning the elections of the Chief Executive and the legislature.

Because the authority which possesses the power to interpret and amend the Basic Law has the final say in the law's application, not surprisingly, Beijing keeps this last line of defense firmly under its control. Article 158 stipulates that the power of interpretation is vested with the Standing Committee of the National People's Congress (NPCSC), while Article 159 provides that the power of amendment is controlled by the National People's Congress. Note that although Hong Kong has its own deputies to the NPC, they have never been democratically elected. Instead, they are chosen mainly by the members of the Election Committee of the Chief Executive.[14] As such, Beijing can ensure that election outcomes would not go awry. But this also implies that the political representation of these NPC members is even lower than that of some local people's congresses in China (Kamo and Takeuchi 2013; Manion 2008).

The NPCSC exercised its power of interpretation soon after the retrocession. On January 29, 1999, the HKSAR's Court of Final Appeal ruled in *Ng Ka Ling v. Director of Immigration* that people born outside Hong Kong have the right of abode in the special administrative region, even though their parents had not been Hong Kong permanent residents at the time of their birth. The government and many Hong Kong people feared that the court's decision would open the floodgates to hundreds of thousands of mainland immigrants, depleting Hong Kong's public resources, if not also jeopardizing its prosperity (Chan et al. 2000, pp. 222–224). The Chief Executive later submitted a request to the NPCSC for an interpretation of the relevant provisions of the Basic Law. The NPCSC ruled that the Court of Final Appeal's interpretation is inconsistent with the legislative intent and thereby overrode the court's decision.[15]

The power of interpretation is also useful for dealing with the highly contentious democratization issues. Annex I and II expressly provide the methods for the formation of the legislature and for the selection of the Chief Executive prior to 2007, which are not universal suffrage. In 2004, the NPCSC again exercised its power of interpretation, in the absence of a request from the HKSAR authorities, ruling out the application of universal suffrage in the 2007 Chief Executive Election

---

[14]For a detailed discussion of the composition of the Hong Kong deputies to the NPC, see Young and Cullen (2010).

[15]The NPCSC ruled that people born outside Hong Kong do not have the right of abode unless their parents had already become Hong Kong permanent residents at the time of their birth. This interpretation drastically reduced the number of potential right of abode holders.

and in the 2008 LegCo election. Moreover, the interpretation also changed the procedure for initiating political reforms stipulated in Annex I and II by adding two new steps extraneous to any provision of the Basic Law.[16] This arrangement allows the NPCSC to intervene in any proposed political reform of Hong Kong at an early stage. The NPCSC did, in fact, exercise its self-imposed authority by making a decision in 2007 to rule out the possibility of amending the methods for selecting the Chief Executive and for forming the LegCo in 2012.

In addition to the power of interpretation and the power of amendment, the NPCSC also has the power to nullify the HKSAR's domestic legislation (Article 17). Article 18 also stipulates that the NPCSC may declare a state of emergency, when the HKSAR government fails to contain turmoil that endangers national unity. Under such circumstances, the Central Government can apply national laws in Hong Kong.

3.3 Last Years of the Colonial Administration

Chinese officials have taken pride in Deng Xiaoping's creative institutional design of the "one country, two systems" principle, manifested itself in the Basic Law (Xiao 1990). Indeed, as demonstrated in the foregoing discussion, the Basic Law has produced a postcolonial political system that curiously combines a high degree of economic freedom, as well as civil liberties, with subtle and all-encompassing top-down controls. Hong Kong observers aptly dub such a system "birdcage democracy" (Weng 1998; Kuan et al. 1999).

This institutional birdcage has ancestral roots in the British colonial administration. Chinese officials in the 1980s were deeply impressed by the colonial political system in Hong Kong, which was characterized by strong executive authority and a small but efficient government. This system, as many believed, underpinned Hong Kong's great economic success in the postwar era. The Basic Law was therefore modeled upon that very system, except changing the name of the sovereign (Scott 2000; Lee 1999). Xu Jiatun, the highest ranking Chinese government official stationed in Hong Kong in the 1980s, pointed out, "when designing the Basic Law. . . we ought to. . . utilize the British system of administration" (Xu 1993).

Note that democratic accountability was never part of the equation in the highly esteemed colonial administration. One major reason is that the popular demand for democratic accountability was relatively low. As previously mentioned, Hong Kong had long been a "refugee society." The refugees had greater tolerance of colonial rule or at least found it bearable; otherwise, they would not have chosen themselves

---

[16]See "The Interpretation by the Standing Committee of the National People's Congress of Article 7 of Annex I and Article III of Annex II to the Basic Law of the Hong Kong Special Administrative Region of the People's Republic of China," adopted at the eighth session of the Standing Committee of the tenth National People's Congress on April 6, 2004.

to arrive in Hong Kong in the first place. In addition, such a migrant population tended to be more individualistic, self-reliant, and pragmatic (Lau and Kuan 1988). They were more interested in making money than making their voices heard. Political apathy, as many believed, is a defining feature of the people of colonial Hong Kong (Miners 1995; Lau 1984). Although this view has been challenged in more recent studies (Lam 2004; Degolyer and Scott 1996), evidence from public opinion surveys does show that local support for democratization was feeble prior to 1989 (Sing 2004). Elite newspapers such as the *Hong Kong Economic Journal* and the *Ming Pao Daily News* were also skeptical at universal suffrage, fearing that it would favor the poor and give rise to a welfare state and class politics (see, e.g., Lam (1984, p. 449) and Cha (1984, pp. 248–251)).

This is not to say that the colonial government ignored the voices of its subjects completely. On the contrary, the colonial government did make an effort to incorporate local views into the policy-making process by establishing grassroots government offices to improve state-society communication. However, the colonial administrators' attempt was not to integrate ordinary people into the political system but to depoliticize their rising demands by converting them into administrative problems to be tackled by bureaucrats. King (1975) names such co-optation effort the "administrative absorption of politics." King's account is consistent with the blueprint of Beijing, who believed that transplanting the colonial political order to postcolonial Hong Kong will work just as fine.

The fact that the colonial administrators were able to use administrative means to solve political problems may not necessarily imply the superiority of the colonial political system. Rather, it may well be the case that the problems they faced were not acute enough. Real tests emerged in the 1980s, when Hong Kong witnessed dramatic social transformations and political challenges unseen in the previous decades. First and foremost, a younger generation of Hong Kong people with different thinking emerged. Unlike their parents, many of whom were former refugees, this younger generation had a stronger attachment to the city and did not identify themselves as sojourners. They were more educated, more vocal, and more conscious of their rights, creating pressure for the government to improve its service provision in both qualitative and quantitative terms.

Starting from the 1970s, the colonial administration did expand its welfare provision. For example, Governor MacLehose announced in 1972 an ambitious ten-year housing program, aiming to construct enough public housing to accommodate 1.8 million Hong Kong citizens within ten years.[17] Then in 1978, the government offered a nine-year free and compulsory education for Hong Kong residents. The welfare expansion provided residents more direct experiences with government bureaucracy, further raising the public's demands for better governance (Lau 1981).

To Hong Kong people, the greatest stimulant to political participation in the 1980s was the issue of reunification. Hong Kong people were not formally consulted

---

[17]The population of Hong Kong in 1971 was 3.94 million (Census and Statistics Department of Hong Kong 2012).

during the Sino-British negotiation over Hong Kong's future due to Beijing's rejection of the British government's request to include Hong Kong representatives in the talk. Feeling betrayed and uncertain about the future,[18] some Hong Kong prodemocracy activists advocated the "use of democracy to counter the Communist" (*minzhu kanggong*). That is, instead of counting on the outgoing British colonists to protect Hong Kong, they endorsed that Hong Kong people should help themselves by pushing for democratization, because democratic institutions would be the most powerful bulwark against the Chinese authoritarian state after the retrocession.

This view received immense public support after Beijing's suppression of a peaceful student-led prodemocracy movement in 1989. Witnessing the brutal crackdown through a live TV broadcast, the entire city of Hong Kong was flabbergasted, indignant, and most of all horrified. So (2011) succinctly describes Hong Kong people's anxiety at the time: "Hong Kong people figured that if the Communist Party could send tanks to suppress the peaceful protests of students, they could do the same in Hong Kong." A record-high one million Hong Kong citizens took to the streets in one demonstration to vent their anger at, if not also to express their fear of, the military crackdown. Employees of Chinese state-owned firms based in Hong Kong or pro-Beijing individuals also voiced out their disapproval of Beijing's ruthless measures. Most notably, soon after the crackdown, Leung Chun-ying, who later became Hong Kong's Chief Executive, made public statements in newspapers to condemn the central authorities.

But of all the social repercussions following the 1989 prodemocracy movement, the most far-reaching one was probably the birth of the Alliance in Support of Patriotic Democratic Movement of China (ASPDMC), which is an umbrella organization consisting of over a hundred civil society groups in Hong Kong. At the height of the movement, the ASPDMC provided financial supports for the student protesters in Beijing. After the crackdown, it helped smuggle student leaders out of the country. Every year since 1990, it organizes a candle night vigil in Hong Kong's Victoria Park in commemoration of the victims of the June 4 Incident. As one of the central tenets of the ASPDMC is to "end one-party dictatorship [in China]," some Beijing leaders viewed the ASPDMC as a subversive united front controlled by foreign governments (Xu 1993, p. 395). Major leaders of the ASPDMC later formed a prodemocracy opposition party, the Democratic Party, which had been for many years Hong Kong's flagship opposition party.

The June 4 Incident accelerated the pace of political liberalization by the colonial administration. For much of Hong Kong's colonial history, the colonial administrators had shown little interest to share political power with its subjects. In the 1980s, as the British government prepared for its graceful retreat from Hong Kong, they began to allow for limited political liberalization. The first LegCo election took place as late as in 1985, and the first elected members were selected from functional constituencies that represented no more than 1 % of the population

---

[18] A prevailing view at that time was that "Great Britain is not reliable and the Chinese Communist is not trustworthy" (*yingguo bu kekao, zhonggong bu kexin*) (Lam 1984, p. 461).

(Scott 2000, p. 42). The June 4 Incident created domestic and international pressure for the British government to do something to protect Hong Kong against the authoritarian state of China. For example, in 1991, the colonial legislature passed a bill of rights. From then on, any government agency in violation of human rights can be tried by courts.

The most dramatic change came in 1992, when the British government appointed Christopher Patten as the new – and the last – governor for Hong Kong. Unlike his predecessor, David Wilson, who was a diplomat with training in sinology, Patten was a career politician and a former chairman of the Conservative Party. His unprecedented populist political style impressed the Hong Kong public, who had never seen a governor equally friendly and amicable. In defiance of Beijing's harsh criticisms, Patten implemented what Beijing considered radical political reforms, including the lowering of the voting age from 21 to 18, the extension of the franchise of functional constituencies to 2.7 million eligible voters, and the adoption of the plurality rule as the electoral formula for the election of the last colonial legislature. Moreover, Patten never shied away from confronting with Chinese officials in an open and antagonistic manner.

The Patten administration left two important legacies. The first is that his political reforms significantly empowered the prodemocracy opposition. As discussed, the winner-take-all nature of the plurality rule marginalized the less popular pro-Beijing parties. The flagship opposition party, the Democratic Party (DP), managed to capture the largest number of seats in the last colonial legislature. The second legacy of Patten, which is arguably more far-reaching, is that his populist, prodemocracy stance and willingness to defy the Chinese authorities further politicized Hong Kong's society. Although the majority of the seats were not popularly elected, the last legislative election was the most democratic ever in Hong Kong's entire colonial history. This inevitably raised the public's expectation of the postcolonial political system, particularly because of Beijing's repeated emphasis of how the future of Hong Kong would be brighter after its glorious return to the motherland.

Not surprisingly, Patten's provocative moves met severe criticisms from Chinese authorities. From Beijing's perspective, the political liberalization introduced by the colonial government in its final years was a British conspiracy to turn Hong Kong into an "independent entity" (Qian 2004, p. 293) or an anti-CCP bridgehead after 1997 (Qiang 2008, pp. 176–178).[19] Regardless of what motivated the British government, the aforementioned political changes have fundamentally reshaped Hong Kong's state-society relations. Suffice it to say, by the time the PRC took over Hong Kong, the political landscape of the city witnessed a sea change from what it had been in the early 1980s.

---

[19]There exist other explanations for the colonial government's unlikely political liberalization since the mid-1980s. Some argue that the British government believed the CCP would fall soon after the June 4 Incident (Lu 2009, p. 70). Others point out that Patten had an incentive to present himself as a freedom fighter for Hong Kong, which would bring him considerable political credential back home after 1997 (Lo 1994, p. 194).

First and foremost, Hong Kong people became far less politically apathetic than before, due to the exposure to competitive elections and the experience of mass mobilization in 1989. Second, a popular prodemocracy opposition emerged as a formidable political force in Hong Kong politics. Third, the colonial administration's accelerated political liberalization also facilitated the development of political activism. People became accustomed to expressing their political opinions as well as disapproval of political figures through the media and public demonstrations. *Apple Daily*, a prodemocracy newspaper unabashedly critical of Beijing, was founded in 1995 and has become one of the most popular newspapers in Hong Kong to this day.

The Basic Law was designed in the image of the British colonial administration prior to the mid-1980s, at a time when Hong Kong's civil society and political society were both in their infancy. By the time the PRC gained its sovereignty over Hong Kong – that is, the time the Basic Law came into force – the infants had grown considerably. Postcolonial institutions, originally intended to be bespoke suits, now looked more like a straitjacket. State-society conflicts emerged soon after the retrocession and have plagued the postcolonial administration ever since.

3.4   After 1997

On July 2, 1997, the second day after Hong Kong's transfer of sovereignty, Thailand gave up its fixed exchange rate because its government failed to defend its currency after months of speculative attacks. Following the announcement, the value of Thai baht fell precipitously, deepening the country's financial crisis. In the subsequent months, Thailand's crisis propagated to other Asian economies, Hong Kong included, and later culminated into the well-known Asian Financial Crisis.

The Asian Financial Crisis punctured the bubble of Hong Kong's housing markets, which had begun to develop from 1995. Hot money flew out of the economy, followed by a rapid decline in property prices. Many homeowners found their apartments now worth less than their mortgages, becoming the so-called negative equities. Bank foreclosures skyrocketed, as more and more homeowners and home speculators failed to meet their monthly mortgage payments. Private consumption plummeted, while unemployment soared. The newly founded HKSAR government needed to deal with an economy in disarray.

Tung Chee-hwa, the son of a business tycoon, was selected by the Beijing-controlled selection committee as Hong Kong's new political leader. Unlike the last colonial governor Christopher Patten, Tung was neither charismatic nor eloquent, although this nondemocratically elected leader did enjoy considerably high approval rating in the beginning of his term. His political honeymoon ended quickly, however, as he failed to rescue the faltering economy. In fact, some even linked his administration to the worsening economic situations.

The first controversy of his administration was his ambitious housing plan announced two months after he assumed the Chief Executive office. At the height of the housing bubble, many in Hong Kong lamented the soaring housing prices.

In response to their complaints, Tung vowed to provide 85,000 housing units on an annual basis. His plan was ill-timed, because Asian economies at that point were already mired in deep financial troubles. Housing markets in Hong Kong also started to crumble. According to the data of the HKSAR Rating and Valuation Department, housing prices dropped 38 % a year after the announcement of Tung's anachronistic housing plan. Not surprisingly, many pinpointed Tung as the culprit of the housing crisis, if not of other economic problems as well.

It took seven years for the economic downturn to bottom out. Those hard days were punctuated by Tung's incessant policy blunders and political mistakes. In late 1997, Hong Kong went into a public health crisis, as the government decided, after days of delay, to kill all local chickens – one million of them – to contain an unprecedented bird flu that first recorded human infections. The operation was swift, but the chicken carcasses were left unattended for days, causing unnecessary worries, if not also defeating the purpose of the operation. In mid-1998, Hong Kong's new airport went into operation. What made international headlines was not its grand opening but a combination of technical and management problems that resulted in serious flight delays and logistical chaos. It took two months to restore normal airport services. Then in 1999, the Tung administration rode the wave of the global Dot-Com Bubble to announce the plan to build a local Silicon Valley named Cyberport. The Cyberport project was part of Tung's larger plan to revive the city's economy. This supposedly credit-claiming developmental project turned out to become another blame-taking fiasco because the government contracted out the project to a scion of a Hong Kong business tycoon without going through the standard procedure of competitive tendering. Worse still, the media found that the scion could pocket billions from developing a luxurious residential compound in Cyberport, leaving a bad public impression that the technology project was nothing but a collusion between the government and the real estate elite.

There was also Tung's weakness in public communication manifested in his remark on the controversial housing policy during a television interview in 2001. He said that his target of building 85,000 housing units per year had long been shelved. "It ceased to exist because I no longer mentioned it," he had confided. His remark, which was perhaps intended to boost the confidence of the investors in the lackluster housing markets, triggered an immediate public outcry. Many believed that the housing doldrums persisted because of Tung's pledge to maintain abundant housing supply. Now the public came to realize that the government had kept them in the dark all along.

In sum, the first term of the Tung administration exposed the Chief Executive's poor leadership, ineffective communication skills, and lack of political savvy. The executive-led model conferred by the Basic Law turned out to be a curse rather than a blessing, as too much power was vested in an incompetent leader. But to many Hong Kong people's dismay, Tung, despite his low popularity, was able to get reelected in 2002 under Beijing's auspices.

The problems of Tung, together with his uncontested reelection, raised the public's awareness of the importance of universal suffrage, which is promised by the Basic Law as the ultimate method for selecting the Chief Executive but has never been put into practice. Many were upset by the fact that they had no power to remove a political leader whose incompetence had contributed, directly or indirectly, to their city's long-standing economic plight. Public discontent gradually built up.

Although ordinary people were unable to vote out Tung, thanks to the city's high degree of civil liberties, they could still actively exercise their freedom of speech to vent anger at Tung and at the larger political system through phone-in radio programs and online forums alike. Radio hosts, such as Albert Cheng and Wong Yuk-man, achieved high ratings by inveighing against the government, while newspapers critical of Tung became the most widely read.

Opposition parties tried to turn the growing public discontent to their advantage. Although the Basic Law severely constrained the power of the legislature, whose role became no more than "a talking shop and a rubber stamp" (Scott 2000, p. 36), elected opposition leaders had at least one political asset that should have made Tung jealous: popular mandate.[20] They turned their subdued position into a weapon of the weak by using each legislative session to question, challenge, criticize, and at times, ridicule the Tung administration, in hopes of attracting media coverage and spreading their political message. During elections, they also took advantage of the government's declining popularity by changing their campaign strategies from attacking Beijing, which had been a salient issue in the last colonial legislative elections,[21] to attacking the HKSAR government (Ma and Choy 2003, pp. 103–199).

Suffice it to say, by the time Tung was reelected, Hong Kong's society was engulfed in a deep sense of hopelessness and powerlessness. The economic outlook was bleak, while political accountability was nowhere in sight. Complaints and resentment dominated public discourse. People became more and more restive. Politically, Hong Kong had all the requisite conditions for a perfect storm. All it needed was a trigger, which presented itself in 2003.

3.5 July 1, 2003

The first draft of the Basic Law, which came out in April 1988, contained a national security provision (Article 22): "The Hong Kong Special Administrative Region shall prohibit by law any act designed to undermine national unity or subvert the Central People's Government." This version was criticized for being too vague and too broad as to invite arbitrary interpretations. In a subsequent draft released in February 1989, this article was revised to replace the vaguely worded offenses with more specific ones such as treason and secession. After witnessing Hong Kong's massive protest turnout and the emergence of the ASPDMC in 1989, Beijing

---

[20]Most of the elected opposition legislators gained their office popularly elected through geographical constituencies.

[21]For the effects of the "China factor" in pre-transition elections, see Leung (1991, 1996).

decided to toughen this provision by rolling back the concept of "subversion" and adding a reference to "foreign political organizations" (Petersen 2005, pp. 17–18). Article 23 of the Basic Law in its final version states:

> The Hong Kong Special Administrative Region shall enact laws on its own to prohibit any act of treason, secession, sedition, subversion against the Central People's Government, or theft of state secrets, to prohibit foreign political organizations or bodies from conducting political activities in the Region, and to prohibit political organizations or bodies of the Region from establishing ties with foreign political organizations or bodies.

Article 23 does not specify the time for the enactment of the national security laws. During the first few years after the retrocession, this legislation was also not on Tung's political agenda. But in 2002, Beijing leaders hinted that the time was ripe during Tung's second term (Ma 2005). Shortly after his reelection, the Tung administration began the preparation work by announcing a consultation paper that contained some proposed legislations for Article 23. The consultation paper caused an uproar in Hong Kong. There were three major reasons. First, a large portion of Hong Kong people still had a deep-seated distrust of the authoritarian state of the PRC. They saw the related legislations not as a tool to protect national security but more as an instrument for Beijing to limit their civil liberties (Ma 2005, p. 476). Second, the offenses suggested in the consultation paper were largely based on obscurely worded or vaguely defined terms and concepts that allowed for an arbitrary interpretation by the state, leaving individual liberties unprotected (Ma 2005, pp. 467–472). Finally, government officials did a poor job of mobilizing public support for the proposed legislations. For example, on one public occasion, someone asked Elsie Leung, then the Secretary for Justice, whether the legislation of Article 23 would create a "white terror" in Hong Kong. Instead of taking the opportunity to allay public fears, Leung bluntly replied that "a knife has already been hung over your head." Her reply was taken as the government's confirmation that the widely perceived threats against civil liberties brought by the national security laws were real.

Civil society mounted strong opposition to the proposed legislation. Journalists, legal professionals, and academics voiced out their worries and disapproval by issuing public statements and organizing concern groups. For instance, a group of the former chairpersons of the Hong Kong Bar Association formed the "Basic Law Article 23 Concern Group," which frequently challenged the government's positions on the national security laws. Even the Catholic Church in Hong Kong aired a high-profile objection, because it, too, could fall victim to the offense of having links with the proscribed organizations, given its ongoing communications with many "underground" churches in the mainland. Despite widespread social opposition, the government showed no sign of backing down. The Tung administration and the civil society became locked in a stalemate.

Meanwhile, a mysterious epidemic struck Hong Kong. The disease, known as severe acute respiratory syndrome (SARS), was first identified in Hong Kong in February 2003. At the beginning of the outbreak, the public had little knowledge about the disease or its cause, fatality rate, and effective cures. All they knew was that each day there were dozens more new cases, while the death toll increased. The disease also seemed dangerously contagious, as healthcare workers who were in touch with SARS patients also contracted the disease. On March 12, the World Health Organization issued a global alert. Three days later, the Centers for Disease Control and Prevention of the United States issued a travel advisory for travelers from Hong Kong and the nearby Guangdong Province.

At that point, the city was thrown in a state of panic. People took unusual steps to enhance their daily personal hygiene. Many developed a new habit of rubbing hands with alcoholic sanitizers on a regular basis. Almost everyone put on surgical masks whenever they stayed outdoors. The best way to avoid the invisible killer, of course, was not to go out at all. People reduced social gatherings of all sorts. Streets lost their jostling crowds. Cinemas and restaurants were empty. On March 27, the government even announced a temporary suspension of schools. As no one wanted to visit an epidemic-ridden city, tourism, one of the major pillars of Hong Kong's economy, badly suffered. In sum, the disease disturbed the city's daily social order and brought devastating impacts on its ailing economy.

The epidemic was subdued within two months. On May 23, the WHO lifted the travel advisory against Hong Kong. The metropolis gradually regained its vitality. Yet while new life was breathed into the city, the political deadlock remained unchanged. The Tung administration continued to push for the passage of the National Security Bill, which was scheduled for the Second and Third Reading in the LegCo on July 9, 2003. But the government now faced a society that was no longer the same.

Perhaps having gone through a dreadful epidemic gave citizens new strength and community spirit. Perhaps the way the Tung administration handled the epidemic wiped out Hong Kong people's remaining hope for the government (DeGolyer 2004, pp. 126–127). No matter what the main reason was, suffice it to say, after the SARS outbreak, Hong Kong people could no longer suppress their fury at the Tung administration. Their anger culminated in a massive social outcry. On July 1, 2003, which was the public holiday in commemoration of Hong Kong's return to China, half a million Hong Kong people – or one in ten adults – took to the streets to demand Tung's resignation and the suspension of the National Security Bill.

The Basic Law provides the freedom of demonstration. Hong Kong people did not shy away from exercising this right even after 1997. In the summer of 2000 alone, street demonstrations had been organized by healthcare professionals, teachers, social workers, and civil servants. Protests were so frequent that the *Washington Post* once named Hong Kong the "city of protests" (Washington Post 2000). However, no protest in postcolonial Hong Kong matched the July 1, 2003 protest in terms of the turnout. Indeed, it was the second largest mass mobilization in the history of the city.[22]

---

[22]The largest one took place immediately after Beijing's brutal crackdown on the student-led prodemocracy movement in 1989.

The massive turnout shocked almost everyone, including the protest organizers, who, prior to the March, estimated that the turnout would be 100,000 at most (Lee and Chan 2011, p. 43). Some government official even thought that 30,000 would be the maximum.[23] Caught unprepared, and possibly dumbfounded, Tung had not been ready to take any of the reporters' questions when he showed up in his office the very next day, except to say "Good morning." He called several Executive Council meetings immediately, but to many people's surprise, no official announcement of the meeting's results was released for the following three days. The dissension within the ruling elite gradually surfaced. James Tien, an Executive Council member who was also the chairman of the pro-Beijing Liberal Party, openly supported a postponement of the reading of the bill, while Tung insisted that it would go ahead as scheduled. The political crisis took a dramatic turn on July 6, when James Tien announced his resignation from the Executive Council. The following day, the government, at long last, acquiesced in the postponement. Within ten days, two key ministers of the Tung administration resigned. One of them, Secretary for Security Regina Ip, was responsible for the promotion of the legislation of Article 23. Tung himself stepped down two years later, without finishing his second term. Although he attributed his premature departure to health problems, many believe that his resignation, which required Beijing's ultimate approval, was to a large extent a result of his incompetence, particularly his inability to handle the aftermath of the July 1, 2003 protest.

3.6 Conclusion

While many worried that Hong Kong's civil liberties would be suppressed after the city's reunification with the single-party dictatorship of the PRC, it seems that the civil society of postcolonial Hong Kong has survived, if not also thrived. There are two reasons for this positive development. First, when Beijing drafted the Basic Law, the mini-constitution that laid down the fundamental political order of the HKSAR, it had a clear goal in mind: to preserve Hong Kong's prosperity that was largely based on free market capitalism. For this reason, the Basic Law was designed in the image of the late British colonial system, which had been noted for its high degree of civil liberties that were considered essential to the operation of a free market. The second reason is that political developments since the late 1980s have significantly politicized Hong Kong's society. The June 4 Incident, the colonial government's long-overdue political liberalization, and the protracted economic downturn after 1997 all had direct and profound impacts on the Hong Kong people's way of life, forcing them to come to terms with an uncertain future

---

[23]Siu-kai Lau, head of the HKSAR's official think tank, gave that conservative estimate.

and a harsh political reality. It was no longer possible for Hong Kong people to remain silent and docile. As they became significantly more politically active, a vibrant civil society came to life.

The rise of a vocal civil society has clashed with another salient characteristic of the Basic Law: a low degree of democratic accountability. The Basic Law vests a wide range of power with the Chief Executive, who is not popularly elected, while reducing the role of the more democratic legislature to a talking shop. This institutional arrangement was also modeled upon the pre-1984 colonial political order, which was notorious for its lack of democracy. Although the Chinese authorities from time to time emphasize that the HKSAR government is more democratic than the colonial administration in any period,[24] the institutional straitjacket prescribed by the Basic Law no longer satisfied Hong Kong people's rising demand for greater democratic accountability.

At times, the postcolonial administration attempted to tame the assertive civil society. The proposed legislation of Article 23 was a case in point. But the administration ended up suffering a humiliating defeat, as half a million Hong Kong residents took to the streets on July 1, 2003 to protest against the proposed national security laws. After the show of people's power in the historic July 1, 2003 protest, Beijing came to realize that governing Hong Kong is by no means an easy task. Politically, Beijing has constrained itself by designing the Basic Law to confer upon Hong Kong a high degree of civil liberties. Socially, the civil society in Hong Kong has grown increasingly vocal and untamable. Economically, crushing by brute force Hong Kong's civil liberties, including freedom of the press, runs counter to the fundamental objective of preserving the city's prosperity.

Facing all these constraints, what can Beijing do to advance its own interests in Hong Kong? How can it counter the popular pressure for political liberalization? As I discussed in the previous chapter, the key lies in building grassroots political organizations, a skill that the Chinese Communist Party has long mastered. In the next two chapters, I will examine how the prodemocracy opposition coalition changed in the wake of the July 1, 2003 protest and how Beijing-sponsored parties fine-tuned their political strategies in response to the rising challenges of civil society.

---

[24]For instance, the "Decision of the Standing Committee of the National People's Congress on Issues Relating to the Methods for Selecting the Chief Executive of the Hong Kong Special Administrative Region in the Year 2007 and for Forming the Legislative Council of the Hong Kong Special Administrative Region in the Year 2008" states: "[S]ince the establishment of the Hong Kong Special Administrative Region, Hong Kong residents have enjoyed democratic rights that they have never had before."

Chapter 4
Power to the People: Changing Electoral Strategies of the Prodemocracy Opposition Elite

One week after the historic July 1, 2003 protest, a key member of the Tung administration, James Tien, resigned from the Executive Council, parting ways with the government for its refusal to shelve the controversial legislation of the national security laws. His resignation caused a dramatic turn in the political saga; the government, which had all along seemed to be unyielding, announced an indefinite postponement of the legislation. Not surprisingly, many interpreted the government's abrupt acquiescence as a triumphant success for the protest. The term "the victory of people's power" immediately hit the headlines of local newspapers.[1] This optimism in the people's power was reinforced again by the subsequent resignation of two ministers, including the one responsible for the promotion of the legislation of the national security laws. Some also considered Tung's resignation, which happened two years later, as a direct consequence of the July 1, 2003 protest (Lo 2007).

The devastating political effects brought by the July 1, 2003 protest were beyond the wildest imagination of any political player, including the opposition parties. Never had anyone been able to override government policies so rapidly and so radically. The July 1, 2003 protest presented to the opposition parties an alternative means to change government policies, or even the government itself, that was not made available to them inside the institutional birdcage. The demonstration of people's power in the historic protest opened up new possibilities for the opposition's prodemocracy struggle. To understand how the July 1, 2003 protest shaped the subsequent movement of the opposition parties, one needs to grapple

---

[1] See the A1 headline of the *Hong Kong Daily News* on July 7, 2003, as well as the A4 headline of the *Apple Daily* and the A9 headline of the *Ming Pao Daily News* on July 8, 2003.

© Springer Science+Business Media Singapore 2015
S.H.-W. Wong, *Electoral Politics in Post-1997 Hong Kong*,
DOI 10.1007/978-981-287-387-3_4

with the main characteristics of the protest. There were two salient features of the protest that have been highlighted time and again in mainstream media and in academic studies:

(1) Peacefulness and orderliness

Although the 500,000 protesters who showed up in the march were driven by disappointment and anger at the government, the protest nonetheless did not end in chaos and violence. No government official was assaulted. No shop was looted, and no tires were burned. Not even a single glass window of government buildings was broken. The most expressive acts of the protesters were merely the waving of placards and the chanting of anti-Tung slogans. This degree of orderliness was remarkable, considering that the unexpected high turnout made the procession of the march extremely slow. The weather was also unkind to the protesters, as the outdoor temperature in the afternoon reached 31 °C . Hundreds of thousands of the participants were stuck in the crowd sweltering under the burning sun for three hours before being able to actually march (Ming Pao Daily News 2003).

The exact reason why the protest remained peaceful and orderly is an interesting question that requires a more systematic analysis, which is beyond the scope of this chapter. But I highlight two possible contributing factors here. The first is that the protesters were highly educated; 56 % of the respondents of an on-site survey reported that they had education at the college level or above (Chan and Chung 2003). In addition, less than 4.6 % of the respondents were unemployed. If the sample of the survey was representative of the population of the protesters, one can see that to many of the protesters, the cost of engaging in political violence was simply too high (e.g., losing a decent job).

The second possible reason is that owing to the existence of the rule of law and a relatively liberal media environment, human rights conditions in Hong Kong were generally good. Police brutality was largely absent. Social grievances that Hong Kong people endured pale in comparison with those faced by mainland Chinese. However irritated they were at the Tung administration, the protesters experienced little of gross violations of human rights in their everyday life. Perhaps for this reason, they were able to observe self-restraint and the protest did not lapse into a massive riot.

Regardless of the reason, the peaceful self-expression of the protesters was lauded by the mainstream media. What emerged from public discourse is a view that identifies Hong Kong people as rational, civil, mild, and self-disciplined (Ku 2007). This view was not wholly different from the long-standing image of Hong Kong people: "economic animals" with no enthusiasm for politics. In fact, Lee and Chan (2011) find that some protesters were eager to downplay their political activism by claiming how politically apathetic they were.

This kind of self-denigration in some ways helped promote the cause of the protesters. For one thing, the lack of a mob quality made it difficult for the government to deal with the demand of the protesters in a heavy-handed way. In fact, the emphasis on the protesters' political apathy undermined the government's position by creating an impression that the only reason for driving such a docile population to mass mobilization is that the government was truly inept. In other words, the peacefulness and orderliness of the July 1, 2003 protest were not considered a sign of weakness, but rather, they represented a powerful tool to constrain the government because citizens were only making a lawful articulation of their rights enshrined in the Basic Law. In this respect, the July 1, 2003 protest resembled what O'Brien and Li (2006) call the "rightful resistance," a tactic widely deployed by Chinese peasants in their struggle against abusive local governments.

(2) The Media as an agent of mobilization

The organizer of the July 1, 2003 protest was the Civil Human Rights Front (CHRF), which was an umbrella organization consisting of, at the time of the protest, some 40 loosely connected civil society groups. Because these groups joined the CHRF on a voluntary basis and because they were nonprofit with diverse issue concerns, the CHRF was neither a hierarchical nor a disciplined organization. As a result, although the CHRF helped coordinate the protest by setting the date, time, and theme, the role that it actually played in mobilization was rather limited. Lee and Chan (2011) provide an interesting example to illustrate this. In late 2002, when CHRF asked its constituent members to report the number of people they were able to mobilize, surprisingly, the total added up by these forty groups was merely 5,000 (Lee and Chan 2011, pp. 47–48).

If the central organizer could mobilize only 1 % of the eventual turnout, who made the remaining 99 % of the protesters throw themselves into the protest? Many studies point out that the media played a crucial role. First, consider traditional media. Based on his content analysis of newspapers' coverage of the proposed national security laws, Clement So, a professor of journalism, finds that only three pro-Beijing papers with rather low readership in Hong Kong overtly supported the legislation of Article 23 (So 2003a,b). In contrast, reports and commentaries carried by popular newspapers such as the *Apple Daily*, *Ming Pao Daily News*, and *Oriental Daily* were in various degrees critical of the proposed legislation. For example, Lam Hang-chi, the owner of an elite paper the *Hong Kong Economic Journal*, confided in one commentary that he might close down the paper if the proposed national security laws were passed, for fear of the looming threat of government censorship.

The outspoken *Apple Daily* had no hesitation in campaigning for the July 1 protest. In the days leading up to the protest, the paper was swamped with articles and commentaries either criticizing the Tung administration or directly urging readers to take to the streets. Table 4.1 displays protest-related A1 headlines in the 10 days leading to the protest. As may be seen, these sensational headlines indicate the paper's unabashed support for the protest. On July 1, the paper even distributed posters calling for Tung to resign. The paper's active involvement in the mobilization made it an inseparable part of the movement, which was arguably a calculated decision of the paper's management. In one interview, an *Apple Daily* senior executive admitted that its paper's mobilization effort was "more like a brand-building exercise with more people linking our name to a popular cause" (Lai 2007, p. 167). From the paper's point of view, its effort paid off hand-somely, as 49.5 % of the protesters identified themselves as readers of *Apple Daily* (Lee and Chan 2011, p. 56).

Table 4.1 *Apple Daily*'s A1 headlines in connection with the July 1, 2003 protest from June 21, 2003 to July 1, 2003

Headline	Date
White House: US Opposed Article 23	June 21
Article 23 Stifled Creativity Filmmakers Will Protest on July 1	June 24
Wen Jiabao Will Stay Hong Kong on July 1 to Feel Public Sentiment	June 26
Legislator Asks Tung: How Many Protesters Needed for Government to Back Down	June 27
US House Against Article 23, Voting Result 426:1	June 28
Premier Wen: Please Listen to Me [the people]	June 29
Hong Kong People Against Article 23 Will Make History Tomorrow	June 30
Take to the Street, See You There	July 1

Note: Wen Jiabao, then the premier of the PRC, paid a visit to Hong Kong between June 29 and July 1 to attend events in celebration of Hong Kong's sixth handover anniversary

Newspapers were not the only media channel that helped mobilize citizens to participate in the protest. Another crucial mobilizing agent was talk radio. Chan and Chung (2003) conducted an on-site survey during the protest and found that 65.2 % of the respondents considered talk radio as an important factor that influenced their decision to protest, not much different from those who answered newspapers with 65.6 %. Of all the talk radio programs, the most influential one was *Teacup in a Storm*, a program of *Commercial Radio Hong Kong*. Its host, Albert Cheng, was renowned for his confrontational, if not sometimes disrespectful, approach toward government officials, whom were often called upon to respond to phone-in complaints. On one occasion, Cheng addressed a responding official as a "dog" (*gou guan*), causing controversy. Despite – or perhaps because of – his bluntness, his program was reportedly then the most popular program of *Commercial Radio Hong Kong* of all time (Ming Pao Daily News 2004b). Some even called Albert Cheng the "Chief Executive of Hong Kong before 10 am" (Lee 2011, p. 181) because his program, which ran from 7 to 10 in the morning, set the issue agenda of the city on each day (Ma and Chan 2007, p. 19).

The way Albert Cheng as a talk radio host contributed to the mobilization of the July 1, 2003 protest was less straightforward, but perhaps no less important, than the way *Apple Daily* did. The government was most probably very bothered. As the broadcast license of *Commercial Radio Hong Kong* was due to expire in August 2003, a rumor went that the government decided to shorten the license period from twelve to three years to punish the company for hiring the polemical Cheng. In the last two weeks leading up to the July 1 protest, Albert Cheng announced that he would take an indefinite leave of absence. The abrupt departure of the extremely popular talk show host left a bad impression on the public. Many took it as evidence of the government's undue pressure. Such an impression, not surprisingly, fueled more public discontent against the already unpopular government.

In addition to traditional media, new media also played an important role in organizing the July 1, 2003 protest. Back in 2003, social media had yet to become widespread, but the Internet had already demonstrated its potential as a mobilizing tool. In weeks prior to the protest, numerous political satires and cartoons mocking Tung Chee-hwa and his administration were circulated in the online world through emails (Chung and Chan 2003). Although these multimedia creations were produced by a handful of activists, ordinary people played an important role in receiving as well as redistributing them to their acquaintances, which helped spread the protest message at an exponential rate. It is therefore difficult to distinguish between the mobilizing agent and the one being mobilized. In fact, Chan and Chung (2003) find that 93 % of the protesters took to the streets with their friends, family, or acquaintances and 50.7 % of all these "group" protesters could not recall whether it was they or their acquaintances who first proposed the protest idea. In this respect, Lee and Chan (2011) contends that the July 1, 2003 protest epitomized the idea of "self-mobilization." Apparently, this self-mobilization could not be made possible without the available information technology (Chan 2005).

In summary, the media played a crucial role in mobilizing the July 1, 2003 protest. This could happen only because Hong Kong has a relatively liberal media environment, under which antigovernment messages could be freely transmitted. Hong Kong people also did not need to worry about political persecution as a result of reading or sharing antigovernment information. The short-term, explosive power that the media of Hong Kong could unleash is something that dictators fear. What would be the long-term effect of such a liberal media environment on the prodemocracy movement? This is what I will discuss in the following sections.

4.1 Political Developments After the July 1, 2003 Protest

For many prodemocracy opposition politicians at the time of the protest, they had developed their first political credentials by serving grassroots constituencies. Their political ascendancy had been inextricably linked to Hong Kong's political development prior to the sovereignty transfer. As discussed in the previous chapter, the colonial administration had gradually liberalized the political system from the early 1980s. It introduced in 1982 the first ever popular election for the District Boards, a new administrative rung at the grassroots level. In 1983, competitive elections were extended to the next higher administrative level, the Urban Council. Many members of the present-day opposition elite entered politics in these early local elections. For example, Frederick Fung, who founded the political party Association for Democracy and People's Livelihood (ADPL), was elected to the Urban Council in 1983. Leung Yiu-chung, founder of another political party, the Neighborhood and Workers Service Centre (NWSC), became a District Board member in 1985. Lee Wing-tat and Sin Chung-kai, core members of the Democratic Party, entered the District Boards in the same election. These budding politicians accumulated practical experience in running election campaigns, providing constituency services, and fostering grassroots political support in the subsequent years. When the colonial administration further extended popular election to the Legislative Council, they could utilize their hard-won reputation and local connections to facilitate their bid for the higher elected offices. These grassroots political elite would later become the major opposition force in the HKSAR legislature.

The July 1, 2003 protest opened up opportunities for a new generation of prodemocracy elite. Most notably, Alan Leong and Ronny Tong, who are both former chairmen of Hong Kong Bar Association and members of a civil society group, the Basic Law Article 23 Concern Group, earned their reputation as human rights activists by mounting challenges against the national security laws. Riding on their wave of popularity built during the July 1, 2003 protest, they stood for the 2004 Legislative Council election and won. Another notable example was the charismatic talk radio host Albert Cheng who also managed to capture a seat in the legislature in the 2004 election. Unlike the first-generation opposition elite, these political newcomers had no experience of local elections, let alone grassroots constituency services. Their meteoric rise was almost entirely attributed to the extraordinary fame they developed during the citywide movement against the national security laws.

The anti-establishment effect of the July 1, 2003 protest also carried over to a local election. A few months after the historic protest, an election for the District Councils was held. The pro-Beijing camp witnessed a resounding defeat. In particular, the Democratic Alliance for the Betterment and Progress of Hong Kong (DAB), the flagship Beijing-sponsored party, lost a quarter of their seats. Its chairman, Jasper Tsang, stepped down as a result. The clear winner of this election was the prodemocracy camp (also known as the pan-democratic camp), but the victory was not confined to the well-established parties such as the DP. For instance, Civic Act-Up, a prodemocracy political group established after the July 1, 2003 protest, fielded five candidates and captured three seats in this grassroots election. Remarkably, their candidates, all District Council novices, had begun meeting their constituents only a few weeks before the election (Apple Daily 2003).

The electoral success of this new generation of prodemocracy elite suggests that there exists an alternative route to enter politics other than the traditional means based on grassroots constituency services. This is particularly true for the legislative elections with respect to the geographical constituencies, because their electoral formula is proportional representation and some constituencies have a fairly large district magnitude. For instance, in the 2012 Legislative Council election, a prodemocracy party with only 6 % of the vote was able to gain a seat in the New Territories East constituency, which had a total of nine seats. Because the vote share required for getting elected is rather low, prodemocracy candidates, however politically inexperienced, stand a good chance, as long as they enjoy some kind of citywide reputation. The key question is how to achieve such a reputation. Given that Hong Kong has maintained a relatively high degree of media freedom and given the enormous mobilizing power of the media as demonstrated in the July 1, 2003 protest, this task does not seem insurmountable. The political trajectory of two new opposition parties that emerged after 2003 attests to this point.

4.1.1 Emergence of New Parties

Two important opposition parties emerged after 2003, and none of them was a service-oriented type of party. The first one is the Civic Party (CP), which was founded in 2006. This party has been led by renowned barristers affiliated with the Basic Law Article 23 Concern Group. It, therefore, earned a nickname, the "barristers' party." Because the membership of this party has been overrepresented by professionals such as lawyers and engineers, it is able to carve out a professional image, which has helped it gain support among middle-class voters. As soon as this party was established, it was already the second largest opposition party in the LegCo. It is worth mentioning that none of the LegCo members of this party captured the elected office as a result of grassroots services, and grassroots services have never been part of the party's branding. This can be seen from the ratio of its District Council members to LegCo members (DC-to-LC ratio). A high ratio reflects a party's attention given to the District Councils. Table 4.2 shows that its DC-to-LC ratio has been one of the lowest among all opposition parties. In general, pan-democratic parties established after 2003 have a significantly lower DC-to-LC ratio than those established before 2003.

A political gaffe made by Alan Leong, the party leader, may mirror the party's abhorrence of grassroots services. After the 2011 District Council election, when a reporter asked Leong to explain his party's dismal showing, he bitterly replied that it was because of the pro-Beijing parties' mysterious ability to dole out *shezhai bingzong*, a derogatory term for trivial giveaways, which literally means "snake

Table 4.2 District Council (DC) and Legislative Council (LC) seats by pan-democratic party

	2007–2008			2011–2012		
	DC	LC	DC-LC ratio	DC	LC	DC-LC ratio
Party established before 2003						
ADPL	17	1	17	15	1	15
CTU	0	1	0	.	.	.
DP	59	8	7.38	47	6	7.83
Frontier	3	1	3	.	.	.
NWSC	4	1	4	5	1	5
Party established after 2003						
Civic Act-Up	0	1	0	.	.	.
CP	8	5	1.6	7	6	1.17
Labor	.	.	.	0	4	0
LSD	6	3	2	0	1	0
ND	.	.	.	8	1	8
PP	.	.	.	1	3	0.33

Notes: District Council elections were held in 2007 and 2011, respectively, while Legislative Council elections in 2008 and 2012. Legislative Council seats include both geographical constituencies and functional constituencies soups, vegetarian dishes, festival cakes, and dumplings." He further added that "our problem is to ask rising barristers or engineers to spend a dozen of hours each day working for a District Council constituency, when we see no hope of becoming a ruling party one day." Leong's candor may have offended some citizens who are beneficiaries of the constituency services provided by their District Council members. Yet, Leong may have spoken out on a dilemma confronting his partisans. In my interview with one District Council member from the CP, he confided that the income of his main employment was ten times more than his salary as a District Council member.[2]

Another opposition party that emerged after 2003 is the League of Social Democrats (LSD). Although the LSD is less elitist than the CP, the electoral appeal of this party does not lie in grassroots services either. Similar to the CP, the founding members of the LSD include some "celebrity" political activists. For example, Leung Kwok-hung, also known as "Long Hair," is a long-time Marxist-cum-street protester well known for his maverick activism style. Another founding member, Wong Yuk-man, was a famous talk radio host and a vitriolic critic of the government. Like Albert Cheng, Wong, who openly encouraged his listeners to participate in the July 1, 2003 protest, reportedly quit hosting his popular radio program due to political pressure (Sing Tao Daily 2005). The party has positioned itself as "truly leftist" (Hong Kong Economic Journal 2006), advocating fair redistribution of wealth. Despite its professed grassroots orientation, the LSD's performance in grassroots elections has been far from impressive. In the 2007 District Council election, only 6 of the 30 candidates from this party were able to capture an office. Of the six winners, only one was not an incumbent. In the 2011 District Council election, all of its 27 candidates were defeated.

In 2011, Wong Yuk-man split from the LSD and formed another political party, People Power (PP). Wong's departure significantly weakened the LSD, as the number of its LegCo members dropped from three to one. Like the LSD, PP has shown little interest in developing local support networks through the provision of constituency services. In 2013, Wong Yuk-man left PP.

4.1.2   Rise of Contentious Politics

While these new parties' constituency services are unremarkable, this does not prevent them from reaching out to voters, thanks to the existence of a relatively liberal media environment. Since their establishment, these parties have been able to maintain a high media exposure. This is not only because they have many political "celebrities," but also because their actions are colorful and, at times, controversial. First, consider the LSD. Its LegCo members have frequently engaged in disruptive behavior during the legislative sessions. Throwing objects and shouting slogans are

---

[2]Personal interview with a District Councillor on January 31, 2012 (Code: 22).

common tactics. On one occasion, Leung Kwok-hung released a helium balloon attached with a slogan that insulted the Chief Executive, who was to make his annual policy address in the legislature. Leung was expelled from the legislature for the disruption, but his helium balloon ascended to the roof of the chamber. Because the ceiling of the chamber was high, the balloon could not be removed immediately, forcing the Chief Executive to face the insulting slogan during the whole time of his policy address.

Starting from 2012, filibuster has become a new tool of disruption for Leung Kwok-hung and Wong Yuk-man alike. As discussed in the previous chapter, the HKSAR legislature has a unique characteristic that permits government bills to be passed by a simple majority of the entire legislature, while requiring private bills to be passed separately in the functional and geographical constituencies. Under this separate voting system, opposition parties, who are always the legislative minority by design despite their majority position in the directly elected geographical constituencies, have little recourse against unpopular government bills. For this reason, there were attempts by opposition parties to use filibuster to delay the voting of bills.[3] But the most publicized use of filibuster occurred in 2012, when Wong Yuk-man and other pan-democratic lawmakers initiated a marathon filibuster by proposing over a thousand amendments to a bill concerning by-election arrangements. Their effort failed to prevent the passage of the bill, as the President of the Legislative Council unilaterally terminated the legislative debate that lasted for more than 33 h.

The elitist CP has not involved in overt acts of disruption in the legislature. But its members have engaged in various dissident tactics that are no less disruptive from the point of view of Beijing and the establishment. Perhaps chief among them was the quasi-referendum the CP helped trigger in 2010.

In response to the government's public consultation on political reforms in the late 2009, the LSD, tired of years of endless and fruitless negotiation with the government over political liberalization in the past years, proposed an innovative move to pressure the government to make a concrete step toward democratization; it suggested to the pan-democratic coalition to choose one legislator in each of the multimembered geographical constituencies to resign. Their simultaneous and collective resignation would trigger a citywide by-election, which can be viewed as a de facto referendum on political reform. The proposed quasi-referendum received an enormous amount of media coverage because of the establishment's fierce condemnation. Some officials called it "radical," "unconstitutional," or even an "act of declaring independence" (South China Morning Post 2010; Wen Wei Po 2010a; Takungpao 2010; Wen Wei Po 2014b). Behind these criticisms was Beijing's fear that this de facto form of direct democracy would develop into a practice, providing a convenient weapon for the opposition to blackmail the Hong Kong government,

---

[3]For instance, filibuster was reportedly used to obstruct the readings of the proposed national security laws in 2003 and the approval of the funding for the construction of the high-speed railway in 2010.

if not Beijing as well. To some observers' surprise, the CP, which had not been considered a radical prodemocracy party, supported the quasi-referendum idea by agreeing to have two LegCo members resign. The movement, however, ended up failing to achieve its intended effect, as pro-establishment parties, probably under Beijing's pressure (Apple Daily 2010b), announced that they would boycott the by-election.[4] Because there was no pro-Beijing candidate to pit against, the by-election lost its referendum purpose, resulting in a dismal turnout at 17.1 %. The quasi-referendum movement came to an uneventful end, as all resigned legislators were re-elected.

The CP was also allegedly involved in a number of controversial legal cases against the government. The construction project of the Hong Kong-Zhuhai-Macau (HZM) Bridge is a case in point. The HZM Bridge, which is one of the most important infrastructure projects in Hong Kong in the past years, was intended to embed Hong Kong more closely into the economic system of the Guangdong province by linking the city to the west bank of the Pearl River Delta. Like other large infrastructure projects, the construction of the bridge involved a potential environmental hazard. The Environmental Protection Department of the HKSAR government assessed the environmental impacts and concluded that the impacts fell within the acceptable limits stipulated by law. However, soon after the construction began, a senior citizen living in the affected area filed an application for judicial review of the Environmental Protection Department's assessment. The government won the case a year later, but officials lamented that the delay resulted from the court case cost taxpayers hundreds of millions of dollars due to the inflation of the construction costs. Blame was heaped upon the senior litigant, who was perceived to abuse the legal process and obstruct Hong Kong's development. More importantly, the Civic Party was accused of being the "evil backstage manipulator" of the whole saga (Wen Wei Po 2011a; Ming Pao Daily News 2011a), because the litigant used to be a party volunteer and members of the Civic Party had provided her legal advice all along. The Civic Party denied the charges, insisting that the senior citizen was exercising her legal rights to hold the government accountable for environmental problems (Ming Pao Daily News 2004a). But the litigant later told the media that "someone" instructed her to get involved in the case, which was an issue she, as an elderly woman, did not fully understand. Although she refused to specify who that "someone" was, her reply had already called into question the party's alleged innocence.

Another controversial judicial review occurred around the same time. Two Philippine domestic helpers challenged the immigration law that denies foreign domestic helpers of the right of abode. In Hong Kong, foreign domestic helpers are not granted citizenship, regardless of their length of employment in Hong Kong. Because they were legally represented by a barrister who is a member of the Civic Party, pro-Beijing media charged the party with supporting foreign

---

[4]Initially, some pro-establishment parties had expressed interest to participate in the by-election (Sing and Tang 2012; Hong Kong Economic Times 2010).

domestic helpers to gain permanent residency (Wen Wei Po 2012a,b; Ta Kung Pao 2011), an accusation that the Civic Party did not deny initially. The court case caused an uproar in Hong Kong, because many feared that labor competition and welfare spending would increase once these foreign workers were granted equal citizenship as the locals. The public's anxiety escalated, as the government hinted that family members of the domestic helpers or half a million foreigners would arrive in Hong Kong en masse if the government lost the case (Wen Wei Po 2011b). Not surprisingly, this fear developed into resentment against the Civic Party in some quarters.

The foregoing discussion explains why these post-2003 opposition parties have been able to maintain a high media exposure. Their colorful confrontations with the establishment, ranging from throwing objects to getting involved in judicial reviews, have attracted the media, which are more interested in reporting conflicts rather than consensus. To see the extent to which these parties capture the media's attention, I collected data from WiseNews, a company that provides online access to all articles that have appeared in major Hong Kong newspapers since the late 1990s. Figure 4.1 shows that within the opposition camp, the CP, LSD, and the PP collectively have enjoyed the lion's share of media coverage, which used to belong to the DP prior to 2006, exactly the year when the CP and the LSD were founded.

It is important to note, of course, that being reported is not tantamount to being popular. As discussed, their political activism often causes controversies. From their own perspective, what they have done is certainly legitimate, justifiable, and perhaps lofty. For example, Leung Kwok-hung considers his object throwing as an effective

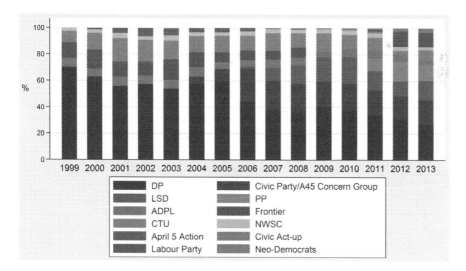

Fig. 4.1 Overtime change of media coverage by party within the opposition camp. Notes: The data include only political parties or groups that have been reported in more than a hundred news articles in two consecutive years. Because many of the founding members of the Civic Party came from the Basic Article 45 Concern Group, these two groups are combined into one category. (Source: WiseNews)

way to expose the injustices of the political system (Lam 2012). Leaders of the Civic Party and the LSD see the quasi-referendum as a population-wide prodemocracy movement (Lam 2012) and a means to raise public awareness of the lack of universal suffrage (Sing and Tang 2012). However, non-prodemocracy media interpret their actions in a different way. The LSD's disruptive acts in the legislature are often framed as a willful destruction of the order in the legislature (The Sun 2010) and a bad influence for young people (Ta Kung Pao 2012). Some even mock Leung as a crook who earns a good salary by causing a mess in the legislature (Ta Kung Pao 2009). For the quasi-referendum, pro-Beijing media inveighed against the CP and LSD for wasting taxpayers' money on a meaningless by-election (Sing and Tang 2012). In short, the confrontational approach of these parties' political activism is not wholly indisputable and is likely to alienate non-radical voters who support the prodemocracy camp.

But from these parties' strategic electoral calculation, the alienation of non-radical voters is not a problem insofar as doing so could consolidate the electoral support of their target constituents, namely, radical voters. The outcome of the 2010 quasi-referendum illustrates this point. As discussed, the turnout rate of this quasi-referendum was merely 17.1 %. This figure is considered low only when compared with a regular election with two camps pitted against each other. One may arrive at a different conclusion if one sees the quasi-referendum as a promotional campaign of two opposition parties. Note that for LegCo elections, getting a seat in the geographical constituencies requires as few as a single digit of vote share. The fact that these parties were still able to mobilize 17.1 % of the voting population to participate in a by-election that lacked its intended referendum content may suggest a very successful political campaign. Perhaps more importantly, they achieved this result without relying on an elaborate grassroots support network; using the media alone was sufficient for mobilizing their supporters. Wong Yuk-man did admit that the by-election outcomes, however disappointing, were actually good for his party. Because the LSD received 120,000 more votes than in the last election, he was confident that his party would be able to carry at least half of these new votes to the next election. In addition, the mobilization effect of the quasi-referendum helped them recruit a large number of volunteers, which could not have been otherwise accomplished with its weak local organization (Hong Kong Economic Journal 2010b).

This tradeoff between moderate and radical voters' support is seen from the performance discrepancy of these parties in elections between different levels. The total number of seats captured by the CP, LSD, and PP in the 2011 District Council election dropped from 14 to 8, while their seats in geographical constituencies in the LegCo increased from seven to nine in the 2012 election. A major reason for this discrepancy is that the District Council election runs the single-member district

(SMD) as the electoral formula. Because the SMD formula produces one winner per district, it disadvantages radical parties, whose supporters are almost always in the minority. In contrast, in LegCo elections, where the PR rule is used, radical voters would be duly represented, rather than marginalized. The tradeoff here suggests a potential dilemma for Hong Kong's political parties; they face a stark choice between constituency services and media attention. If a party opts for the latter as a way to reach out to voters, it needs to exploit controversies. But if it engages in controversial activism, it is likely to alienate moderate voters from whom it could woo support by providing constituency services. In other words, the two vote-getting tactics are not interchangeable because they appeal to different constituents.

Knowing that their political messages would be misrepresented in the mass media, these parties also built up their own media outlets to help promote their causes directly. In addition to economical tools such as Web sites and a *Facebook* fan page, these parties have also explored more costly options, the most major being online radio broadcasting. In fact, after the July 1, 2003 protest, Hong Kong witnessed a proliferation of activist online radio stations. For example, the activist barristers from the Basic Law Article 23 Concern Group set up *a45radio.com*, which aimed to stimulate public discussion of Article 45 of the Basic Law concerning universal suffrage of the Chief Executive. Although *a45radio.com* was later shut down, members of the Civic Party have involved themselves in another online platform: *OurTV.hk*, which provides both radio and television programs on current affairs. Opposition politicians are invited to host these talk shows.

One of the most successful online radio stations is *hkreporter.com*, owned by businessman Stephen Shiu. It was reported that its popular broadcast programs had a weekly audience size of 30,000 (Ip 2009, p. 230). In 2008, *hkreporter.com* merged with *myradio.com*, another popular online radio station run by Wong Yuk-man of the LSD. From then on and until Wong Yuk-man left the LSD, *hkreporter.com* became an important media channel for the LSD to promote its ideology and attract followers (Ip 2009, p. 237).

The advantage of online radio broadcast is that it falls outside of the scope of the existing laws (Ip 2009, p. 232).[5] This means that not only is a broadcasting license not required, but also that the content need not observe regulations pertaining to standard radio broadcasting. Talk show hosts of radical online radio stations could therefore freely use profane language to attack government officials and political enemies. This unusual form of freedom encourages an unrestrained expression of anger, which has a strong appeal to ideological voters. It is worth noting, however, that these online media channels offer more than political programs. For example, one of the most popular shows in *hkreporter.com* was a horror-story program *Kongbu Zaixian*. *OurTV.hk* also produces soft news programs on entertainment. Presumably, these programs are intended to broaden its listenership, as politics, after all,

---

[5]Not all prodemocracy activists go for the online option. Tsang Kin-shing, a member of the LSD, has continuously run a traditional radio broadcast station, Citizens' Radio, in defiance of repeated crackdowns by the government on the charge of illegal broadcasting.

might not be an interesting topic for many people. Despite these efforts, these online broadcast programs have yet to achieve the audience size of traditional broadcasting. Part of the reason is that it can reach only a small subset of the population, who are comfortable listening to the radio or watching television on their computers. Yet from the perspective of radical parties, this limitation is perhaps less of a concern because ordinary voters are not their target constituents in the first place.

4.1.3 Rise of Internal Strife Within the Opposition Camp

Although the new opposition parties discussed in the previous analysis are more interested in using eye-catching and noisemaking media tactics to promote themselves, their emergence has posed a grave challenge to the first-generation opposition parties, whose political support is largely based on relatively mundane constituency services. First, these new parties have gradually edged out their senior counterparts with respect to media exposure. The most noticeable example is the DP. As may be seen in Fig. 4.1, 70 % of the news coverage of the opposition camp in 1999 went to the DP. This dropped to less than 30 % by 2013.[6]

To the moderate opposition parties, especially the flagship party DP, the most serious challenge posed by these new parties is probably their virulent attacks. The difference in tactics to fight for democracy between the moderate and the radical wing of the opposition camp has evolved over the years into a competition for ideological purity. Although the DP was once labeled by Chinese officials as a "radical prodemocracy force" (*jijin minzhupai*) (Xu 1993, p. 394), it is not interested in throwing objects in the legislature or in committing acts that are expressively disruptive. When it comes to bargaining with the establishment, the DP is also more pragmatic, as it is willing to accept partial improvement over the status quo, however small it is. Whether the radical parties are any more effective at extracting concessions from the government than the DP remains unclear, but the former's confrontational and uncompromising attitude does look daring and heroic, at least in the eyes of ideological voters. On the other hand, the DP's insistence on a "peaceful, rational, nonviolent, and gentlemanly" approach (*heli feifei*) may appear too timid and lame. This contrast allows the radical parties to claim a moral high ground vis-à-vis the DP and other moderate parties. At times, the radical parties and their

---

[6]It is important to note that the decline is in part due to the DP's decreasing seat share in the legislature. In 1998, the DP occupied nine out of the 20 seats for geographical constituencies, while in 2012, it could only capture four. But seat share is not the only factor affecting a party's media exposure. For example, the LSD in 2013 had only one LegCo seat, but its news coverage in that year was four times that of the ADPL and seven times that of the NWSC. The two latter parties also have one seat each in the LegCo.

supporters openly question the moderate parties' political integrity. For example, Leung Kwok-hung on one occasion excoriated the DP for cheating its prodemocracy supporters for 19 years (Oriental Daily 2010).[7]

There is no need to assume that the DP leaders are ideologically less radical than their LSD counterparts. But as the largest party in the opposition camp and the central pillar of the city's prodemocracy movement in the past decade, the DP cannot deviate too much from the ideological position of ordinary prodemocracy voters. After all, a widely shared impression of Hong Kong's ordinary prodemocracy citizens is their peace-loving and law-abiding character, an image that has been reinforced by the peacefulness and orderliness of the July 1, 2003 protest. This moderate character was also considered a laudable quality in 2003.

Attacking an ally from within the same political camp also makes electoral sense because supporters of one's ally likely share an ideology akin to one's own supporters. An electoral implication is that grabbing votes from an ally's support base is easier than votes from an opposing camp's. The 2008 LegCo election offers one telling example that shows how outflanking an ally can be translated into one's own electoral gains. In the Kowloon West district, where 14 party lists competed for five seats, the CP candidate, Claudia Mo, was initially leading Wong Yuk-man, the LSD candidate, by 7 % points. In a couple of television debates, Wong launched fierce attacks on Mo, rather than on pro-Beijing candidates who were also present in the event. Wong lambasted Mo for "telling lies" and described the CP "an evil force of democracy, monopolizing the representation of democracy." Failing to present a convincing rebuttal to Wong's charges, Mo was seen as a major loser in the debates. More interestingly, the way Wong berated Mo was so inflammatory as well as entertaining that the debates received over 100,000 views on YouTube. In a space of one month, the popularity ratings of the two candidates almost reversed. At the end, the party list led by Wong finished with the second most votes, whereas the Mo's failed to get any seat.

The internal strife within the prodemocracy camp became more acute as the idea of the quasi-referendum surfaced in 2009. Proponents of the movement urged opposition parties to join the fray. Moderate parties, however, were unimpressed by the idea. Frederick Fung of the ADPL and Leung Yiu-chung of the NWSC pointed out that the benchmark for winning and losing the quasi-referendum was not clear enough to avoid an arbitrary interpretation of the outcome. Their worries were not unfounded, as victory can be determined by the total number of votes received or the total number of seats retained or both. Voter turnout also matters. In many countries with a statutory referendum procedure, a referendum is considered valid only if it

---

[7]Ironically, Leung Kwok-hung, who joined a Trotskyist vanguard party in the 1970s, is now viewed by his ultraleft comrades as a "traitor of the revolution" because of his association with the establishment (Xu 2013, p. 174).

meets a certain turnout threshold. Hong Kong has no legal provision for referendum and therefore no agreed benchmark to determine the result of a quasi-referendum. Without a clear benchmark for success, it is difficult to motivate voters to participate as well as to legitimize the referendum outcome.

The proponents of the quasi-referendum were aware of the pitfalls of their movement. To allay the skeptics' worries, they initially adopted a demanding benchmark for success: defeat the opponents in the total vote share and achieve a turnout of 50 % (Ming Pao Daily News 2010a). A spokesperson of the CP added that the movement should be considered a failure if not all resigned legislators are reelected (Hong Kong Economic Journal 2010a).

Skeptics remained unconvinced, however. Party heavyweights of the DP counter-argued that Hong Kong people's support for democratization has been evidenced by the prodemocracy camp's past electoral success in the geographical constituencies of the LegCo. There was no need to hold a quasi-referendum to prove the obvious. In addition, Beijing was unlikely to accelerate the pace of democratization even if the quasi-referendum supporters are able to present new "evidence." At worst, if some legislators failed to win the by-election, the entire prodemocracy camp would suffer because it might lose a "critical minority" in the legislature and hence lose the veto power of constitutional amendments (Sing and Tang 2012, p. 149).

The unsupportive attitude of the moderate opposition fueled the radicals' resentment. Wong Yuk-man lamented that he would not recognize the NWSC as his prodemocracy ally (Wen Wei Po 2010b). Leung Kwok-hung suggested that the relationship between the DP and the quasi-referendum campaign was analogous to an appendix to a human body, implying that the DP should be removed in order for the campaign to move on (Sing Pao 2009).

The rift between the moderate and the radical opposition elite deepened in the wake of the quasi-referendum. On the one hand, the CP-LSD alliance refused to concede defeat, even though the turnout was far lower than their proclaimed benchmark for success.[8] The Pro-Beijing media criticized the "referendum" legislators for their lack of principle and proclaimed that Hong Kong people deserted the "radical approach" (Hong Kong Commercial Daily 2010; Wen Wei Po 2010c).

On the other hand, soon after the quasi-referendum saga, the moderate opposition engaged in closed-door meetings with Chinese authorities. They quickly struck a deal, as both sides were willing to work out a compromise. In particular, Beijing agreed to add ten seats to the legislature, evenly split between the geographical constituencies and functional constituencies. The five new functional constituency seats would represent the District Councils, and constituents for these five new seats are Hong Kong citizens who previously held no vote in the functional constituencies, or over 90 % of the voting population. In a nutshell, these five new functional constituency seats are de facto geographical-constituency seats. This change effectively tipped the balance slightly in favor of the prodemocracy camp with the lowering

---

[8]The CP-LSD alliance had unilaterally lowered the benchmark for victory, as the by-election neared. But the turnout rate still failed to meet their lowest target.

of the actual seat share of the functional constituencies. The deal later became the government's political reform bill that was sent to the LegCo for passage.

The CP-LSD alliance showed no appreciation for the DP, despite its success in extracting political concessions from Beijing. Rather, some deemed the limited concessions as too small and too humiliating (Sing Pao 2010b). Others maintained that the deal would only justify and perpetuate the existence of the functional constituencies, which are widely perceived to be the stumbling block to democ-ratization (Sing Pao 2010a). The DP was also under attack for holding closed-door meetings with Beijing. Some worried the deal made in the smoke-filled room was an indication that the DP had been co-opted (Sing Tao Daily 2010). Others went so far as to accuse the DP of being a "traitor of democracy" by not supporting the quasi-referendum in exchange for a chance to negotiate with Beijing (Ming Pao Daily News 2010d).

Despite its allies' fierce objections, the DP went ahead and voted for the government's political reform bill. With DP's support, the bill, which required a two-thirds vote of the LegCo to be passed, was successfully passed on June 24, about a month after the quasi-referendum. But the DP paid a high price for its pragmatism. One DP legislator quit the party just before the bill's passage. A few months later, a group of DP District Councillors left and set up a new party, the Neo Democrats. Perhaps more importantly, a backlash against the DP gradually surfaced. For example, during the debate of the bill, thousands of protesters besieged the legislature to voice out their objection to the reform. When the DP's chairman, Albert Ho, left the building, he was greeted by angry protesters who threw objects at him and shouted insulting phrases.

The anti-DP sentiment also manifested itself in the annual July 1 protest of that year. The DP, a long-standing supporter of the rally – and possibly the beneficiary as well – was transformed into a target of the protesters. The DP marchers were ridiculed and insulted along the way. The LSD capitalized on the resentment by mobilizing protesters to shout anti-DP slogans.

To the media, the mudslinging among the opposition elite was too sensational to miss. For decades, the most salient political cleavage in Hong Kong had revolved around the prodemocracy camp versus the pro-establishment camp. Never had Hong Kong people seen such an intense infighting among the reputed democracy fighters. Conceivably, the mockery, smearing, and stinging criticism received disproportion-ate attention in the media. How the DP defended its pragmatism and the advantages of the partial reform largely went unnoticed. In short, the mass media provided little room for an in-depth and sober discussion of the pros and cons of the DP's actions.

The political bickering among the opposition elite reached its peak during the 2012 LegCo election. The DP was a major target of blame. In numerous television debates, the fiercest attacks the DP received came not from the pro-establishment camp but from the pan-democrats, particularly People Power's candidates. To characterize more systematically this intra-camp political bickering, I ran a content analysis of election news that appeared in major newspapers three months prior to LegCo elections. I first classified news articles that had mentioned the name of any pan-democratic party into two groups: those involving blaming and those that did not. Of those "blaming" news, I further examined the patterns of blaming. The results are displayed in Table 4.3. Several features stand out from the table. First, since 2003, "blaming" has become an increasingly important component in electoral news that involve pan-democrats. In 2004, about 20 % of pan-democratic references are related to blame. The figure increased to 39 % in 2012. A plausible explanation is that pan-democratic parties increasingly rely on negative campaigns.

Another striking feature is a remarkable increase of blame within the pan-democratic camp in 2012. Of the 1701 "blame" references, 21 % are related to other pan-democratic parties. Table 4.4 displays a more detailed pattern of blaming within the pan-democratic camp. The table is a matrix that shows the number of times one party (on the vertical axis) criticizes another party (on the horizontal axis).

As expected, the DP took a lot of blames. The single most critical DP basher is People Power, which has blamed the DP for 67 times. The DP also suffers from serious internal strife, which has captured 70 references in the news.[9] The HKSAR

Table 4.3 Blaming between political parties during legislative elections, 2000–2012

Year	2000		2004		2008		2012	
Total number of newspapers	9		9		13		14	
Total number of news articles with pan-democratic references	1114		3141		2261		2554	
	No blame	Blame	No blame	Blame	No blame	Blame	No blame	Blame
	1031	400	3027	738	2887	1041	2676	1701
a. Blame involving pro-establishment		340		631		914		1385
b. Blame involving pan-democrats		72		119		155		364
a/b		4.72		5.3		5.9		3.8

Source: WiseNews

Notes: The unit of observation is the reference to a pan-democratic party. For instance, in 2000, there are 1,431 references of pan-democratic parties in 1,114 news articles that come from nine newspapers. Of these 1,431 references, 400 are involved with blaming. Of the 400 "blame" references, 340 are associated with pro-establishment parties (either a pan-democratic party blaming the establishment or a pro-establishment party or a pan-democratic being blamed by the establishment or a pro-establishment party), while 72 with another pan-democratic party. "Blame involving pro-establishment" and "Blame involving pan-democrats" do not add up to the total number of blame references because a pan-democratic party can blame both a pro-establishment party and a fellow pan-democratic party at the same time

---

[9]Much of the internal strife was caused by a DP District Councillor, who quit the party in an attempt to apply for a high-ranking government position.

Table 4.4 Blaming within the pan-democratic camp, 2012

	Pan-democratic parties								Establishment		
	ADPL	CP	DP	LABOUR	LSD	ND	NWSC	PP	Beijing	HKSAR govt	Pro-establishment parties
ADPL	0	0	0	0	0	0	0	3	9	56	29
CP	1	58	1	0	0	0	0	4	41	145	56
DP	0	20	70	0	2	1	0	60	36	383	67
LABOUR	0	1	0	0	0	0	0	3	5	92	12
LSD	0	4	3	0	0	0	0	4	64	116	50
ND	0	0	8	0	0	0	0	0	1	15	3
NWSC	0	1	0	0	0	0	0	0	9	19	0
PP	8	9	67	0	2	0	0	2	13	85	35

Source: WiseNews

Notes: In the above matrix, rows indicate blamers, while columns those being blamed. For instance, CP blamed the ADPL once and PP four times. The main diagonal represents within-party conflicts. For example, the DP has 70 news references related to its internal strife

Table 4.5 Blaming within the pro-establishment camp, 2012

	Pan-democratic parties					Establishment		
	DAB	FTU	LP	NPP	Others	Beijing	HKSAR Govt	Pan-democratic parties
DAB	0	0	1	0	2	2	94	116
FTU	8	0	2	0	0	0	70	32
LP	2	0	0	11	3	0	21	4
NPP	0	0	10	0	0	0	2	28
Others	0	0	6	0	0	0	14	9

Source: WiseNews

Notes: In the above matrix, rows indicate blamers, while columns those being blamed. The main diagonal represents within-party conflicts. Others include Civil Force, Economic Synergy, Kowloon West New Dynamic, and Professional Forum

is by far the most frequent target of blame for these opposition parties, which is not surprising. What is astonishing is that four out of these eight pan-democratic parties criticized their pan-democratic allies more frequently than their pro-establishment rivals. In particular, People Power faulted the DP almost twice as much as it did to all pro-establishment parties combined. Such a phenomenon may well suggest that two forces are simultaneously at play. The first is that pan-democratic parties are vying for similar votes, which makes intra-camp competition keener than that between opposing camps, while the second is that pan-democratic infighting captures more media attention than between-camp bickering.

As a comparison, Table 4.5 shows the blaming pattern within the pro-establishment camp. Several features also stand out from this chart. First, these parties tended to blame the pan-democratic rivals more than their pro-establishment fellows. Only the LP engages more frequently in within-camp blaming. Second, unlike the pan-democrats, within-party conflicts are nonexistent among pro-establishment parties. Finally, the HKSAR is a usual target of criticisms by these parties, except for the NPP. This result should not come as a surprise. These pro-establishment parties, by definition, support the establishment, which may weaken their appeal to voters who are dissatisfied with the government's performance. During election campaigns, therefore, these parties have an incentive to distance themselves from the government, in order to expand their electoral support. One way to do it is to criticize the government and present themselves as parties responsible for monitoring the government.

In summary, compared with pan-democratic parties, pro-establishment parties are less inclined to use the blaming strategy. When they do, they tend to target parties of the opposing camp or the HKSAR government itself. As a result, unlike the pan-democrats, internal strife among pro-establishment parties is far less visible.

The extent to which the backlash against the DP carried over to the 2012 LegCo election remains unclear, however. Although the DP's total geographical-constituency vote dropped by 20 % (total votes approximately down from 312,000 to 247,000), the party fielded two lists to compete for the newly added functional constituencies (also known as the "super seats"), which were decided by over 90 % of the voting population. With two votes in hand (one for the geographical constituency and one for the functional constituency), some prodemocracy voters may vote strategically by allocating one vote to the DP in the "super seat" functional constituency and another vote to a non-DP opposition party in the geographical constituency. As a result, it is difficult to determine the DP's exact vote loss. What is certain, though, is that radical opposition parties were major gainers within the opposition camp. The LSD and the breakaway PP together received about 260,000 votes, 67 % up from what the LSD obtained in 2008.

4.2   Key Developments of Civil Society

After the July 1, 2003 protest, civil society in Hong Kong was awash in optimism. As Ku (2007) vividly describes, "a sense of empowerment and solidarity was heightened in society giving rise to a self-congratulatory discourse of a rising civil society (p. 196)." Lee and Chan (2011) have a similar observation, "[b]y the end of 2003, 'July 1' has already been totemized in public discourse as a condensation symbol for a set of social values, a type of political power, a kind of 'spirit,' and a beginning of a 'new era' (p. 9)." Indeed, the historic protest had breathed new life into Hong Kong's civil society. One indicator is the formation of new societies. In Hong Kong, establishing a new society requires registration with the Police Licensing Office or application for an exemption from registration. Between July 1997 and June 2003, the total number of new societies registered or exempted from registration was about 8,100 (HKSAR 2006, p. 115), or 1,350 per year on average. Since 2005, the annual number of newly formed societies had increased from around 2,000 to almost 3,000 (see Table 4.6).

Table 4.6 New societies and public order events in Hong Kong, 2004–2013

Year	2004	2005	2006	2007	2008	2009	2010	2011	2012	2013
New societies		1950	2205	1980	2489		2718	2923	2824	
Public order events	1974	1900	2228	3824	4287	4222	5656	6878	7529	6166

Sources: HKSAR (2012, Table 13), HKSAR (2013), Hong Kong Police Force
Notes: "New societies" refer to the annual number of new societies registered or exempted from registration. "Public order events" include public processions and public meetings

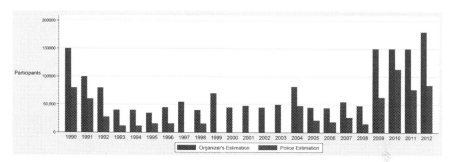

Fig. 4.2 Number of participants in the candlelight vigil in commemoration of "June 4" victims (Source: Ming Pao Daily News, June 5, 2012)

Hong Kong people also seem to become more inclined to take part in public demonstrations to express their preferences over political and social issues. Table 4.6 shows that the number of public processions and gatherings has increased drastically since 2005. The annual candlelight vigil in commemoration of the June 4 Incident is particularly revealing. After 1989, each year tens of thousands of Hong Kong citizens gathered in the Victoria Park on the night of June 4, raising a candle for the victims of the prodemocracy student movement in Beijing in 1989. The number of participants in this event increased slightly right after 2003 but has reached new heights time and again since 2008 (see Fig. 4.2).

A series of social movements have broken out since 2003. Of all these social movements, two were particularly important given their massive turnouts and amount of media coverage. The first is the "Anti-High Speed Rail Movement" that occurred between the late 2009 and early 2010. The Hong Kong government proposed in 2008 the construction of the Express Rail Link, which would connect to the high-speed rail network in the mainland. The railway project was controversial because the government planned to situate the terminus at a prime residential zone. According to one report prepared by railroad experts affiliated with a civil society group, Professional Commons, the proposed site was suboptimal with respect to its cost (Hung et al. 2010). The location was also criticized for being inconvenient to most Hong Kong residents (except wealthy residents who lived near the site) and required the demolition of villages. Students, social activists, environmentalists, and affected villagers alike jointly organized protests, petitions, and hunger strikes. To show their resolve, some supporters even went on a prostration march, a form of mortification akin to a religious ritual. Their activism attracted an enormous amount of media attention, although it failed to reverse the government's decision.

The second important social movement is the "Anti-Patriotic Education Movement" that took place in 2012. The government was planning to introduce a new school curriculum, "Moral and National Education," to primary and secondary schools starting from September 2012. Many worried that the new curriculum, which was compulsory, was a form of indoctrination, aiming to instill political propaganda into the minds of students. The publication of a government-sponsored teaching manual exacerbated the public's worries, as it contained biased views in favor of the Chinese Communist Party such as describing it a "progressive, selfless, and a united ruling coalition." Concerned parents and students threw themselves into a series of activism in protest of the curriculum including organizing mass demonstrations and student walkouts. The movement, which gradually gained momentum in the summer of 2012, culminated into an occupy-government event. From the late August, activists camped out in the plaza outside of the government headquarters and began to go on a hunger strike. In the days that followed, tens of thousands of citizens flocked to the government headquarters after work to show solidarity with the activists. At one point, the government office was besieged by over 120,000 protesters chanting anti-patriotic education slogans. On September 9, the government announced an indefinite suspension of the compulsory implementation of the new curriculum and hence ended the political crisis.

There are some significant differences between these post-2003 movements and the July 1, 2003 protest. Most notably, young activists played a leading role in these social movements. The "Anti-High Speed Rail Movement" actually popularized the term "post-80s generation," which refers to people who were born after 1980, because most of the leaders of the movement were in their twenties at the time. In the case of the campaign against the "Moral and National Education," an activist group called "Scholarism," which is basically composed of secondary school students, had a ubiquitous presence throughout the course of the movement.

Another difference is that activists of these new social movements became increasingly dissatisfied with the conventional tactic of resistance, namely, a peaceful and orderly procession, which symbolized the July 1, 2003 protest (So 2008, p. 248). They were more willing to utilize alternative resistance actions to make their voices heard. For example, the "post-80s" activists in the "Anti-High Speed Rail Movement" blockaded roads and clashed with the police on a number of occasions.

Although these high-profile social movements differ from the July 1, 2003 protest in the above respects, they all share an important similarity with their predecessor: self-mobilization. Thanks to the proliferation of online communication channels such as social media, concerned individuals were able to quickly discover each other's presence, so that joint actions among strangers were made possible. Communication technology also facilitated the dissemination of their ideas and the recruitment of followers. For example, the activists of the "Anti-High Speed Rail Movement" were actively using *inmediahk.net*, an online citizen media platform created by organizers of the July 1, 2003 protest, to promote their cause. As for the "Anti-Patriotic Education Movement," the *Facebook* page "National Education Parents Concern Group"[10] served as a central portal for activists and concerned citizens to connect and share information among each other. Because the activists were able to stage, sometimes spontaneously, a large-scale social mobilization by dint of their own efforts, they did not seek organizational assistance from opposition parties, let alone a long-term collaboration with them.

In fact, activists of these movements consciously distanced themselves from political parties for two reasons. The first is to protect their cause from smear campaigns by the pro-Beijing media. Take the "Anti-Patriotic Education Movement" as an example. Their demand, namely, calling a halt to political propaganda, is itself highly political. Some pro-Beijing newspapers portrayed the movement as a secret political agenda by the opposition camp, who, as their conspiracy theory went, sought to boost its electoral support by sabotaging a well-intentioned education policy of the government (Wen Wei Po 2012d). For this reason, in order to prevent their movement from lapsing into a fight between political camps, the organizers of the movement from the very beginning had framed their movement as a "saving the children" campaign. They identified themselves as "concerned parents," who wanted to protect their children from bad influences. They staged a protest march, the participants of which were predominantly parents and their babies in prams. The parent activists also organized a press conference, in which they answered reporters' questions while they had their young children sitting on their lap. These were gestures intended to depoliticize their demand, in hopes of broadening the reach of their cause.[11]

The second reason for the distance between these movements and political parties is that social activists in Hong Kong have a deep-seated aversion to party politics. In his study of Hong Kong's young activists, Ma (2008) finds that they were heavily influenced by the wave of "New Social Movement" (NSM) that occurred in Western democracies in the postwar period. The NSMs emphasized autonomy from the state and focused on identity politics related to postmaterialist issues such as gay rights and environmental protection (Offe 1985), rather than political democratization. To many NSM activists, they are dissatisfied with contemporary representative democracies, which are thought to limit political participation by ordinary citizens (Pichardo 1997). Being influenced by the NSM paradigm, the young activists in Hong Kong often dismiss parties "as part of the establishment and electoral machines intent on seizing power" (Ma 2008, p. 164). In my interview with Bobo Yip, a social activist who had participated in the "Anti-High Speed Rail Movement" and served as the spokesperson for the "Anti-Patriotic Education Movement," she succinctly pointed out a general impression held by many social activists: "politicians are seen as selfish, while social activists as altruistic."[12] Similarly, Yan-ho Lai, a former student activist and the former convenor of the

---

[10]https://zh-cn.facebook.com/parentsconcerngroup

[11]Personal interview with a member of the group on May 16, 2014.

[12]Personal interview with Bobo Yip on March 27, 2014 (Code: 30).

CHRF, shared a similar observation: "There is a common perception (among social activists) that social activists represent the people, and political parties should listen to the people. That is why political parties should listen to social activists."[13]

Note, however, that this kind of anti-politics and anti-party sentiment seems to have existed even before the 1990s. Back in the 1980s, when the colonial administration introduced elections at grassroots level, a debate emerged among activists of liberal civil society organizations (Ma 2012); while some refused to join the establishment of the colonial government, others who were inspired by Gramsci (1971) believed that they needed to fight a "war of position" by competing for key institutional resources to empower their movement. Many of the latter took part in the elections and subsequently became the first-generation opposition elite.

To some activists, they are averse not only to political parties but also to organizations in general (So 2008, p. 247). Note that two types of organization skeptics exist. The first type opposes only hierarchical organizations. They value participatory democracy and deemphasize the distinction between organizers and participants. Horizontal organizations, cross-class alliance, and coalitional politics are acceptable to them. The second type is fundamentally against organizations of all forms. Bobo Yip points out that the "Anti-High Speed Rail Movement" consists of many second-type skeptics,[14] who pride themselves on their adherence to "de-organization" (*qu zuzhihua*). Asserts an activist in one television interview: "We have no organization. The only tool we use is the Internet. We start pages and groups on *Facebook* and *Twitter*, and people just show up on the day of the protest without prior arrangement" (cited in Lam (2012, p. 214)).

Based on my interviews with some social activists, I find that the underdevelopment of organization is actually a pervasive phenomenon in liberal civil society groups. Mirana M. Szeto, a university professor who has led various conservation movements in Hong Kong since 2005, bluntly puts it: "Hong Kong has many activists, but few organizers."[15] In a similar vein, an NGO worker, who has been involved in gender, labor, and environmental activism, makes a bitter comment, "Hong Kong has no social movement, only social gatherings."[16] The problem is, as she contends, that civil society groups seldom develop membership. "When they need to organize a protest," she explains, "their only mobilization strategy is to send out a mass email. But you would be amazed by how short their email list is."

These liberal civil society groups' organizational structure, or the lack thereof, may explain their ideological chasm with some opposition parties. As many of them are formed spontaneously in response to a single, ad hoc issue, the activists involved care less about the groups' long-term development, which implies that they have no incentive to develop and maintain an enduring membership, and lack a broad and well-defined constituency to whom they need to answer. From the establishment's

---

[13] Personal interview with Yan-ho Lai on August 11, 2014 (Code: 47).

[14] Personal interview with Bobo Yip on March 27, 2014 (Code: 30).

[15] Personal interview with Szeto May on May 15, 2014 (Code: 32).

[16] Personal interview with an NGO worker on May 12, 2014 (Code: 31).

perspective, these groups are difficult to deal with because unlike opposition parties who have to negotiate with the government from time to time, these social activists deal with the government often on a one-off basis. There is little need to foster mutual respect, let alone mutual trust. The relationship between the government and Scholarism, the student activist group which played a prominent role in the "Anti-Patriotic Education Movement," is illustrative of this lack of mutual trust. Tommy Cheung Sau-yin, a former student leader of this group confided that while the government may occasionally approach liberal civil society groups privately to build rapport, it refrained from establishing any private communication channel with Scholarism. "The reason is," he explains, "government officials fear that we would tap the conversation and make it public."[17]

Conceivably, liberal civil society groups tend to refuse to compromise during negotiations with the government. When their activism succeeds to pressure the nondemocratically elected government to reverse a policy, they would rise to fame and become the darlings of the media as well as heroes of society. When their activism fails, they can safely return to their everyday life as long as their activism does not involve any criminal offense. To these social activists, defeat is no less glorious than victory because they can always occupy the moral high ground by being a fighter against the undemocratic regime. This unique incentive structure affords them an uncompromising militancy against the establishment.

It is erroneous to conclude that all liberal civil society groups are organizationally weak. A notable exception is the Hong Kong Professional Teachers' Union (PTU), which employs about 180 full-time staff members to serve more than 80,000 union members. It is highly self-sufficient, holding HK$100 million in cash savings as of 2010 (Szeto 2011, p. 193). The PTU has been a staunch supporter of the prodemocracy movement in both Hong Kong and the mainland. Although the PTU is not a political party, it has sent candidates to contest and capture the functional constituency seat of the education sector in every single election. But the political significance of the PTU manifested itself long before there were functional constituencies. The CCP has reportedly attempted to infiltrate into this teachers' union as early as in the 1970s (Szeto 2011, pp. 204–211). Note, however, the organizational strength of the PTU is really an exception. Few liberal civil society groups have ever been able to achieve a fraction of its membership and wealth.

4.3 Conclusion

Since the historic July 1, 2003 protest, collective political resistance has shown no sign of abatement in Hong Kong, a place that was long perceived to be nothing but an economic city. Opposition parties organize mass protests and social movements to draw political support. Liberal civil society groups stage public demonstrations

---

[17]Personal interview with Tommy Cheung Sau-yin on June 5, 2014 (Code: 34).

and other innovative forms of political activism to rally for their causes. These colorful movements could not be made possible without a relatively free media environment, which is prescribed by the Basic Law. In essence, the media provide a low-cost and effective means for organizers of these movements to promote their messages, attract followers, and connect with each other. A notable example is the quasi-referendum movement in 2010. Despite its insignificant grassroots organization, the CP-LSD alliance was still able to mobilize 17 % of the voting population to take part in a by-election that fell short of its intended "referendum" effect. Similarly, mass social movements, such as the "Anti-High Speed Rail Movement" and the "Anti-Patriotic Education Movement," were able to achieve an unusually high turnout even in the absence of an established support network in the community. The media, both traditional and new, online and offline, have served as a crucial mobilizing agent in all these examples.

In this regard, it can be said that the relatively free media environment of the city has facilitated – or even provided a necessary condition for – the aforementioned social movements. While media freedom may have strengthened Hong Kong's civil society, its effect on the city's prodemocracy movement has not been wholly positive. For one thing, the moderate opposition parties, namely, those who rely on grassroots organizations rather than controversial campaigns to build political support, have been sidelined in one way or another. As I discussed in the previous sections, the voice of such parties has been marginalized in the media, as media companies pay significantly more attention to radical opposition parties, who are maverick, polemical, and more vociferous. The moderate opposition parties cannot pursue similar tactics to compete for media attention because they are constrained by their supporters' ideological position. Interestingly, the ideological position of these supporters is partly defined by the July 1, 2003 protest, which has been touted as a manifestation of the "peace-loving and law-abiding nature" of Hong Kong citizens.

The plight of the moderate opposition parties is a matter of not only declining media attention but also of losing the moral high ground. Because radical opposition parties have their eyes on more or less the same constituency as the moderate parties, i.e., prodemocracy voters, these radicals could improve their electoral support at the expense of their moderate allies. As may be seen in the 2012 LegCo election, the most virulent criticisms of the moderate opposition parties often came from radical opposition candidates, who liked to bash the moderate's pragmatic approach to democratization. The radical's hardliner position and unyielding attitude helped them develop an image of ideological purity and hence claim the moral high ground, at least in the eyes of ideological voters. The outcomes of the 2012 LegCo election did show that radical opposition parties were the major winner within the prodemocracy camp.

Civil society in Hong Kong has become more vocal and vibrant since 2003, but this does not seem to benefit moderate opposition parties. Social activists have little incentive to collaborate with the moderate opposition elite, because they can stage large (perhaps larger) protests without the assistance of the opposition's organizational networks at the grassroots level. In fact, many liberal-minded activists are staunch supporters of democratization, but, paradoxically, they also despise political parties, if not organization in general. They are proud of being able to mobilize like-minded people to join their movement using the latest communication channels such as *Facebook* and *Twitter* (Apple Daily 2010a), instead of a top-down, hierarchical organization. Conceivably, the political bickering among opposition parties would further discourage liberal social activists from developing a close rapport with the moderate opposition elite, for fear of being criticized by the radical opposition elite.

In brief, Hong Kong's prodemocracy movement since 2003 has experienced a period characterized by strong mobilization and weak organization. Incidents of collective political resistance are abundant due to the existence of a relatively free media environment and the improvement of communication technologies. The incentive to build grassroots organizations to support the movement, however, has been consistently undermined. A major consequence of this is alienation of a large group of citizens who are neither active in social movements nor ideologically committed to the cause of democratization. It is this group of voters whose support is what some pro-Beijing parties have been fanatically seeking.

Chapter 5
All Politics Is Local: Grassroots Strategy of Beijing-Sponsored Parties

The Chinese Communist Party has a long history of political organization in Hong Kong. The party was founded in 1921. By 1925, the CCP had successfully developed its membership in the former British colony (Kiang 2011, p. 52). As the KMT's purge of the CCP escalated in 1927, many mainland Communist members such as Zhou Enlai and Ye Jianying fled to Hong Kong for temporary sojourn. After the World War II, Hong Kong again became a refuge for many Communist and left-wing intellectuals, who escaped from the KMT-controlled areas in the mainland. Their arrival gave rise to the Ta Teh Institute, a college established by the CCP in Hong Kong in 1946. This institute produced more than 500 students who ended up joining the CCP in its military struggle against the KMT.

During the Chinese Civil War between 1945 and 1949, the CCP also took advantage of Hong Kong's freedom of the press and freedom of entry to expand its united front work. For example, the CCP sponsored a number of political parties to attract social and political elite who opposed the KMT. Of the eight "democratic parties" supported by the CCP, five were founded in the former British colony. Despite the KMT's rigorous border surveillance, the CCP was able to smuggle more than a thousand pro-CCP dignitaries through Hong Kong to the mainland in preparation for the establishment of the PRC. These dignitaries later became delegates of the first Chinese People's Political Consultative Conference and high-ranking officials of the new Chinese government.

The importance of Hong Kong can be seen from the establishment of the CCP Hong Kong branch (*zhonggong xianggang fenju*) in 1947. All party organizations in the Guangdong and Guangxi provinces were under the leadership of this branch, which also supervised party organizations in neighboring provinces. In particular, the Hong Kong branch consisted of the Urban Work Committee (*chengshi gongzuo weiyuanhui*) and various local party committees (*diqu dangwei*) responsible for underground party activities and armed insurgencies in Southern China

© Springer Science+Business Media Singapore 2015
S.H.-W. Wong, *Electoral Politics in Post-1997 Hong Kong*,
DOI 10.1007/978-981-287-387-3_5

(Kiang 2011, p. 206). In the same year, the CCP also established the Xinhua News Agency Hong Kong Branch, which would later become a semiformal representative of the PRC in Hong Kong.[1]

In most cases, the Communists in Hong Kong kept a painstakingly low profile to avoid persecution by the colonial administration as well as the KMT. Instead of organizing activities in the name of the CCP, the Hong Kong Work Committee (*xianggang gongwei*), which was under the leadership of the CCP Hong Kong branch, helped set up a plethora of social organizations and companies to promote the CCP's ideology and recruit followers. In addition to the aforementioned Ta Teh Institute, examples include, but not limited to, secondary schools (e.g., Pui Kiu Middle School), trade unions (e.g., the Hong Kong Federation of Trade Unions), newspapers (e.g., Ta Kung Pao, Wen Wei Po), and movie production companies (e.g., Great Wall Movie, Feng Huang Motion Pictures). Note that the CCP assumed a leadership role in at least some, if not all, of these social organizations.[2] Although the colonial administration's attitude toward these CCP-sponsored entities was far from friendly, as evidenced by its forceful shutdown of the Ta Teh Institute, together with 92 pro-CCP schools in 1949 (Li 1997, p. 38), it did permit many of them to survive until 1997.

As for the KMT, it could not openly carry out anti-Communist missions in this British colony, but it did send intelligence agents and mobilized its affiliated groups to sabotage and subvert the CCP-affiliated organizations in Hong Kong. Most notably, the KMT made a number of attempts to assassinate CCP cadres who were stationed there (Kiang 2011, pp. 212–214).

Part of the reason for the colonial administration's unfriendly attitude is that CCP cadres had used Hong Kong as a strategic base to provide support, often clandestinely, for their armed struggles in the mainland as well as in the city. In the late 1920s, Nie Rongzhen, one of the ten Great Marshals of the People's Liberation Army, ran a military course in Hong Kong to train cadres (Nie 2005, p. 83). In 1929, the CCP set up an underground radio broadcast station in Kowloon to facilitate the communication between various revolution bases in Southern China (Zi 2004, pp. 58–59). During World War II, the Eighth Route Army under the command of Mao Zedong and Zhu De established an office in Hong Kong to create an anti-Japanese guerrilla troop known as the Hong Kong-Kowloon Brigade (*gangjiu zhidui*) (Qiang 2008, p. 23). Declassified documents of the PRC government also indicate that Beijing secretly aided Hong Kong's transport workers who went on strike in 1950 (Central Committee of the Communist Party of China Party Literature

---

[1] The actual job responsibilities of the Xinhua News Agency were far more than representing the PRC. As its former director, Zhou Nan, recounts, the agency was responsible for publicity, political organization, grassroots work, and united front work in Hong Kong (Zong 2007, p. 347).

[2] Zhang Junsheng, the former vice director of the Xinhua News Agency Hong Kong Branch, confides in his memoir that pro-Beijing newspapers such as *Wen Wei Po* and *Ta Kung Pao* could not openly admit the fact that they were led by the CCP (You et al. 2011, p. 136). In the memoir of Ng Hong-man, the former principal of Pui Kiu Middle School, he revealed that he as the school principal had to take orders from the Xinhua News Agency Hong Kong Branch.

Research Office 1998, p. 224). In addition, there were reported cases of Communist infiltration into the Hong Kong Police Force. One known case was Tsang Siu-fo, a high-ranking Hong Kong police officer, who was deported to the mainland in 1961 for conducting espionage operations in the former British colony (Kiang 2012, pp. 102–107). Owing to the variety of missions and operations assigned by higher authorities, Communist members in Hong Kong were expected to observe a doctrine laid down by Mao Zedong: hiding professionally, lurking indefinitely, accumulating power, and waiting for opportunities (*yinbi jinggan, changqi maifu, jixu liliang, yidai shiji*) (Mao 1976). They were not allowed to disclose their party membership unless their superiors instructed them to do so (You et al. 2011, p. 144).

Given its extensive underground activities in the former colony, one would expect that the CCP would not shy away from meddling in Hong Kong's affairs after gaining the city's sovereignty. Interestingly, this is not the case. While pro-Beijing organizations and groups still exist and proliferate, CCP cadres have continued to maintain an invisible presence in the city. There is no formal office representing the CCP in Hong Kong. Nor is there any official figure of CCP membership in the city. A primary reason for this anomaly is that the June 4 Incident has severely tarnished the legitimacy of the CCP, which became a synonym for "unjust," "illiberal," and "brutal." For CCP cadres who want to seek an elected office in Hong Kong, their membership has lapsed into a political liability, rather than an asset.

Yet low visibility does not equal weak influences. Having spent decades infiltrating into Hong Kong's society and conducting united front work and other political operations, the CCP had acquired at least a basic knowledge of Hong Kong society at large and an extensive experience of fostering local support networks to advance its political interests. It was waiting for a harvest time, which arrived in 1997. In this chapter, I examine how Beijing has relied on its sponsored parties to undermine the prodemocracy opposition in postcolonial Hong Kong.

5.1   The Pro-Beijing Camp: Changes and Continuities

In Hong Kong, there are many pro-Beijing parties, which are collectively known as the pro-establishment camp. On major political issues, the pro-establishment camp votes faithfully along the lines of Beijing in the LegCo. A notable example is to ban the motion to vindicate the student activists of the 1989 prodemocracy movement in Beijing. This motion, which is moved by prodemocracy legislators every year before the anniversary of the June 4 Incident, has never been passed since the retrocession due to the pro-establishment camp's steadfast opposition. On the issue of political liberalization, the pro-establishment camp has also from time to time voted against bills proposed by prodemocracy opposition parties. In the eyes of many prodemocracy voters, therefore, the pro-establishment camp is a stumbling block to democratization.

It is erroneous, however, to treat all pro-establishment parties as a monolithic entity. Some parties are arguably closer to Beijing than others. An example of parties with a close relationship with Beijing is the Hong Kong Federation of Trade Unions (FTU), a pro-Beijing labor union-cum-party, which was founded in 1948. Its core members were fervent believers of Communism and disciples of the CCP, at least in the early years. For decades, they were known as the "leftists," who helped promote CCP's doctrines in Hong Kong. Organizationally, the FTU had cozy, albeit opaque, linkages to the CCP. Xu Jiatun, the former head of the Xinhua News Agency in the 1980s who defected to the United States after 1989, exposed the cryptic connection by pointing out that "'leftist' unions [in Hong Kong] are under the leadership of the CCP" (Xu 1993, p. 148). Its intimate connection with the CCP can also be reflected from how it was treated by the colonial administration during the Cold War. In the year after its establishment, a number of unionists of the FTU were deported back to the mainland, as the colonial administration decided to clamp down on the Communist movement in the city (Hong Kong Federation of Trade Unions 2013, pp. 21, 34–35).

Another party close to Beijing is the Democratic Alliance for the Betterment and Progress of Hong Kong (DAB). When Beijing finalized the Basic Law in 1990, it was clear that party politics would be unavoidable in postcolonial Hong Kong, as the Basic Law allows for a fair number of popularly elected legislative seats. Beijing, thus, needed to foster a local party to serve as its proxy in the emerging party politics. In 1992, the DAB was founded. Its founding members all had an impeccable "leftist" pedigree. The first chairman, Jasper Tsang, was the principal of a preeminent "leftist" secondary school, Pui Kiu Middle School. The vice-chairman, Tam Yiu-chung, was a leader of the FTU. Chan Yuen-han, DAB's standing committee member, also came from the FTU. The Party Secretary, Cheng Kai-nam, taught at Pui Kiu Middle School. One of the Central Committee members, Elsie Leung, who later became the HKSAR's first Secretary for Justice, was a student of Chung Wah Middle School, a "leftist" school set up by her grandfather.[3] A cogent indicator of the DAB's political significance is that in the very month when it was established, its leaders were invited to Beijing to meet with Jiang Zemin, the then General Secretary of the CCP.

In contrast, the Liberal Party (LP), a pro-Beijing party that represents the interests of the business elite, has relatively weak ties with Beijing. Historically, the business elite in Hong Kong had not been close to the CCP for a good reason; the ideology of the CCP had been fundamentally against capitalism. It was not until the 1980s, when Chinese leaders implemented domestic economic reforms and dealt with Hong Kong's sovereignty transfer, did Beijing begin consciously co-opting Hong Kong's business elite (Wong 2012). To Beijing, these elite served two important functions. First, they could provide capital and technological know-how to modernize the PRC's economy. Second, Hong Kong witnessed a massive emigration wave in the

---

[3]The colonial administration decided to permanently close Chung Wah Middle School after the "1967 Leftist Riots" (Bickers and Yep 2009).

1980s, as many Hong Kong people lacked confidence in the reunification with the PRC. Beijing needed to seek the economic elite's support to halt capital flight (Qiang 2008, p. 177). From the business elite's perspective, they also had an incentive to switch their allegiance from Great Britain to Beijing, because they wanted to preserve their business interests beyond 1997.

The resulting alliance between Beijing and Hong Kong's business elite is therefore grounded in mutual benefits, rather than shared ideologies.[4] Perhaps for this reason, the bonding between Beijing and the LP has never been as tight as that of between Beijing and the FTU or the DAB. The political fallout of the July 1, 2003 protest attests this point. The Tung administration was forced to suspend the legislation of the national security laws to a large extent because the maverick chairman of the LP, James Tien, unexpectedly resigned from the Executive Council. To some members of the traditional pro-Beijing elite, James Tien's political integrity is questionable (Li 2010, p. 67), as he could desert a political ally in times of emergency. In this respect, one can reasonably assume that Beijing is likely to find the LP less reliable than the traditional "leftist" elite or what I call "Beijing-sponsored parties."

This distinction is crucial in the following discussion. It tells us who in the pro-establishment camp is more likely to win Beijing's trust. Simply put, of all the pro-establishment parties, Beijing-sponsored parties are the ones that Beijing would turn to when the need arises, given their ideological affinity and potential organizational linkages with mainland authorities such as the CCP. What can these parties offer to Beijing? They have at least two functions. The first is to safeguard Beijing's interests in Hong Kong, which include assisting the HKSAR government to govern effectively and thereby increase public support for the HKSAR government as well as for the PRC. Their second function is to provide updated information to Beijing, so that Beijing can devise appropriate policies for Hong Kong.

This is not to say that the interests of Beijing-sponsored parties and those of Beijing are always aligned. Scholars of Chinese politics have long observed that local officials are able to find ways to circumvent policy directives imposed by the Central Government (*shangyou zhengce, xiayou duice*) (O'Brien and Li 1999). The relationship between Beijing and the pro-Beijing elite in Hong Kong is not immune to this principal-agent problem. The most illustrative example is the "1967 Leftist Riots."

In 1967, the Cultural Revolution was sweeping China. Inspired by the mainland's radical mass movement, the "leftists" in Hong Kong orchestrated a series of mass mobilization events, in hopes of undermining, if not overthrowing, the colonial administration. They called upon the masses to take part in street protests, strikes,

---

[4]Li Xiao-hui, a deputy editor-in-chief of the pro-Beijing mouthpiece Wen Wei Po provides one ideological distinction between the traditional leftist elite and the conventional pro-establishment elite. He argues that the traditional pro-Beijing elite (*qingzhongpai*) support the socialist system in the mainland and the CCP leadership, whereas some conventional pro-establishment elite only show respect to the PRC's socialist system, which they do not totally agree with (Li 2010, p. 56). Li's view may reflect how Beijing authorities see the pro-establishment camp in Hong Kong.

and school walkouts, which were met with the colonial government's heavy-handed repression. Some "leftist" activists retaliated by resorting to terrorism; they planted homemade bombs near police stations, government offices, banks and on busy streets, causing some casualties and seriously disrupting social order. Ordinary Hong Kong citizens balked at the extremism of the "leftists," who seemed to bring more harm to local Chinese than to colonists. A heavily cited example of the atrocity associated with the "1967 Leftist Riots" was the murder of a Chinese radio talk show host, who did nothing but making satirical comments about the "leftists."

The mess that the Hong Kong "leftists" created annoyed the then premier Zhou Enlai, who had no intention to disturb the political status quo of the former British colony. He summoned leaders of the Hong Kong Work Committee (*xianggang gongwei*) to Beijing to "sober their minds" (Kiang 2012, p. 266). As the major organizers were made to stay in Beijing for about two months, the riots in Hong Kong gradually died down. The 1967 Leftist Riots were later termed as a serious "left-leaning adventurism mistake" (*zuoqing maojin zhuyi*) (Ng 2011, p. 178). The riots disturbed Beijing's grand overarching strategic plan with respect to Hong Kong, i.e., "long-term planning and full utilization" (*changqi dasuan, chongfen liyong*).[5] In addition, the identities of many underground Communists or CCP supporters were exposed during the riots, making them the victims of the colonial administration's subsequent repression (Ng 2011, p. 85). Worse still, their extremism alienated the majority of Hong Kong citizens, severely tarnishing the reputation of the pro-Beijing elite in Hong Kong. To this day, the riots remain a social stigma in Hong Kong.

In 1976, Liao Chengzhi, the person-in-charge of Hong Kong affairs in Beijing, called up a meeting to rectify Beijing's Hong Kong policy. The meeting censured the ultraleft elements behind the 1967 Leftist Riots and reaffirmed a pragmatic approach (Li 1997, p. 64). A new institution, Hong Kong and Macao Affairs Office of the State Council, was established as a result. This new office, headed by Liao himself, was responsible for administering and supervising Hong Kong affairs. From then on, pragmatism triumphed over ideology in Beijing's Hong Kong policy. Class struggle was brushed aside, while united front work was emphasized. In his memoir, Xu Jiatun recollected what Deng Xiaoping told him to do as the head of the Xinhua News Agency in Hong Kong during the 1980s, "Dare to be a great rightist, a great spy" (Xu 1993, p. 122), implying that Xu was expected to mingle with the rich and powerful in Hong Kong, with the ultimate aim of co-opting them in preparation for the city's eventual unification with the PRC. This policy change makes eminently good sense, as what Beijing needed to achieve by the 1980s was to win the hearts and minds of Hong Kong people, rather than pestering an outgoing colonial government.

It is important to note that the 1967 Leftist Riots were the exception rather than the rule. "Leftists" in Hong Kong adhered to Beijing's political lines most of

---

[5] Hong Kong as a British colony at that time provided a crucial outlet for the PRC's exports. Chinese leaders, therefore, had no plan of changing the political status quo of the city.

the time. Especially in the 1980s and beyond, Hong Kong's reunification with the mainland became an important item on the national agenda. Beijing kept a close eye on Hong Kong's political development. It would be difficult for these local agents to deviate from their assigned roles even if they wanted to do so. At the same time, and perhaps more importantly, the "leftists" in Hong Kong have gone through difficult times that helped transform themselves. First, the ultraleft faction lost much ground after the 1967 Leftist Riots. Second, Beijing's brutal crackdown of the peaceful student-led prodemocracy movement in 1989 further disillusioned many of those who had once been staunch supporters of the CCP. Some decided to leave the "leftist" camp permanently, while many of those who chose to stay were humbled and changed from ideologues to pragmatists.

Because Beijing-sponsored parties follow Beijing's political lines more closely than other parties within the pro-establishment camp, if one wants to study how Beijing makes use of its local proxies to shape Hong Kong politics to its desired direction, one cannot avoid analyzing these Beijing-sponsored parties. In addition, they occupy more legislative seats and have far more members and supporters than other pro-establishment parties, so they are an important subject of study in their own right. The focus of this chapter is therefore on these Beijing-sponsored parties.

5.2   Building a United Front at the Grassroots

As mentioned, Beijing has been attempting to co-opt Hong Kong's social and economic elite since the 1980s, in hopes of soliciting their political support, or at least neutralizing them, so that they would not be in opposition to Beijing. However, co-opting the rich and powerful alone was insufficient for allaying Beijing's fear because it was clear by the early 1990s that the HKSAR government would inherit from the colonial government a strong opposition force. Indeed, by the end of the colonial rule, the Democratic Party (DP) emerged as a formidable opposition, as its prodemocracy ideology had an enormous appeal in the former British colony. Thanks to the winner-take-all nature of the plurality rule, an electoral formula adopted by the colonial government in its last legislative election, the DP managed to capture 12 of the 20 directly elected seats. Together with additional seven indirectly elected seats of the functional constituencies, it became the largest political party in the colonial legislature. This was not an outcome that the Beijing government wanted to see for good reason. The leading members of the DP such as Szeto Wah were simultaneously controlling another political group, the Alliance in Support of Patriotic Democratic Movement of China (ASPDMC), whose central tenets included "ending one-party dictatorship [in China]" and "building a democratic China."

To curtail the political influences of the DP, Beijing unilaterally declared that the term of the DP-dominated legislature was over and replaced it immediately after the handover with a provisional legislature whose members were supported by Beijing. Although an election of the Legislative Council was held a year later,

Beijing changed the rules of the game; it replaced the plurality rule with proportional representation. As a result of this rule change, the seat share of pro-Beijing parties significantly increased. In addition, the Chinese government continued to allow the existence of the functional constituencies. Because the playing field of the functional constituencies has been skewed heavily toward the business elite, rather than ordinary citizens, Beijing has been able to exert more influence on the election outcomes.

By dictating the rules of the election, Beijing might have reduced the opposition politicians' presence in the legislature, but it achieved little against their overriding popularity in the city. As mentioned, the prodemocracy opposition enjoyed a wide appeal in Hong Kong, especially after the June 4 Incident. A concurrent political development in Hong Kong during the 1980s was gradual liberalization of the political system for local participation. Many Hong Kong people came to see that building a democratic institution was perhaps the only effective way to check the Chinese Leviathan state. Conceivably, such a political environment was favorable to the opposition elite, whose prodemocracy stance won it immense popular support in successive elections.

Beijing could not challenge the political credentials of the prodemocracy camp without building its own political support base. However, it has been hamstrung by the institutional setup it designed for Hong Kong; under the "one country, two systems" principle, Chinese officials or members of the CCP are not supposed to meddle with Hong Kong's internal affairs. In addition, the June 4 Incident reinforced the political stigma that the CCP had carried in this former colony, where a significant portion of the population consisted of refugees who fled Communist China. Under such circumstances, Beijing, for many years, had tried to avoid any overt intervention in the city's politics, for fear that such an action would alienate, rather than appease, the Hong Kong public.

These political constraints are not insurmountable, however. Given its extensive experience of mass movement, Beijing overcame these constraints by forging a grassroots united front in support of its interests, with the help of the pro-Beijing force it has fostered for years. Qiang Shigong, a law professor of Peking University, argues that introducing democracy to Hong Kong worries Beijing because Hong Kong people tended not to identify themselves with the state of the PRC. For this reason, as Qiang points out, Deng Xiaoping laid down a rule of thumb for governing Hong Kong: fully utilize the function of the united front work to empower the pro-Beijing elements in the city (Qiang 2008, p. 183). Indeed, as early as in 1982, when Deng Xiaoping was receiving a delegation of Hong Kong social and economic elites in Beijing, he made it clear that Hong Kong needed to have political organizations to produce the city's own ruling elite (Li 1997, p. 80). Deng reiterated the same point when he met the Hong Kong delegates to the second session of the Sixth National People's Congress held in 1984 (Ng 2011, p. 188). The key to strengthen the united front, according to Deng, is to consolidate the "grassroots work" (*jiceng gongzuo*) (Zong 2007, p. 346). Later in 1990, when Jiang Zemin gave a speech on united front work, he stressed that the CCP should unite as many Hong Kong people as possible, in order to pave the way for the PRC's takeover of the city (Zhonggong Zhongyang

Wenxian Yanjiushi 1991, p. 1128). A month later, the CCP issued a notice, calling for an aggressive expansion of united front work in Hong Kong, using organizations and multiple channels to unite people from all walks of life (Zhonggong Zhongyang Wenxian Yanjiushi 1991, p. 1209).

Beijing-sponsored parties have responded positively to the PRC leaders' calling. The FTU set up its first District Services Center (*diqu fuwuchu*) in 1992 and expanded to 16 by 2013. This union-cum-party is candid about their electoral concerns behind the establishment of these centers: "Districts... are an important base for electoral votes... For this reason the FTU has given high priority to district works" (Hong Kong Federation of Trade Unions 2013, p. 136). The same is true for the DAB. As mentioned, many of the founding members of the DAB actually came from the FTU. Not surprisingly, this party also shares a similar vision with respect to grassroots organizations. Indeed, one of the stated missions of the DAB is to provide services at the grassroots level (DAB 2013b). Its first chairman, Jasper Tsang, points out that prior to 1997, party resources were directed to the development of local district offices, and he takes pride in that strategy (Yuen 2011, p. 11).

5.3 Beijing-Sponsored Parties' Incentives

As discussed, the central-local relations in China are often plagued by the principal-agent problem. But on the issue of developing grassroots networks, the interests between Beijing and Beijing-sponsored parties converge. The reason is that in order for Beijing-sponsored parties such as the DAB to compete with the pan-democrats over the directly elected seats in the legislature, they need to maximize their popular support. But one of the most salient electoral cleavages in the post-1997 Hong Kong has been democratization (Ma and Choy 1999; Ma 2007a). Pan-democratic candidates have frequently exploited this ideological cleavage in times of elections. They urge the government to implement universal suffrage of the Chief Executive and abolish the functional constituencies, while criticizing the pro-establishment camp as a hurdle to democratization. In this intensely ideological confrontation, pro-establishment parties have difficulties presenting a convincing counterargument against the pan-democrats' call for political liberalization (Sing 2010).

One of my interviewees, a District Councillor who belongs to the pro-establishment camp, bluntly puts it, "Society has become too ideologically polarized now. The pro-establishment camp cannot play the ideology card against the pan-democrats. What ideology can pro-establishment parties sell to voters? Patriotism? No way. Hong Kong people don't buy that."[6]

Indeed, many pro-establishment legislators themselves were the beneficiaries of the political status quo; they managed to enter the LegCo through the non-directly elected functional constituencies. Any reason raised by these legislators in

---

[6]Personal interview with a District Councillor on January 11, 2013 (Code: 15).

opposition to further political liberalization is easily perceived by voters as a defense of their vested interest, rather than as a genuine concern for the well-being of Hong Kong society.

"To compete against the pan-democrats," the District Councillor explains, "pro-establishment parties need to avoid the talk of ideology, and focus on practical works [community services]." His remark explains why some pro-establishment parties have an incentive to undertake grassroots works. Because they can hardly challenge the pan-democrats' position over the dominant cleavage of democratization, they have to exploit other issue areas to distinguish themselves and to attract political support. Grassroots service is a natural choice for three reasons.

First, grassroots service is instrumental in building a close relationship with local constituents. One District Councillor points out that during his first term, he organized an apartment renovation project for a housing estate in his district.[7] The project required a home visit to the apartment of the interested home owners to check the renovation needs. After this project, he got to know the majority of the residents. More importantly, he obtained contacts and some important household demographic information through the home visit. This information is useful not only for getting out the vote on election day but also for finding volunteer helpers, the kind of human resources that are vital to his general service undertakings.

Second, citizens who value or have a strong demand for grassroots constituency services tend to be the least ideological. I have been told by more than one District Councillor[8] that of all the demographic groups, the elderly is by far the "easiest catch." This is in part because elderly people do not need to leave the district for work or for study. As they always stay in the neighborhood, they are likely to notice the variety of services that the District Councillor offers. In addition, many senior citizens are indifferent to politics, let alone the ideological confrontation between the two dominant political camps. There are reported cases where senior citizens vote for someone whose name they could not utter; all they know about the person is his candidate number because this is the only piece of information they received from some pro-Beijing group that organized a day-trip for these elderly people on election day (Apple Daily 2012a).

Third, pro-establishment parties have a comparative advantage of offering grass-roots services because of their ample resources. Take the leading pro-establishment party, the DAB, as an example. The DAB is arguably the wealthiest political party in Hong Kong. The political donations it received in 2013 reached HK$97 million, while the two largest prodemocracy parties, namely, the DP and the Civic Party, combined received only about a fifth of that amount. More remarkably, the DAB's income, as may be seen from Fig. 5.1, has skyrocketed since 2003, dwarfing its pan-democratic counterparts.

---

[7]Personal interview with a District Councillor on January 31, 2013 (Code: 20).

[8]Personal interviews with District Councillors on January 2, 2013, January 9, 2013, and January 23, 2013 (Code: 9, 13, and 19).

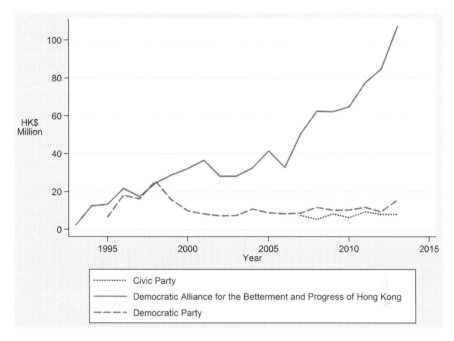

Fig. 5.1 Annual income by party (Source: Annual financial statements of the respective parties, retrieved from the HKSAR Companies Registry)

The great discrepancy in resources partly results from the business sector's reluctance to offer political donation to the prodemocracy camp for fear of provoking Beijing. This severely constrains the prodemocracy parties' ability to raise financial resources. In contrast, Beijing-sponsored parties seem to have little difficulty raising funds from the business sector. For example, in its 2012 fundraising dinner, the DAB received nearly HK$20 million donations from local tycoons (Wen Wei Po 2012c). During the same event in 2014, the DAB even raised HK$68.38 million(Wen Wei Po 2014a). Remarkably, the director of the Liaison Office of the Central People's Government in the HKSAR, the successor of the Xinhua News Agency Hong Kong Branch, openly assisted with fundraising by singing a song on stage and donating his own calligraphy work, which raised HK$11 million and HK$13.8 million, respectively. Many speculate that political contribution to Beijing-sponsored parties helps the donors gain Beijing's trust, if not also gain more business opportunities.

Beijing-sponsored parties are rich not only in financial capital but also in human resources. The DAB has over 20,000 members, while the DP only has around 700. The FTU offers another illustrative example. This labor union-cum-party has 300,000 members. It has set up a team of volunteer workers for community services in virtually every single district. Four of these volunteer teams contributed over 10,000 man-hours to do community services in 2002 (FTU 2002). As a comparison, the DP is unable to afford setting up a local party branch in every district, and some of the local branches it has do not even have a regular office.

The disparity is not surprising. As a Beijing-sponsored party, the DAB and FTU can offer many tangible and intangible benefits to its members, ranging from perks and privileges to business connections in the mainland (Wen Wei Po 2009). In contrast, members of the opposition movement face censure and ostracism directly and indirectly from Beijing. For instance, many members of the Democratic Party are denied entry to the mainland (South China Morning Post 2013). Many business groups would not place advertisements in prodemocracy news media for fear of displeasing Beijing (Ma 2007b).

The three reasons discussed above suggest that Beijing-sponsored parties share congruent interest with Beijing in fostering grassroots political networks. While Beijing needs a local support coalition to counter the political influences of the pan-democrats, Beijing-sponsored parties require such networks to provide grassroots service, which in turn helps them develop an alternative issue ownership to compete for the geographical constituencies. Of course, their ambition may not be confined to the geographical constituencies only. One of my interviewees, a District Councillor of the DAB,[9] candidly admits that his party's aggressive expansion at the grassroots level aims to prepare itself for taking over the government in the future (*quanmian zhizheng*).

5.4 Beijing-Sponsored Parties' Grassroots Strategy in Action

A good starting point of studying Beijing-sponsored parties' grassroots strategy is the District Councils, which are the lowest administrative rung of the HKSAR government. Because the office of the District Councils is elected, this government tier is a battlefield between pro-establishment parties and the pan-democratic camp. In particular, Beijing-sponsored parties have devoted an enormous amount of resources to expand their turf in the District Councils. Thus far, their efforts have paid off, as they have gradually crowded out the pan-democrats. Table 5.1 shows the number of seats controlled by different political camps over the years. As may be seen from the table, the seat share of Beijing-sponsored parties has increased from 101 in 1999 to 147 in 2011. Note, however, this is the most conservative estimate of the power of the pro-establishment camp in the District Councils. If the definition of the pro-establishment camp includes self-proclaimed independent District Councillors who have close ties with pro-establishment social groups such as the Heung Yee Kuk, this camp actually controls 315 seats or three quarters of the total District Council seats in 2011. In contrast, the seat share of pan-democratic parties dropped from 106 to 83 in the same period.

The political ascendancy of Beijing-sponsored parties at the District Council level requires two factors: (1) they are able to defend the District Council Constituencies they have already occupied, and (2) they are able to encroach on the District Council Constituencies that their rivals are occupying. I discuss each factor in this section.

---

[9]Personal interview with a District Councillor on January 3, 2013 (Code: 11).

Table 5.1 Number of District Council seat by political camp

	1999	2003	2007	2011
Beijing-sponsored parties	101	76	115	147
Pro-establishment parties	128	105	147	175
Pro-establishment parties and individuals	129	166	238	315
Pan-democratic parties	106	128	95	83

Source: Electoral Affairs Commission

Notes: Beijing-sponsored parties include the Democratic Alliance for the Betterment and Progress of Hong Kong (DAB), the Hong Kong Federation of Trade Unions (FTU), and the Hong Kong Progressive Alliance (HKPA). The HKPA merged into the DAB in 2005. Pro-establishment parties include the Civil Force, the Liberal Party (LP), the New People's Party (NPP), and all Beijing-sponsored parties. Some self-proclaimed independent District Councillors may be considered as pro-establishment or pro-Beijing due to their affiliation with pro-establishment social groups such as the Heung Yee Kuk. Pan-democratic parties include the Association for Democracy and People's Livelihood (ADPL), the Civic Act-Up, the Civic Party (CP), the Hong Kong Confederation of Trade Unions (CTU), the Citizens Party, the Democratic Party (DP), the Frontier, the League of Social Democrats (LSD), the Neo Democrats (ND), the Neighborhood and Workers Service Centre (NWSC), and People Power (PP)

5.4.1 Defending Their Own Turf

In order to grasp pro-establishment parties' strategies to defend their occupied seats, it is important to understand the nature and function of the District Council office. The British government planned to introduce some democratic practices to Hong Kong toward the end of its colonial rule (Lau and Kuan 2000). The establishment of the District Boards in 1982 was the first step of this limited democracy reform (Ma 2007a). Although the District Boards served only grassroots constituencies, their political significance was far reaching, for they were the first government body in the colony that experienced a democratic election.[10] Their long-lasting impact is evidenced by the fact that many politicians from the prodemocracy camp, such as Lee Wing-tat and Sin Chung-kai, carved out their political careers first in the District Boards, where they developed their political support base through the articulation of grassroots interests (Ma 2007a). It is also noteworthy that although the British government had no intention of using the District Boards to promote party politics (Lau and Kuan 2002), this elected body did give rise to some grassroots prodemocracy political parties, for example, the Association for Democracy and People's Livelihood (Ma 2012), which remains active in the legislature to this day.

After 1997, the District Boards were renamed the District Councils. There are altogether eighteen districts in Hong Kong, each of which consists of dozens of

---

[10]Only one-third of the members in the District Boards were democratically elected in 1982, with the rest of the seats occupied either by government appointees or officials. The number of directly elected seats gradually increased afterward. In 1994, all District-Board seats became popularly elected.

District Council members (also known as District Councillors).[11] The majority of these members are individually elected from subdistricts known as District Council Constituencies using the single-member district formula. The geographical area that these subdistricts oversee is very small. Each District Council Constituency (DCC) is supposed to house around 17,000 dwellers. But given the city's high population density, the actual physical size of a District Council Constituency may span no more than a dozen of apartment buildings. The tiny size of the District Council Constituencies severely limits what District Councillors can deliver.

In addition to the geographical factor, District Councillors are also constrained by the formal function of their office. According to the District Council Ordinance, a council has only two functions:

1. It advises the government:

    I. on matters affecting the well-being of people in the district;
    II. on the provision and use of public facilities and services within the district;
    III. on the adequacy and priorities of government programmes for the district;
    IV. on the use of public funds allocated to the district for local public works and community activities.

2. District Councils can undertake the following items in the district when funds are allocated by the government:

    I. environmental improvements in the district;
    II. the promotion of recreational and cultural activities in the district;
    III. community activities in the district (Registration and Electoral Office 2011).

In other words, the law stipulates that a District Council provides nothing more than an advisory role to the government (Cheng 2004). As an advisory body, District Councillors have no formal administrative power over policies – even policies related to their tiny constituency. District Councillors can propose a policy recommendation to the government, but whether the policy is implemented or not is entirely up to the government.[12]

The only area where a District Councillor can have a more solid control is government subventions. Each District Councillor is entitled to a monthly subsidy worth about HK$24,000 that can be used to pay for her office expenditure and local activities. Meager as it is, it provides many pan-democratic District Councillors a stable source of income to finance community services. In addition, there are two government subventions at the District Councils' disposal.[13] One is an

---

[11] As of 2012, there were 412 District Councillors who were directly elected.

[12] For instance, several pro-establishment and prodemocracy District Councillors in East Kowloon had advocated, respectively, a project to develop a business district in their constituencies; but their suggestion had remained on paper for more than a decade. It was not until 2011, when the Chief Executive announced to implement the "Kick-Starting the Development of East Kowloon," which incorporated their suggestions by providing more office spaces in the district.

[13] There are many more public funds for community development not tailored for the District Councils, although District Councillors may also apply for them.

earmarked subsidy program for community activities.[14] Another is the "District Minor Works Program." District Councillors can apply for this program in order to "improve local facilities, living environment, and hygiene conditions (Home Affairs Department 2012b)," such as adding rain shelters over bus stops and chess tables in playgrounds.[15] In 2013, District Councils received a windfall: the government allocated a one-off HK$100 million to each of the 18 districts to implement the "Signature Project Scheme" to "address the needs of the district[s]." Note that any proposed use of these earmarked funds requires the approval of a District Council. Because pan-democratic District Councillors have already been reduced to a minority in all 18 District Councils, pan-democratic parties have basically no control of how these funds are used.

With this constrained decision-making power and limited geographical reach, the services that District Councillors are able to bring to their constituencies are often particularistic in nature. In general, such services can be classified into two types: (a) welfare and recreational activities and (b) problem-solving.

(a) Welfare and Recreational Activities

First, consider welfare and recreational activities. A popular expression with a certain derogatory connotation for such activities is "snake soup, vegetarian dishes, cakes, and dumplings" (*shezhai bingzhong*). Indeed, many District Councillors I have interviewed regularly organize discounted banquet dinners (for some reason, such feasts often feature snake soups), run day-trips to local tourist attractions, offer free flu shots, and distribute complimentary cakes and dumplings to local residents during traditional Chinese festivals.[16] These services are popular among grassroots citizens who may be otherwise unable to afford them at a regular price. Through these activities, the District Councillors can reach out to more local residents. Perhaps more importantly, they can obtain their contacts, which are crucial for election campaigns.

Shrewd District Councillors may even make use of these activities to discipline disloyal residents. In their study of the Mexican authoritarian state under the PRI, Diaz-Cayeros, Magaloni, and Weingast find that the state would punish localities electing the opposition by cutting off their perks and privileges (Diaz-Cayeros et al. 2003). We heard a similar story from a pro-establishment District Councillor, who confided that some pro-establishment District Councillors in the vicinity of his constituency threatened to end services offered to local residents who were simultaneously receiving giveaways from their political rivals.[17]

---

[14]The earmarked subsidy is worth about HK$3,200 million to be distributed among the eighteen districts (Home Affairs Department 2012a).

[15]During the financial year of 2014–2015, the provision for this program is HK$340 million for the eighteen District Councils.

[16]Personal interviews with District Councillors on January 2, 2013, and January 9, 2013, and January 23, 2013 (Code: 8, 14, and 17).

[17]Personal interview with a District Councillor on January 3, 2013 (Code: 10).

Organizing all these activities requires significant financial resources. A common impression is that pro-establishment parties are good at delivering such activities because they are rich (Oriental Daily News 2011). This impression is not entirely accurate, as District Councillors do not always need to spend their own money organizing these activities. Many business corporations have a budget for the underprivileged in the community as part of their corporate social responsibility. For example, Towngas, a public utility company, formed a partnership with the District Councils to dispense more than 230,000 moon cakes to the elderly in 2010 (Towngas 2010). District Councillors can also apply for earmarked government funds, such as the Community Investment and Inclusion Fund, to finance community activities. The single most important resource that District Councillors need is perhaps labor, because they need helpers to hunt out corporate or government sponsorships and to assist the running of these activities. In this respect, pro-establishment parties no doubt enjoy a comparative advantage over the pan-democrats, not only because they have more party members but also because pro-Beijing social organizations may at times mobilize their members to assist these parties as voluntary workers.[18]

Because of the strategic importance of these social organizations, their nature and function deserve close attention. The formation of these organizations is usually based upon different social relationships, such as kinship, gender, occupation, class, education, and common interests. Examples include the Shatin Women's Association, North District Resident Association, and Hong Kong Taekwondo Action Association. They are officially registered as "charitable institutions," and they attract followers by providing members free or subsidized services, ranging from yoga classes and language courses to day care for kids and occupation training. Organizationally, they are led by a regional or city-level pro-Beijing association. For a list of these associations, see Table 5.2. Lo et al. (2002) point out that these organizations, together with their leading mass associations, assist pro-Beijing elements to penetrate into Hong Kong's society.

As shown in the table, these five leading mass associations expanded rapidly within a decade. For instance, the number of members of the New Territories Associations of Societies (NTAS) exceeded 210,000 in 2012 (Ming Pao Daily News 2013b). With the aid of 300 affiliated subsidiary organizations throughout the New Territories, it aimed to recruit 20,000 new members in 2013.

These social organizations play an important role in helping pro-Beijing incumbents build their social networks through co-organizing welfare or recreational activities. A common example is to distribute giveaways. A pro-establishment District Councillor of the New Territories area claimed that the NTAS has secured a stable supply of rice donation from some wealthy businessmen. As a pro-establishment District Councillor, he has been invited by the NTAS to allocate the

---

[18] I also heard that Chinese state-owned enterprises would send their Hong Kong workers to help Beijing-sponsored parties in elections.

Table 5.2 Pro-Beijing mass associations in Hong Kong

	Hong Kong Federation of Trade Unions (FTU)	New Territories Associations of Societies (NTAS)	Kowloon Federation of Associations (KFA)	Hong Kong Island Federation of Associations (HKIF)	Federation of Guangdong Community Organizations (FHKGCO)
Founding Year	1947	1985	1997	1999	1996
Number of members in 2004	310,000	70,000	30,000	25,000	100,000
Number of affiliated organizations in 2004	173	128	43	121	179
Number of affiliated organizations in 2012	246	307	148	147	250
Target membership	Working class	Community groups in New Territories	Community groups in Kowloon	People and groups in Hong Kong Island	Guangdong communities in Hong Kong

Sources: Ma (2007a) and the homepage of these associations

rice to his constituents once in a few months.[19] Occasionally, these organizations even directly fund recreational activities organized by District Councillors.[20]

It is important to note that not all pro-establishment parties are able to benefit from the assistance of these mass associations. My interviewees from non-Beijing-sponsored pro-establishment parties lament that resources of these mass associations funnel only to Beijing-sponsored parties such as the DAB, although they may sometimes be invited to jointly host some local events with the mass associations.[21]

In addition to their direct help in organizing welfare and recreational activities, the mass associations also aid major pro-establishment parties by crowding out the pan-democrats in service provision. While District Councillors of all political stripes have an incentive to organize recreational activities for their constituents, local recreational facilities are always in short supply. Because many public facilities such as community halls are allocated based on casting lots, whether one can reserve a facility depends on how many other individuals are also interested in the same venue at the same time. In one of my interviews,[22] a prodemocracy District Councillor complained that the pro-establishment camp intentionally crowded him out by mobilizing numerous mass organizations to submit applications for public

---

[19]Personal interview with a District Councillor on January 2, 2013 (Code: 9).

[20]Personal interview with a District Councillor on January 2, 2013 (Code: 9).

[21]Personal interview with a District Councillor on January 9, 2013 (Code: 13).

[22]Personal interview with a District Councillor on June 14, 2012 (Code: 2).

facilities all year round. A similar example is that the Tseung Kwan O Kai Fong Joint Association, a subordinate group of the NTAS, applied for a community hall to hold yoga classes along with seven friendly organizations under the NTAS (Ming Pao Daily News 2012a). Its application failed, but it managed to hold the classes in the facility anyway because one of those friendly organizations who had already successfully obtained the time slots passed the use right to this association.

A similar tactic has been applied to the competition for public funds. As mentioned, the District Councils have the power to allocate an earmarked government fund for community activities (Home Affairs Department 2012a). Similar to recreational facilities, the application for this fund is open to all social groups, but no group can be funded twice in a given year. As a result, social groups have sprung up all over the place in the past years. A DAB interviewee who chairs seven social organizations acknowledges that he mobilized every friendly organization to apply for this fund. Eventually, each organization received a subvention of around HK$8,000 in the financial year of 2012/2013.[23]

(b) Problem-solving

In her study of machine politics, Stokes highlights a quintessential voter-commitment problem that plagues clientelistic parties: how to ensure voters do not renege on the implicit deal where the party offers private benefits and the recipients vote for the party (Stokes 2005). Indeed, multiple pro-establishment District Councillors[24] point out that voters are becoming smarter, such that they would attend the pro-establishment camp's discounted banquet dinner today and join the day-trip organized by a pan-democratic District Councillor of a nearby neighborhood tomorrow.[25] For this reason, as pointed out by a number of pan-democratic District Councillors, welfare and recreational services alone are unable to win political support, despite the popular impression that the District Council politics is all about such trivial activities.

A more reliable way to win residents' support is to help them solve practical daily problems. The problems, or caseworks, that District Councillors have to handle include, but not limited to, family disputes, public bus rescheduling, applications for welfare allowances, building maintenance, and general legal consultation alike. A typical District Councillor of a public rental estate may receive from several hundreds to a thousand cases per year, depending on the neighborhood's demographic structure and how industrious the District Councillor is. By helping residents solve a problem, a District Councillor can build an intimate relationship with the residents, as the latter would identify the former not merely as a service provider but as a

---

[23]Personal interview with a District Councillor on January 2, 2013 (Code: 9).

[24]Personal interview with District Councillors on January 2, 2013, January 3, 2013, and January 23, 2013 (Code: 9, 10, and 17).

[25]This kind of indiscriminate consumption of party services may have been popularized by a slogan proposed by a radical pan-democratic party, the League of Social Democrats (LSD): "Enjoy the DAB's largess, Vote for the LSD."

friend or a trustworthy companion. One interviewee sees problem-solving this way, "Whether I can find a solution to the problem in hand is not really important. What is important is that you have walked through the difficult situation with the constituents."[26]

There are different ways to accomplish caseworks. But it is generally true that District Councillors are unable to solve a problem single-handedly, given the limited formal power they have. Oftentimes, they have to contact government authorities on behalf of the concerned residents to seek solutions. To what extent they can pressure government authorities depends on the political resources they are able to mobilize. Almost all pro-establishment parties have members occupying key government positions, such as the Executive Council.[27] Pro-establishment District Councillors concur that when these members step in, they would have an easy time pushing government officials to get the job done. "With their help," a pro-establishment District Councillor explains,[28] "even the head of a government department would come down to my district to listen to the residents."

This is not to say that all these District Councillors need to do is to give a phone call to a senior party member and let him handle the cases once and for all. In fact, they cannot abuse their senior party members' assistance by passing the buck all the time. District Councillors need to be selective and sometimes may need to learn how to package cases. A District Councillor told us that when he received a case from an individual resident, he would ask other residents if they encountered a similar problem.[29] If an individual problem can be packaged as a district-wise problem, then he can attract media attention and stand a good chance of getting government authorities to respond.

Of course, not all District Councillors are equally diligent. More sinister ways to market one's problem-solving ability do exist. Some pan-democratic District Councillors[30] reveal that one trick that their pro-establishment counterparts may use is to obtain insider information about local policies (e.g., the creation of a public park) that the government will soon implement.[31] Then, prior to the public announcement of such policies, these pro-establishment councillors would put up street banners telling residents that they are "negotiating" with government officials about those policies. Once the policies really come into effect, they can then

---

[26]Personal interview with a District Councillor on March 7, 2013 (Code: 23).

[27]The Basic Law stipulates that "[t]he Executive Council of the Hong Kong Special Administrative Region shall be an organ for assisting the Chief Executive in policy-making" (Hong Kong Government 2012). Thus, the Chief Executive consults the Executive Council before making a major decision in public policies (Li 2012).

[28]Personal interview with a District Councillor on January 2, 2013 (Code: 7).

[29]Personal interview with a District Councillor on January 23, 2013 (Code: 18).

[30]Personal interview with District Councillors on October 12, 2012, and March 7, 2013 (Code: 4 and 23).

[31]Thanks to their cozy relationship with the government, such insider information seems not too difficult to obtain.

claim all the credit, despite the fact that the policies would be carried out by the government anyway. A pan-democratic District Councillor even laments that a pro-establishment District Councillor from a nearby neighborhood was so audacious as to steal from him the credit for successfully pressing government authorities to install additional elevators in his housing estate by using such shenanigans.

5.4.2   Invading Rivals' Turf

To bring my analysis into focus, by political rivals, I refer to the pan-democrats. However, it is important to note that pro-establishment parties do compete with each other, and sometimes the competition is just as intense as that among the pan-democrats. The competition among pro-establishment parties often escapes media attention for two possible reasons. The first is that the frequency is relatively lower. Second, these parties try to conceal it for fear of condemnation by Beijing, which is intolerant of infighting among its political proxies.

(a) Newcomers' Actions

The aggressive expansion of Beijing-sponsored parties in the District Councils requires effective strategies to invade its rivals' turf, and effective strategies begin with locating an appropriate District Council Constituency. This is not a simple task because District Council Constituencies vary greatly according to their demographic structure, class composition, residents' dynamics, and, perhaps most importantly, the quality of the incumbent. There is no one-size-fits-all strategy for different constituencies. For instance, some find neighborhood voluntary organizations such as Mutual Aid Committees critical to their electoral success (Kwong 2010, pp. 107–8), while others see them as an unreliable partner.[32] A potential challenger needs to identify a District Council Constituency that matches her ability and personality. DAB District Councillors admitted that they have received great help from the party in this because their party has a structured apprenticeship system,[33] in which mentors, usually seasoned politicians with ample local connections and street knowledge, offer valuable advice to newcomers on identifying constituencies.

What if different Beijing-sponsored parties have an eye on the same constituency? The leaders of Beijing-sponsored parties maintain private communication channels with each other to avoid territorial clashes. The Liaison Office also plays an important role in regulating electoral competition among pro-establishment parties. The bottom line is to resolve all conflicts within the pro-establishment camp before the election year (Au 2015), though this goal is not always achievable.

---

[32]In one interview, a District Councillor points out that precisely because Mutual Aid Committees are an important player in local affairs, if one relies too much on them, one may suffer a great electoral loss when they defect (Code: 20).

[33]Personal interview with District Councillors on January 2, 2012, and January 3, 2013 (Code: 8 and 11).

After identifying a suitable constituency, the next step is to penetrate it. Timing is of paramount importance. My interviewees suggest that in the 1990s, it was not uncommon that a challenger parachuted into a District Council Constituency just a couple of months before the election, then ran a campaign, and defeated the lazy incumbent. As elections have become increasingly competitive, incumbent Councillors these days dare not to slight their constituents. A pan-democratic District Councillor, who has occupied the job for almost two decades, recalls that District Councillors back in the 1990s might not even have a regular office, and it was perfectly acceptable that they met local residents once a week.[34]

"The situation now is totally different," he explains. "The constituents expect you to show up in office every single day."

As a result, now it is nearly impossible to unseat a pro-establishment incumbent with a person unfamiliar to the constituents. A typical newcomer from a pan-democratic party serious about District Council elections would penetrate into her target constituency one or two years prior to the election. As for Beijing-sponsored parties, there have been many cases where newcomers began their district works three years in advance. "Their election machine resumes as soon as an election is over," a seasoned prodemocracy politician observes.[35]

The first thing a newcomer needs to do is to gain publicity. I am told that an effective way to become known in the neighborhood is to greet residents in wet markets or in bus terminals during peak hours everyday. Newcomers would usually take that opportunity to distribute handbills, detailing some long-standing local issues such as sewage problems. The main point of such activities is to leave constituents an impression, however vague it is, that the newcomers are concerned about the well-being of the neighborhood and are extremely diligent.

The single most important task newcomers have to achieve in these preparation years is to forge a robust support network in the target neighborhood. The best way to attract followers is through services. They should start offering constituency services I discussed in the previous section as if they already held a District Council office. The problem is that without a formal position, in what capacity can they offer such services in order to achieve an effective result?

There are three common channels through which newcomers can deliver services. The first is that they work as assistant to an incumbent District Councillor or Legislative Councillor in a neighboring constituency and organize activities that encompass the residents of their target constituency. A pro-establishment District Councillor points out the limitation of this method.[36] "My assistant has already been overwhelmed by the work of my office. I do not think she has much time left for cultivating another constituency," he says.

Another channel is to deliver services as a community worker of the party. The DAB enjoys a superior competitive advantage in this regard. This party has been

---

[34]Personal interview with a District Councillor on January 31, 2013 (Code: 21).

[35]Personal interview on April 11, 2014 (Code: 29).

[36]Personal interview with a District Councillor on January 9, 2013 (Code: 13).

conscious of developing itself into a grassroots party with elaborate local networks since its establishment in 1992. In 1994, it had only nine local branches. By 2012, it has 46 local branch offices, in addition to more than a hundred LegCo and District Council offices (DAB 2013a). As a comparison, each of the two largest pan-democratic parties, the DP and the CP, only has five local branch offices. A DAB interviewee points out the importance of local branch offices during his election campaign.[37] He worked as a community worker in a local party branch, and he found that the proximity of the branch office has significantly lowered his logistic costs, thereby facilitating his services offered to his target constituency.

The third important channel to deliver service is through Beijing-sponsored social organizations. These social organizations help newcomers in a number of ways. A pan-democratic District Councillor[38] told us that as the 2011 District Council election neared, a women's organization affiliated with the NTAS launched a massive service blitz, involving recreational activities such as day-trips, dancing classes, and gift giving in his constituency. These activities were co-organized by a DAB member who ended up being his challenger in that election. He believed that these activities helped his challenger rapidly develop a local support network.

His conjecture is probably right. What a newcomer lacks is the constituents' contacts. This is where the social organizations as local community brokers can offer great help. These organizations reportedly pass the personal contacts of members who joined their welfare and recreational activities to pro-establishment parties for election campaigns (Lo et al. 2002; Ming Pao Daily News 2007). I heard a case where a resident received get-out-the-vote phone calls on election day from the teacher of an FTU yoga class that the resident had taken three years ago. One of my interviewees from the pro-establishment camp admitted that a women's organization affiliated with the NTAS did help him contact its members living in his district to solicit votes.[39] In his study of patron-client politics in District Council elections, Kwong (2010) observes similar electoral functions performed by a local women's organization in another district (pp. 106–107).

Au (2015) even points out that the pro-establishment camp has developed a "household registration" system (*hukou bu*) such that pro-establishment parties and organizations are required to submit a databank of residents' contacts that they collected through grassroots activities to the Liaison Office, who would coordinate the electoral campaign for the pro-establishment camp as a whole.

It is not uncommon that these social organizations provide office space for pro-establishment newcomers. One interviewee, an independent incumbent associated with the pan-democratic camp, told us that his pro-establishment rival, after being defeated, immediately opened an office next to his District Council office under the

---

[37]Personal interview with a District Councillor on January 2, 2013 (Code: 8).

[38]Personal interview with a District Councillor on January 23, 2013 (Code: 17).

[39]Personal interview with a District Councillor on January 9, 2013 (Code: 13).

name of a social organization. With this official position, his rival engaged in district works as if he were the incumbent.[40]

(b) Newcomers' Incentives

Wars are fought by soldiers. Without party members who are willing to engage in mundane and routine district matters, Beijing-sponsored parties cannot execute any of the strategies mentioned earlier. In fact, the ability to attract newcomers is what I find as the most important manifestation of the pro-establishment camp's resource advantage. To understand this, one needs to know the evolution of government tiers in Hong Kong.

Prior to its sovereignty transfer, the Hong Kong government consisted of three elected tiers: the District Boards, the Urban Council/Regional Council,[41] and the Legislative Council. The District Boards were considered a career entry point for many junior politicians with aspirations. After accumulating experiences at the District-Board level, they hoped to get elected into the Urban Council/Regional Council. Given their larger constituency, greater policy-making power, and higher fiscal autonomy, the Urban Council/Regional Council would have further prepared these politicians for the ultimate trophy: the Legislative Council.

In 1999, the government carried out administrative reform, abolishing the two municipal councils. Junior politicians who occupied a District Council office suddenly found themselves stuck in an awkward situation. No matter how hard they worked for their tiny constituency, the political credentials and policy knowledge they accumulated over the years were by no means sufficient to prepare them for a LegCo election. In fact, their reputation could hardly travel beyond their tiny District Council Constituency. Worse still, the LegCo seats open for direct elections were limited, and many senior members, who had devoted themselves to the democracy movement since the 1980s, still occupied the LegCo office.[42]

Not all politicians have an ambition for the LegCo, however. For those who simply want to eke out a living from their District Council post, they are confronted with other problems. Chief among them is that the salary of a District Councillor is uncompetitive. Notwithstanding a recent pay raise, the monthly salary of a District Councillor is HK$22,090 in 2012–2013 (Legislative Council 2012), which is on a par with the wage of a junior secondary school teacher. Unlike school teachers, however, District Councillors have no opportunity of job promotion. Nor do they have statutory pay adjustment that civil servants enjoy. Lateral job transfers are also

---

[40]Personal interview with a District Councillor on June 14, 2012 (Code: 2).

[41]Both the Urban Council and the Regional Council were municipal councils in Hong Kong. While the former council dealt with municipal matters in Kowloon and Hong Kong Island, the latter council provided services for the New Territories.

[42]There are exceptions. Wu Chi Wai, of the DP, is one of the fortunate few, who, after waiting for 13 years as a District Councillor, saw an opportunity in 2012 when his senior retired from the LegCo. The party supported Wu by placing him as the first candidate on the only party list in his constituency. He eventually won a LegCo seat for the first time at the age of 50.

difficult, given that the skill set they have developed does not appeal to private sector employers.[43] District Councillors are also excluded from the Mandatory Provident Fund, a pension system to which all employees in Hong Kong are entitled. In brief, almost all District Councillor interviewees find their job financially unrewarding in the long run. As a result, many have to look for a part-time job, such as being a social worker[44] or a college instructor,[45] to make ends meet.

The meager salary, dismal career prospect, and reelection uncertainties greatly discourage junior politicians from starting their career at the District Council level. In my interviews, many political parties have a difficult time looking for newcomers to stand for District Council elections. Yet this problem is less of a concern to major pro-establishment parties such as the DAB.

Thanks to its unparalleled war chest for party development, the DAB is able to assign full-time paid jobs to its junior members who aspire to compete for District Council seats. After obtaining a bachelor's degree in language education, Wong Ping Fan was hired as an assistant coordinator with a monthly salary of HK$15,000 (Ming Pao Daily News 2010b). Her job duty was to provide community services such as free haircut in her target constituency, Bik Woo. The two-year intensive grassroots services had prepared her for the 2011 District Council election, in which she lost by a slim margin. One of our interviewees from the DAB had had a similar career path except that she successfully unseated a longtime pan-democratic incumbent in the same election.[46]

Beijing-sponsored parties' financial assistance to newcomers may continue even after their electoral success. A pro-establishment interviewee tells me that his friend, who is a District Councillor of the DAB, continues to receive a monthly salary of HK$11,000 for his part-time position in the party.[47] Chan Hok Fung, another DAB District Councillor, reportedly earned a monthly salary of HK$11,500 for working as the assistant of a LegCo member of his party (Ming Pao Daily News 2013a). Together with his District Council salary, his monthly income would be over HK$33,000. It is also worth noting that the DAB no longer requires their District Councillors to make a monthly contribution to the party (Yuen 2011, p. 40), while pan-democratic parties would top slice 5–10 % of their District Councillors' monthly salaries.

This financial arrangement explains why major pro-establishment parties can continue to field newcomers for District Council elections. If party members win, they can keep their salary as party employees. If they lose, they can go back to work as a full-time employee in the party or in affiliated social organizations. "In

---

[43]Personal interview with a District Councillor on January 23, 2013 (Code: 17).

[44]Personal interview with a District Councillor on January 9, 2013 (Code: 13).

[45]Personal interview with a District Councillor on June 15, 2012 (Code: 3).

[46]Personal interview with a District Councillor on January 2, 2013 (Code: 7).

[47]Personal interview with a District Councillor on January 9, 2013 (Code: 13).

the worst case, I can be an instructor for FTU's employee retraining programs in case of losing the election," says an interviewee from the FTU.[48]

In contrast, candidates of the prodemocracy camp seldom enjoy such a luxury. Many prodemocracy parties have difficulties supporting not only defeated candidates but even incumbents who seek reelection. It is reported that a candidate from the DP had to sell his own apartment, in order to raise sufficient funds for running the 2008 LegCo elections (Ming Pao Daily News 2010c). Many of my pan-democratic interviewees have to keep not only a part-time job but also to pursue further studies to maintain their competitiveness in the labor market.[49] To pan-democratic District Councillors, they are fully aware that once defeated, they can count on no one but themselves.

In addition to monetary rewards and career safety nets, Beijing-sponsored parties, with their cozy relationship with the government, can offer their junior members an alternative career path in the public sector. Chan Hak Kan of the DAB is a case in point (Ming Pao Daily News 2011b). He started his political career by winning a District Council seat in 1999. After losing his office in the 2003 elections, the government appointed him as a special assistant to the Chief Executive in 2006, with a monthly salary of around HK$70,000. Another example is Chan Pak Li (Information Services Department 2013). He started his political career by running for the 2007 District Council elections as a DAB candidate. After landslide victories in two successive elections, he was appointed as a political assistant for the Commerce and Economic Development in March 2013, with a monthly salary of around HK$98,000.

The effort of Beijing-sponsored parties in developing its grassroots networks aims to diminish the political influences of the pan-democrats. As we have seen in Table 5.1, it has achieved resounding success at least at the District Council level. Its past success will also make future success more likely. With more seats under its control, it can focus more resources in the remaining constituencies it has yet to capture. In addition, there exists a complementarity effect regarding service provision among constituencies. A pro-establishment District Councillor describes how he and nearby District Councillors of the same party work as a team:[50] "Two of them have legal backgrounds. Together with my expertise in district matters, we have nicely complemented each other's work." If he cannot attend a meeting with local residents, another teammate would show up on his behalf even if the teammate comes from another constituency. "The key is," he emphasizes, "we make the constituents feel that the party is always at their service."

---

[48]Personal interview with a District Councillor on December 18, 2012 (Code: 6).

[49]Personal interview with District Councillors on June 15, 2012, and October 12, 2012 (Code: 3 and 4).

[50]Personal interview with a District Councillor on January 4, 2013 (Code: 12).

5.4.3   Candidate Selection

The strength of Beijing-sponsored parties is reflected in the candidates whom they field in District Council elections. Figure 5.2 offers a glimpse of candidate attributes according to political camp. Since 2003, the average age of Beijing-backed candidates (solid line) has gone down. At the same time, the share of female candidates of these parties has consistently been on the rise. There is no noticeable trend with respect to both age and gender for pan-democratic parties.

A remarkable achievement for pan-democratic parties is its use of novice candidates, defined as those who did not participate in the last election. Its share of novice candidates (dashed line) has increased from 31.5 % in 2003 to almost 50 % in 2011 (see the bottom left panel of Fig. 5.2). Note, however, novelty is not tantamount to quality. Equally noticeable is the appalling decline in the success rate of these pan-democratic novices, dropping from 52 % in 2003 to 6 % in 2011. By contrast, although no drastic change is observed among Beijing-sponsored parties in the share of novice candidates between 2003 and 2011, they have significantly raised the election rate of their new candidates from 8 to 44.5 % (see the bottom right panel of Fig. 5.2).

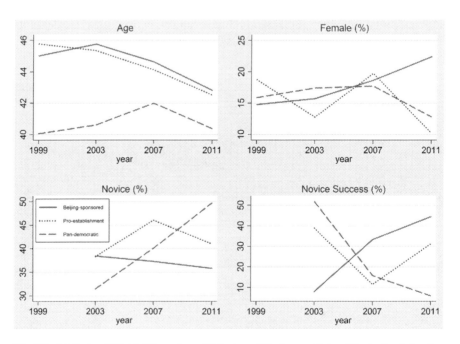

Fig. 5.2 Attributes of District Council candidates by political camp. Notes: "Novice" is defined as candidates who did not participate in the last District Council election. Pro-establishment parties here do not include Beijing-sponsored parties (Source: Author's calculation based on election data from the HKSAR Electoral Affairs Commission)

A crucial reason why Beijing-sponsored parties do not endorse so many novices is that they are able to keep junior candidates working in a district despite initial defeat. One-time loss cannot tell much about the long-run potential of a politician. But the experience of defeat is an important asset to junior politicians, who can grow skillful through past mistakes. In addition, the relationship vote takes time to develop. For this reason, given that they have ample resources to invest in younger members, Beijing-sponsored parties can afford hiring defeated candidates to continue to work in a district. Pan-democratic parties, on the other hand, have difficulty retaining defeated candidates due to the lack of funding. Once defeated, many pan-democratic candidates would end up dropping out permanently. Consequently, pan-democratic parties would have to find many inexperienced new faces for every election cycle.

To examine the discrepancy in the ability to retain talents between Beijing-sponsored parties and the pan-democrats, I conduct probit regression analyses to find out correlates of District Council challengers'[51] dropout decisions based on the election data from 1999 to 2011.[52] In particular, for each political camp, I regress the outcome variable *dropout* on numerous relevant factors.[53] The regression results are presented in Table 5.3.

First, consider the variable *Novice*. The coefficient has a positive sign in both samples, suggesting that new candidates are more likely to drop out of the subsequent election than seasoned candidates. However, the coefficient on this variable is not significantly different from zero in the Beijing-sponsored parties' sample. But as for the pan-democratic sample, the coefficient is both statistically and substantively significant. Converting the probit coefficient (0.448) into probability, I find that the probability for defeated pan-democratic novices to quit a subsequent election is 16% points, higher than defeated pan-democratic veterans.

Next, consider the effect of *Vote Share*. One would expect that a challenger defeated by a narrow margin is less likely to opt out of the next election. In other words, the probability of dropping out should be negatively associated with a defeated candidate's vote share. Indeed, the data support this theoretical expectation, as the coefficient on *Vote Share* is negative across all specifications. Note that in the pan-democratic sample, the effect of vote share is no longer statistically significant once we control for *Novice*. This may imply that those who received a low vote share in the pan-democratic camp are predominantly inexperienced candidates.

In theory, elderly challengers who are defeated are more likely to opt out. This is true with respect to the Beijing-sponsored sample, as the coefficient on *Age* is statistically significant in Specifications (1) and (2). On average, the probability that a defeated Beijing-sponsored candidate would drop out of the next election increases

---

[51]A District Council challenger refers to a candidate who is not a District Council incumbent.

[52]The 2011 District Council election data are used to identify dropouts from 2007. One cannot tell whether a 2011 candidate will drop out until the 2015 election.

[53]The outcome variable is a dichotomous variable that takes a value of "1" if a defeated challenger opts out of the following election and "0" otherwise.

Table 5.3 Probit estimates of challengers' dropout by political camp

	Beijing-sponsored parties' dropout		Pan-democratic parties' dropout	
Dependent variable	(1)	(2)	(3)	(4)
Novice		0.085		0.448*
		(0.256)		(0.244)
Vote share	-0.027***	-0.023*	-0.019**	-0.007
	(0.009)	(0.012)	(0.009)	(0.011)
Age	0.030***	0.044***	0.011	0.014
	(0.008)	(0.012)	(0.008)	(0.011)
Female	-0.105	-0.271	0.303	0.252
	(0.230)	(0.293)	(0.225)	(0.273)
Female incumbent	0.152	0.013	0.222	0.535*
	(0.225)	(0.281)	(0.225)	(0.281)
Age of incumbent	-0.016*	-0.038***	0.003	-0.006
	(0.009)	(0.012)	(0.008)	(0.010)
Pan-democratic incumbent	-0.382*	-0.615**		
	(0.199)	(0.263)		
Novice incumbent	0.049	-0.108	0.110	0.081
	(0.256)	(0.275)	(0.277)	(0.305)
Beijing-sponsored incumbent			0.092	0.019
			(0.167)	(0.214)
Constant	1.403**	2.230**	0.685	4.481***
	(0.707)	(1.078)	(0.671)	(0.948)
N	308	206	284	184
AIC	390.22	261.31	417.66	277.83

Notes: A "dropout" challenger is one who chooses not to compete in the following District Council election given that he or she is defeated in the current District Council election. The dependent variable is a dichotomous variable that takes a value of "1" if a defeated candidate drops out of the subsequent election and "0" otherwise. All specifications control for district and year fixed effects, which are not reported. The data cover District Council elections from 1999 to 2011. Standard errors clustered at candidate level are in parentheses
*<0.10; **<0.05; ***<0.01

by 1.2 % points for each additional year in age. Surprisingly, no significant age effect can be found in the pan-democratic sample. My conjecture is that Beijing-sponsored parties have a certain mechanism to retire senior candidates, especially after their defeats, in order to make room for younger and more promising candidates.

Whether a defeated challenger decides to strike back depends on the incumbent's quality. There is a wealth of literature in American politics that studies how high-quality incumbents are able to deter strong challengers (e.g., Stone et al. 2004). For this reason, I also control for incumbents' gender, age, and political affiliation in the probit regression specifications. There is no compelling evidence suggesting that gender matters. But an incumbent's age is negatively correlated with a defeated challenger's dropout decision. A possible reason is that it is relatively easier to unseat elderly incumbents, which makes defeated candidates willing to spend four more years in a district waiting for their next chance.

Finally, for Beijing-sponsored parties, their defeated challengers are more likely to stay if the incumbent is a pan-democrat. The effect is of both statistical and substantive significance. Take the coefficient on *Pan-democratic Incumbent* as an example. The probability that a Beijing-sponsored defeated candidate would opt out of the next election is 17 % points lower if the incumbent happens to come from a pan-democratic party. This result indicates the conscious aggression of Beijing-sponsored parties on the turf of the pan-democrats. The converse is not true, however. For pan-democratic parties, whether the incumbent comes from a Beijing-sponsored party has little to do with a defeated candidate's dropout decision.

Taking all these together, one can see that Beijing-sponsored parties have a more structured, comprehensive, and organized electoral strategy than their pan-democratic counterparts. They have an established system to protect defeated novices and to retire less competitive senior candidates. Their attack is also more targeted, as they are able to have their defeated candidates to base in the same district to gnaw away at the support of pan-democratic incumbents.

When I asked the pan-democratic District Councillors how they feel about the aggressive expansion of Beijing-sponsored parties in the District Councils, all of them agreed that the effective organizational capacity and superior resource advantage of their rivals have posed a serious threat to the survival of the pan-democratic camp. The majority of them held that the political outlook of their camp was bleak. A couple of them even suggested that an electoral turnaround would only be possible when the pro-establishment camp completely wipes out the pan-democrats. "At that point, voters may yearn for a wholesale change," comments one interviewee.[54]

Perhaps such a turnaround will happen one day. Perhaps the pan-democrats will experience another July 1, 2003 protest that would help them drive the pro-establishment parties out of the District Councils. However even if that day really comes, the pan-democrats' victory is going to be short-lived, if the structural weaknesses of pan-democratic parties as detailed in this chapter remain unchanged. In this sense, my interviewee's hope seems unrealistic at best and defeatist at worst.

5.5 "Independent" Candidates

As discussed in the beginning of this chapter, the CCP has long established its branch in Hong Kong, although its membership has been shrouded in secrecy. Concealing party identity helps CCP members avoid getting into political trouble and achieve various strategic objectives. Would candidates from Beijing-sponsored

---

[54]Personal interview with a District Councillor on March 7, 2013 (Code: 23).

parties also hide their local party affiliation when they compete for District Council seats? One incentive in doing so is to avoid invoking voters' negative feelings about these parties. Although ideology plays a relatively small role in District Council elections, implying that party labels are less important, there exist numerous anecdotal accounts of this practice (Ming Pao Daily News 2012b; Apple Daily 2012b). Such candidates are commonly referred to as "invisible leftists" (*yinxing zuopai*).

Some pan-democratic District Councillors whom I interviewed have also shared their experience of dealing with these "invisible leftists." But a more intriguing personal encounter I heard came from a pro-establishment District Councillor, whose party is not Beijing-sponsored. He confided that a major Beijing-sponsored party had long been anxious to unseat him, although he also belonged to the pro-establishment camp. But it could not do it openly because, as I mentioned previously, Beijing generally disapproves of infighting within the pro-establishment camp.[55] "To escape Beijing's attention," explains the District Councillor, "my challengers first quit their party prior to an election and ran their campaign under an independent label. But they would rejoin the party after I beat them." He has survived such an attack twice. His experience suggests not only an alternative incentive to hide one's political affiliation but also the keen competition within the pro-establishment camp, which often escapes media attention.

5.6   Redistricting

A number of pan-democratic District Councillors whom I have interviewed lament that they have been under constant threat of gerrymandering. Gerrymandering refers to an electoral trick of redrawing district boundaries in order to maximize one's electoral chance. This electoral practice, or malpractice, has been observed in many countries, especially those adopting a "single-member district" electoral formula (Handley and Grofman 2008). Studies on gerrymandering in Hong Kong are woefully inadequate because official data on the government's redistricting policies remain opaque. In principle, the boundary of a district should be redrawn in order to have the district conform to an official population quota (approximately 17,000 people per District Council Constituency).[56] The implementation of the population quota is rather lax. The law allows the Electoral Affairs Commission, the government agency responsible for redistricting, to deviate from the population

---

[55]Exposing elite dissension would reveal the weakness of the ruling coalition and encourage the emergence of challenges from society. This was one of the factors leading to the collapse of the Soviet Union (Dimitrov 2013, p. 310). Perhaps for this reason, the CCP has tried painstakingly to maintain an image of elite cohesion.

[56]For detailed criteria of redistricting in Hong Kong, see Section 20 of the Electoral Affairs Commission Ordinance (Hong Kong Special Administrative Region Government 2013).

quota by as much as $\pm 25\%$. In addition, the bandwidth, albeit sufficiently lax, is also nonbinding. The commission can ignore the population quota altogether on the grounds of "preserving community identity and local ties" (Electoral Affairs Commission 2011), where the terms "community identity" and "local ties" are vaguely defined.

Perhaps for the above reasons, there is no shortage of bizarrely shaped District Council Constituencies. Some pan-democratic District Councillors I have interviewed also suggest that they could not really understand why their districts appear the way they are. What they knew was that they suddenly lost a sizable portion of their constituents because the Electoral Affairs Commission claimed that their districts needed redrawing. Some tried to file a complaint to the commission, asking for a revocation of the redistricting plan, but to no avail. The authorities explained to them that they were responding to suggestions from citizens who requested redistricting. One pan-democratic District Councillor elaborates on this point, saying, "The pro-establishment camp would mobilize their people to file such redistricting requests to the authorities in order to undermine pan-democratic incumbents." I was curious why he did not do likewise. "Because the authorities would not respond to my requests," he sighs.

The uneasiness of my pan-democratic interviewees is understandable. Gelman and King (1994) argue that incumbents are generally averse to redistricting because it "creates enormous levels of uncertainty, an extremely undesirable situation for any sitting politician (p. 541)." Redistricting uproots the constituents whom a District Councillor has served for years and replaces them with someone unfamiliar with the District Councillor's achievement and diligence. Worse still, redistricting in Hong Kong typically occurs only a few months prior to an election. For instance, in 2003 and 2011, the Electoral Affairs Commission announced the redistricting plan six to seven months before the elections, regardless of the statutory deadline prescribed by Section 18 of the Electoral Affairs Commission Ordinance which requires the Commission to make the boundary delimitation recommendations no later than twelve months before an election. With such a short notice, affected incumbents would find it difficult to build connections with their new constituents.

To verify if a systematic bias exists against pan-democratic District Councillors with respect to redistricting, I contacted various government agencies including the Electoral Affairs Commission and the Lands Department for redistricting data. In particular, I wanted to find out the District Council Constituency to which each residential building belongs in each District Council election. Such data are necessary because the extent of redistricting varies significantly from constituency to constituency. To evaluate the systematic bias more accurately, if any, I needed to measure not only the occurrence but also the intensity of redistricting for each District Council Constituency. Quite surprisingly, the government authorities replied that such data are not available. What they could offer me was a set of digital maps that show the demarcation of District Council Constituencies since 2003.

As a result, I had to use a more complicated way to collect the desired data. I took advantage of the fact that for each residential building, its physical location does not change from one election to another. What may change is its District Council

Table 5.4 District change of residential buildings by political camp

t	$t+1$			
	Pan-democratic parties	Beijing-sponsored parties	Others	Total (%)
Pan-democratic parties	83.02	1.42	15.56	100
Beijing-sponsored parties	1.32	96.49	2.2	100
Others	2.56	1.53	95.91	100

Notes: The unit of observations is the percentage of residential buildings. The transition matrix shows the percentage change of residential buildings from one political camp to another between time t and $t+1$. The data are based on three District Council elections: 2003, 2007, and 2011. Beijing-sponsored parties include the Democratic Alliance for the Betterment and Progress of Hong Kong (DAB), the Hong Kong Federation of Trade Unions (FTU), and the Hong Kong Progressive Alliance (HKPA)

Constituency. If I can collect the geo-coordinates of residential buildings, I can then map these geo-coordinates to the District Council Constituency maps, which would allow me to figure out the change of district identity of these buildings.

Using the above method, I ended up identifying approximately 38,000 residential buildings' geo-coordinates, housing 1.98 million apartment units. Because Hong Kong has 2.3 million domestic households (Hong Kong Housing Authority 2012), the dataset covers approximately 84 % of the total household population. The data are not perfect but should provide a reasonably decent estimate of the potential redistricting bias.

Table 5.4 presents a transition matrix, which shows the percentage change of residential buildings from one political camp to another between elections. For instance, pan-democratic parties can carry over 83.02 % of the residential buildings in their districts to the next election. However, Beijing-sponsored parties can retain 96.49 %, which is significantly higher. In fact, even the "Others" category, which consists of other pro-establishment parties and "independent" candidates, is able to hold 95.91 % of the buildings in their districts unchanged. In short, a District Council Constituency controlled by a pan-democratic party has on average 4.86 times more buildings being subject to redistricting than a constituency controlled by a Beijing-sponsored party. The findings provide prima facie evidence to support the conjecture of the pan-democratic District Councillors I interviewed: pan-democratic District Councillors are more likely to fall prey to redistricting, which disrupts their ties with the constituents and hence lowers their chance of getting reelected.

Pan-democratic District Councillors are not completely defenseless, however, in the face of the redistricting risk. A number of them say that they have to provide constituency services not only to residents of their constituencies but also to those living in neighboring ones, so that when redistricting really occurs, the newly added constituents, who are likely residents of neighboring constituencies, would also be familiar with their work. But making a wider web of influence is costly. As mentioned, pan-democratic District Councillors are already facing tremendous financial constraints. Suffice it to say, redistricting would not make their political life and survival easier. Rather, it is likely to compound their plight.

5.7 Conclusion

Grassroots political organizations only get a brief mention in the Basic Law. Article 97 stipulates that "[d]istrict organizations which are not organs of political power may be established in the Hong Kong Special Administrative Region, to be consulted by the government of the Region on district administration and other affairs, or to be responsible for providing services in such fields as culture, recreation and environmental sanitation." Although district organizations are supposedly apolitical, as provided by this article, District Councils, ironically, turn out to be a powerful political tool for Beijing-sponsored parties to challenge the dominant position of the opposition parties. By driving the opposition parties out of District Councils, Beijing-sponsored parties have effectively deprived their rivals of a vital source of financial incomes. Losing local elected offices also implies losing local contacts. Beijing-sponsored parties would be able to uproot their rivals' grassroots political networks.

Thus far, their encroachment on their rivals' turf has been fairly successful. Despite a temporary setback in 2003, as a consequence of the historic July 1, 2003 protest, the Beijing-sponsored parties' dominance over the District Councils has risen unambiguously. This result indicates that the July 1, 2003 protest did not disrupt Beijing's long-term political planning in Hong Kong. On the contrary, Beijing-sponsored parties have redoubled their efforts to consolidate their united front work at the grassroots level (Qiang 2008, p. 185).

A DAB District Councillor points out that the political crisis in 2003 was a wake-up call. "It shows that we lacked a sense of crisis," he explains, "We need to strengthen our district work." Another DAB District Councillor, who is also a member of the party's central committee, confided to me that the DAB invested "at least twice as many resources in grassroots work after 2003." Note that the escalation of investment in united front work is probably not confined to Beijing-sponsored parties. Kwong (2010) finds that a pro-Beijing women's center had also received a huge sum of money from its patrons after the July 1, 2003 protest. The money was used to offer recreational and cultural activities at a discount rate to local residents. Conceivably, this kind of local initiatives is part of Beijing's overarching strategic plan of marginalizing the pan-democrats' social support through the use of vertical patron-client networks.

The enormous united front investment explains the inexorable rise of Beijing-sponsored parties in the District Councils. They enjoy a superior resource advantage over pan-democratic parties. Such an advantage allows them to not only provide highly labor-intensive constituency services but also to cushion the impact of electoral defeats. In addition, political ideology plays little role in District Council elections, which implies that Beijing-sponsored parties can avoid dealing with the ideological confrontation mounted by the opposition that occurs in higher-level elections.

Redistricting may also contribute to the success of Beijing-sponsored parties' District Council strategy. As I have shown in Table 5.4, redistricting occurs with a significantly higher frequency in District Council Constituencies controlled by the pan-democratic District Councillors than those controlled by the pro-establishment camp. The District Councillors whom I have interviewed all agree that redistricting has devastating impacts on their chances of getting reelected because it can sever their ties with the constituents whom they have been serving for years.

The ambition of Beijing-sponsored parties will likely not just be confined to the District Councils. Ultimately, they aim to outflank their pan-democratic rivals in the LegCo, the major battlefield. Does their District Council strategy help them in trying to achieve this larger goal? This is what we will examine in the next chapter.

Chapter 6
Surrounding the Cities from the Countryside: An Empirical Assessment of the Electoral Effects

During its initial armed struggles against the Kuomintang (KMT), the Chinese Communist Party suffered from serious setbacks. Mao Zedong soon came to see the problem as a strategic mistake; the CCP had wrongly placed its focus on urban uprisings. As cities were the KMT's stronghold, the CCP, while in its infancy, stood no chance of defeating the KMT. Mao later adopted an alternative strategy. He jettisoned the urban focus and moved his forces deep into the countryside, in the belief that before his party's military capability grew stronger, it should avoid any head-on military confrontation with the KMT. The rural regions, he reasoned, provide a fertile ground to grow his revolutionary base and a shield against the KMT's aggression. Once the CCP developed a bastion in the countryside, it could mount an offensive against the KMT in cities, the major battlefield.[1] Mao's tactical maneuver is famously known as "surrounding the cities from the countryside," which has been touted, at least by the official rhetoric, as the key to the CCP's ultimate success in conquering the KMT.

In many ways, the Beijing-sponsored parties' policy toward the District Council resembles Mao's military strategy. Their major battleground is the Legislative Council. But these parties have difficulty making inroads into LegCo elections because political ideology plays a strong role in such elections, and their pan-democratic rivals have a solid issue ownership of political liberalization. For this reason, Beijing-sponsored parties shifted their focus to the "rural region," a metaphor for the District Councils. As mentioned in the previous chapter, pan-democratic parties have no strategic advantage of occupying this elected tier. Peripheral as they seem, the District Councils are of paramount strategic importance, as they can act as a bastion against pan-democratic parties' electoral expansion and, ultimately, undermine their support base from the ground up. In this

---

[1] For details of Mao's strategic considerations, see Mao (1952a,c).

© Springer Science+Business Media Singapore 2015
S.H.-W. Wong, *Electoral Politics in Post-1997 Hong Kong*,
DOI 10.1007/978-981-287-387-3_6

chapter, I present empirical evidence to show how capturing District Council seats helps Beijing-sponsored parties "besiege" their pan-democratic rivals in LegCo elections.

6.1 The Causal Mechanisms

There is a popular belief in Hong Kong that prodemocracy voters' behavior in LegCo elections is vastly different from that in District Council elections. In the latter elections, they may support pro-establishment candidates who offer quality constituency services. But when it comes to LegCo elections, these voters would always side with pan-democratic candidates, who are ideologically closer to them. As a result, pan-democratic parties have no need to worry even if they fare poorly in District Council elections. They may lose the battle, but they will win the war.

Not only ordinary citizens[2] but some pan-democratic politicians are also dogged believers in this optimistic view. I heard a party heavyweight of the Civic Party insist that her party was able to retain the same level of voter support, irrespective of its performance in District Council elections.[3] Almost all of the District Councillors I have interviewed, however, believe otherwise.

There are four main reasons why District Council seats are strategically important to a party's quest for higher elected offices:

(1) They provide a stable source of income.

Running a LegCo election campaign is costly. Most pan-democratic parties are short of financial resources, partly because, as discussed in the previous chapter, the business community is reluctant to support these opposition parties for fear of antagonizing Beijing. Under such circumstances, the monthly salary contribution of elected party members, however meager, becomes a stable and important source of income for many pan-democratic parties. Losing District Council seats, thus, has a direct financial impact on a pan-democratic party's ability to compete in LegCo elections.

(2) They foster local support networks.

Behind the aforementioned popular belief about the disconnection between District Council and LegCo elections is an assumption that voters value ideological affinity dearly. To many District Councillors I spoke with, this is a fallacious assumption because personal rapport weighs more heavily than ideology in many voters' minds. Sometimes people vote for a candidate simply because they had a chance to talk to her in person. In order for candidates to make an impression on local residents, they need to establish their contacts first. Collecting constituents'

---

[2]Personal interviews with ordinary citizens on January 7, 2014 (Code: 41 and 42)

[3]Personal communication, October 19, 2012

contacts is, therefore, of paramount importance. Because the population size of the LegCo's geographical constituencies is fairly large,[4] it is not easy for LegCo candidates to obtain their constituents' contacts, let alone their electoral support. In contrast, a typical District Council Constituency consists of only 17,000 residents. District Councillors, therefore, have a crucial role to play, as their local knowledge enables them to act as political brokers for LegCo candidates.

How does a District Councillor acquire the local knowledge? Casework is an integral part of a District Councillor's job. Based on my interviews, diligent District Councillors handle more than a thousand cases related to their constituents each year. In other words, they should be able to accumulate thousands of local residents' contacts over a single term of office. Moreover, they may hold various cultural and recreational activities, through which they can reach out to even more constituents. Suffice it to say, even if District Councillors cannot make themselves a household name in their constituency, no one has more acquaintances in the neighborhood than they do.

District Councillors' local contacts can assist a LegCo candidate's election campaign in several ways. The most straightforward use is canvassing; for example, the District Councillors call their constituents on election day to promote the LegCo candidate. More importantly, their local knowledge helps the LegCo candidate allocate resources more efficiently. Who are the swing voters? How many are they? These are important electioneering questions that a LegCo candidate cannot answer without District Councillors' inputs.

Another important function of District Councillors' local support networks is to supply volunteers. A good rapport with local residents earns District Councillors not only more votes but also more volunteers to assist in their work. In one interview, a DAB District Councillor contends that "recruiting volunteers is the most vital part of the job [of District Councillors]."[5] This is because constituency services are labor intensive and wages in Hong Kong are high. Getting loyal supporters' voluntary help can significantly bolster a District Councillor's chance of getting reelected.[6] In the case of LegCo elections, running an election campaign is no less labor intensive. The number of volunteers LegCo candidates can mobilize is typically very limited, given their relatively weak linkages with the constituency. They, therefore, need to solicit help from District Councillors, who can bring together a large pool of volunteers for their deployment.

---

[4]For instance, in the 2012 LegCo election, the population size of the geographical constituencies ranged from 437,968 (Kowloon West Constituency) to 987,333 (New Territories West Constituency).

[5]Personal interview with a District Councillor on January 3, 2013 (Code: 10)

[6]The law stipulates that voluntary service can be exempted from regulations concerning election expenses. See Sect. 6.2 of the Election (Corrupt and Illegal Conduct) Ordinance.

"My job is analogous to multi-level marketing," a DAB District Councillor describes his role in the party's LegCo election campaigns.[7]

District Councillors have their own incentive to help LegCo candidates from their own parties. Because LegCo elections take place about a year after District Council elections, the result of a LegCo election is indicative of a District Councillor's ongoing performance. One DAB District Councillor points out, "If I can get 80% of the residents I know to support my endorsed LegCo candidate, I would then know that I stand a good chance in the coming District Council election."[8] District Councillors are probably not the only ones interested in knowing how many votes they can contribute to a LegCo election. Party leaders also want to have that figure in order to gauge junior party members' performance. It is plausible that peer pressure exists among District Councillors in this respect.

(3) They facilitate vote-splitting.

A more technical reason why District Councils are able to influence LegCo elections is that District Councillors facilitate vote-splitting in LegCo elections. The electoral formula of LegCo elections is proportional representation (PR) with the largest remainder method. Because the PR system encourages small parties to participate, parties from both political camps field candidates to compete in each LegCo election. Parties from the same political camp court support from similar voters, so intra-camp competition is very much alive. At times, such competitions lead to suboptimal outcomes for the camp as a whole. For instance, when there are three candidates representing three different parties from the pan-democratic camp, all of them may be able to get elected if the votes they received are even. But if a candidate receives more than two-thirds of the votes of the pan-democratic camp, then only one candidate from this camp can get elected, as the votes "in excess" of the winning pan-democrat cannot be transferred to the other two candidates.

For this reason, the current electoral formula benefits the political camp that is able to coordinate votes among its support parties, minimizing the aggregate vote loss due to intra-camp competition. The success of this vote coordination in part depends on how accurately a political camp knows the amount of votes it obtains in a district. With accurate information, the camp can calculate the number of lists to field in a legislative district in order to avoid excessive intra-camp competition. It can also make use of the information to decide how to split votes among the lists. One way to do this is to assign lists to District Council Constituencies (Ma and Choy 2003, pp. 175–179). For instance, if a legislative district consists of 20 District Council Constituencies, 10 of these DCCs are mobilized to support one list, while the remaining 10 to another. Each District Councillor in these 20 DCCs is responsible for mobilizing supporters to vote for their assigned legislative list.

---

[7]Personal interview with a District Councillor on January 3, 2013 (Code: 10)

[8]Personal interview with a District Councillor on January 3, 2013 (Code: 10)

(4) They groom newcomers.

The long-term survival of a political party depends on its ability to continue to produce new candidates to occupy elected offices. Whether a party's new blood is electorally competitive in turn hinges upon experience and tutelage. The District Councils provide a training ground for parties to groom junior members. How to gain local residents' trust? Which government office to contact when a certain problem arises? How to run an effective election campaign? What would attract media attention? District Councillors are confronted with such questions all the time. By solving these questions, they can develop political savvy and practical knowledge, both of which are requisite skills for a potent LegCo member who needs to face a much larger constituency with more complicated issues.

Competition among junior members allows a party to identify promising candidates for LegCo elections. For young District Councillors, an effective way to stand out from their peers is to attract media attention, which is a challenge to most District Councillors, because their job is notoriously mundane and insignificant beyond their DCCs. If a District Councillor is able to bring a media spotlight to her work, she is demonstrating her ingenuity, if not also the potential for a more important office.

The internal competition in Beijing-sponsored parties is more intense because of their ability to recruit new members. Take the DAB as an example. As of 2013, the party has 1,400 members under the age of 35 (Wen Wei Po 2012e). Although this number is small compared with the party's 23,000 members, it surpasses the total membership of the Democratic Party. Another example that illustrates the keen competition among the DAB juniors is that each year the party would organize an in-house training program for young members including the current District Councillors. Admission to the program is fairly selective; the party recruits only one-third of the applicants after multiple rounds of interviews (Wen Wei Po 2013). In addition, it is reported that since 2013, the DAB has introduced a "point system" to continuously appraise its young members who are interested in LegCo seats (Ming Pao Daily News 2013c). This system is analogous to a primary election except that it spans several years. Presumably, a party needs a primary only when it has more candidates than seats available.

Identifying promising candidates is only the first step. The next step for a party is how to promote these rising stars to compete for LegCo seats. The problem of newcomers is a lack of a citywide recognition. The District Councils again have an important role to play.[9] Under the PR system, candidates can gain a LegCo seat as long as they can obtain a small percentage of votes in a LegCo district. This can be achieved with the help of political brokers; as discussed, each District Councillor is able to mobilize at least a fraction of the residents to vote for a LegCo list by dint

---

[9]Personal interview with District Councillors on January 3, 2013 (Code: 10) and on April 11, 2014 (Code: 29), respectively

of their own effort. For this reason, as long as a party has a sufficient number of District Council seats, it does not really need to count on the mass media to promote its own newcomers.

6.2 The Electoral Effects

6.2.1 A First Glance

In the previous section, I show various causal mechanisms that explain why controlling District Council offices can benefit a party in its bid for LegCo elections. Some mechanisms are concerned with a party's long-term survival (e.g., grooming newcomers), while others deal with short-run electoral effect (e.g., facilitating vote-splitting). In this section, I focus primarily on measuring the short-run effect of the District Councils for two reasons. First, the long-term effect is still unfolding; we lack data to evaluate its full impact. Second, the short-run effect is politically important. If a party cannot survive in the short run, it may not have a chance to improve its long-term well-being. Although Hong Kong's political system is not fully democratic, popular elections are nevertheless held on a regular basis, which creates constant reelection pressure for political parties. The reelection pressure shortens the time horizon that a political party faces. A politician may not be impressed to learn that capturing a District Council seat can improve her chance of winning a LegCo seat in the distant future. But she would be concerned to hear that losing her current District Council seat would reduce her vote share in the following LegCo election by 5 % points.

To measure the short-run effects on LegCo elections through occupying District Council offices, I compare the LegCo vote shares of major parties in District Council Constituencies under their control with those not under their control. If the District Council factor does not matter, we would expect to see no significant difference in vote share between these two types of District Council Constituencies.

As may be seen from Table 6.1, the District Council factor actually has an enormous effect. Except for People Power, all parties received a significantly higher vote share in their controlled District Council Constituencies than in the uncontrolled ones. The effect size (uncontrolled DCCs – controlled DCCs) ranges from −6.74 to −29.35 %. More concretely, consider the Democratic Party. Its LegCo vote share in a DCC would increase by 10 % points if the DCCs were under its control. The difference is unlikely due to chance because the difference of means tests are all statistically significant.

The data in Table 6.1 seriously challenges the popular belief that losing District Council seats has no effect on LegCo elections. It also explains why Beijing-sponsored parties are anxious to drive the pan-democrats out of the District Councils; many pan-democratic parties actually demonstrate a stronger ability to convert their District Council seats into an electoral advantage in LegCo elections

Table 6.1 Average vote share received in Legislative Council elections by political party: controlled and uncontrolled District Council Constituencies (DCCs)

Party	Uncontrolled DCCs		Controlled DCCs		
	Average LegCo vote share	Number of observations	Average LegCo vote share	Number of observations	Difference of means test
Pro-establishment camp					
Civil Force (CF)	3.34	63	14.44	12	−11.1(−8.58)
Democratic Alliance for the Betterment and Progress of Hong Kong (DAB)	20.47	765	28.02	242	−7.55 (−12.38)
Hong Kong Federation of Trade Unions (FTU)	10.32	461	19.84	12	−9.52 (−4.03)
Liberal Party (LP)	7.29	588	14.03	18	−6.74 (−5.36)
New People's Party (NPP)	7.94	152	21.15	4	−13.21 (−7.35)
Pan-democratic camp					
Association for Democracy and People's Livelihood (ADPL)	6.43	311	31.98	45	−25.55 (−18.73)
Civic Party (CP)	13.4	676	28.74	15	−15.34 (−7.75)
Democratic Party (DP)	19.5	819	29.79	188	−10.29 (−13.17)
Frontier	16.57	180	25.17	5	−8.6 (−2.55)
League of Social Democrats (LSD)	7.99	630	17.37	6	−9.38 (−3.98)
Neo Democrats (ND)	4.82	68	20.7	7	−15.88 (−12.32)
Neighborhood and Workers Service Centre (NWSC)	9.19	275	38.54	13	−29.35 (−20.57)
People Power (PP)	9.99	329	6.83	1	3.16

Notes: Data come from Legislative Council elections in 2004, 2008, and 2012. Controlled District Council Constituencies refer to constituencies where the District Council seat was occupied by a given political party at the time when a following Legislative Council election was held. The t-statistics are displayed in parentheses in the last column

than their pro-establishment counterparts (most notably, the ADPL and NWSC). To diminish the pan-democrats' presence in the LegCo, uprooting their District Council seats is the first and foremost step that Beijing-sponsored parties have to take.

6.2.2   A Closer Look

Can Beijing-sponsored parties really undermine the pan-democrats' electoral support by capturing more District Council seats? This question is tricky to answer,
despite the seemingly compelling evidence presented in Table 6.1. The reason is that
the data in Table 6.1 only suggests what would have happened to a party's LegCo
vote share had it not been able to occupy a District Council Constituency. Again,
take the DP as an example. If the DP loses a DCC, its vote share in the following
LegCo election is expected to decrease by about 10% points. But Table 6.1 does not
show where the 10% points would go. If 10% of voters end up voting for the CP
or other pan-democratic parties, the DP's loss is not necessarily the pan-democratic
camp's loss.

The DP example suggests the importance of taking into account voters' preferences when estimating the instrumental effect of occupying District Council
offices. More concretely, legislative candidates sometimes get elected because
voters genuinely support their ideology or party (the effect of voter preference).
They may also get elected because, as I argue in the previous section, their party has
successfully captured the District Councils so that their rival's source of income is
disturbed and vote-coordination strategy is disrupted (the instrumental effect of the
District Council office). Note that the effect of voter preference and the instrumental
effect are not mutually exclusive. In fact, the instrumental effect is arguably intended
to influence voter preference in the long run. But because I am primarily interested
in identifying the short-run instrumental effect of the District Councils, I need to
distinguish voters' genuine support from the District Councils' instrumental effect,
in order not to mistake the effect for the cause.

For this reason, showing that pan-democratic parties receive more votes in
districts where they control the District Council seats is insufficient to support
the claim that winning the District Council seats would improve their electoral
support. This is because we cannot separate the effect of voter preference from the
instrumental effect of the District Council office; for example, in a District Council
Constituency where a candidate from a Beijing-sponsored party is elected, voters
may genuinely favor Beijing-sponsored parties over the pan-democrats. As a result,
when it comes to the LegCo election, the Beijing-sponsored party is likely to receive
more votes. The correlation between a political camp's control of a District Council
Constituency and the camp's LegCo vote share in that constituency reflects only the
underlying preference of the voters, rather than the instrumental effect of winning
a District Council office. Because voter preference at the District Council level is
unobservable independent of voting outcomes, one is confronted with a potential
spurious relationship between occupying a District Council seat and the outcomes
of a subsequent legislative election.

The unique institutional setting of Hong Kong allows us to tackle this estimation
problem with a specific research design known as regression discontinuity. The
regression discontinuity design (RDD) is a quasi-experimental research design
that mimics random assignment of treatment and control groups in a randomized

controlled experiment. The details of the application of the regression discontinuity design are discussed in the appendix to this chapter.

The Hong Kong government's Electoral Affairs Commission publishes data on District Council and Legislative Council elections on its Web site. I use the outcomes of the 2003, 2007, and 2011 District Council elections to predict the outcomes of the 2004, 2008, and 2012 LegCo elections. The arrangement of District Council elections differs from that of LegCo elections in a number of respects. Take the 2007 District Council election as an example. There were 405 District Council members elected by the plurality rule from 405 districts. As for the 2008 LegCo election, there were only five LegCo geographical constituencies electing 30 LegCo members by the method of proportional representation.[10] The five LegCo districts (LCD) are supersets of the 405 DCCs, and there is no DCC which cuts across the boundary of LCDs. Because the Electoral Affairs Commission of the Hong Kong government publishes electoral results of the LegCo at the DCC level,[11] this allows me to measure the effect of a party capturing a District Council seat on that party's vote share in a LegCo election.

Note as well that District Council elections are held in November, while LegCo elections take place in September of the following year. A party that succeeds in capturing a seat in a District Council should have at least several months to bring private benefits to its constituency (or a longer time if the party already has an incumbent District Councillor), which may affect its chances of success in the ensuing legislative election.[12]

The statistical results based on the regression discontinuity design are presented in Table 6.2. The table consists of twelve different regression specifications, which vary by their functional forms and variables of interest. In the first four specifications, I regress the pan-democratic camp's vote share in LegCo election on the treatment variable $D_{\text{Beijing-sponsored}}$, which is assigned the value of "1" if District Council Constituencies are controlled by Beijing-sponsored parties and "0" otherwise. Interestingly, the variable of interest is statistically insignificant in three of the four specifications, suggesting that Beijing-sponsored parties cannot reduce, at least in the short run, the electoral support of the pan-democrats by their occupation of District Council seats.

However, if we look at the next four specifications, in which I regress the pan-democrats' LegCo vote share on another treatment variable $D_{\text{pro-establishment}}$, we see a powerful effect of the District Councils emerge. Take the cubic polynomial specification as an example. By capturing a District Council Constituency, a pro-

---

[10]Although incumbent District Council members are allowed to compete for legislative seats, the difference in the seat numbers between these two levels suggests that only a few District Council members can hold a concurrent seat in the LegCo.

[11]The electoral results are available from the Commission's Web site: http://www.eac.gov.hk/

[12]With only a few months, the party cannot undertake large public projects, which may limit what it can offer to its constituency. That said, District Council members have no formal decision power to carry out such projects.

Table 6.2 Effect of controlling a District Council Constituency on a rival camp's vote share in the Legislative Council election: a regression discontinuity design

Dep. var. Polynomial function	Pan-democratic camp's vote share in LegCo election				Beijing-sponsored parties' vote share in LegCo election			
	Linear	Quadratic	Cubic	Quartic	Linear	Quadratic	Cubic	Quartic
$D_{\text{Beijing-sponsored}}$	-4.634*** (1.075)	1.713 (1.547)	-2.479 (2.045)	-1.194 (2.421)				
$D_{\text{pro-establishment}}$	-4.125*** (0.809)	-1.823* (1.074)	-5.378*** (1.228)	-4.714*** (1.340)				
$D_{\text{pan-democrat}}$					-4.779*** (0.591)	-2.752*** (0.740)	-3.657*** (0.779)	-3.409*** (0.801)
Margin$_-$	0.004 (0.010)	-0.224*** (0.057)	0.117 (0.156)	-0.241 (0.303)	-0.024*** (0.008)	-0.168*** (0.041)	0.101 (0.114)	0.043 (0.225)
Margin$_+$	-0.035*** (0.011)	-0.246*** (0.058)	0.037 (0.163)	0.062 (0.319)	-0.031*** (0.007)	-0.113*** (0.043)	-0.024 (0.110)	-0.199 (0.214)
Margin$^2_-$		-0.002*** (0.000)	0.008* (0.004)	-0.011 (0.014)		-0.001*** (0.000)	0.007** (0.003)	0.002 (0.011)
Margin$^2_+$		0.002*** (0.000)	-0.006 (0.004)	-0.007 (0.015)		0.001** (0.000)	-0.003 (0.003)	0.008 (0.010)
Margin$^3_-$			0.000** (0.000)	-0.000 (0.000)			0.000*** (0.000)	-0.000 (0.000)
Margin$^3_+$			0.000* (0.000)	0.000 (0.000)			0.000 (0.000)	-0.000 (0.000)
Margin^4				-0.000 (0.000)				-0.000 (0.000)

Margin^4_+				−0.000				0.000				0.000
				(0.000)				(0.000)				(0.000)
Constant	38.475***	34.412***	36.693***	35.145***	37.520***	35.328***	37.532***	36.564***	42.391***	41.405***	42.545***	42.739***
	(1.029)	(1.359)	(1.682)	(2.024)	(0.959)	(1.135)	(1.366)	(1.592)	(0.913)	(1.001)	(1.201)	(1.407)
N	753	753	753	753	853	853	853	853	753	753	753	753
R^2	0.57	0.58	0.59	0.59	0.55	0.56	0.57	0.57	0.35	0.37	0.38	0.38
AIC	5,227.3	5,200	5,194	5,196.1	5,921.5	5,911.5	5,883.4	5,885.3	4,915.2	4,896	4,887.4	4,889.4

Notes: $D_{\text{Beijing-sponsored}}$ is the treatment status, with the value "1" denoting the District Council controlled by a Beijing-sponsored party and "0" otherwise. $D_{\text{pan-democrat}}$ and $D_{\text{pro-establishment}}$ are similarly defined, with the former variable representing pan-democratic parties and the latter variable the pro-establishment camp. The variable MARGIN refers to the incumbent District Councillor's margin of victory in a District Council election held at time t. The subscript "$+$" ("$-$") denotes margin above (below) the threshold. All regressions control for year and LegCo constituency fixed effects. Standard errors are in parentheses
* <0.10; ** <0.05; *** <0.01

establishment District Councillor – who can be anyone from a Beijing-sponsored party, a non-Beijing-sponsored pro-establishment party, or just a pro-Beijing "independent" – is able to reduce the pan-democrats' overall vote share by 5.378 % points. This effect is not only statistically significant but also substantively important. As mentioned in Chap. 4, the district magnitude of the LegCo geographical constituencies is fairly large. In some LegCo constituencies, a candidate can win a LegCo seat with as low as 6 % of the vote. The effect size of 5.378 % points is therefore too big to ignore by any party or political camp.

The last four specifications reveal a yet more subtle relationship between capturing a District Council Constituency and competing for a LegCo seat. In this set of regressions, I swap the positions of the pan-democrats and Beijing-sponsored parties by regressing Beijing-sponsored parties' LegCo vote share on $D_{\text{pan-democrat}}$, which takes the value of "1" if District Council Constituencies are controlled by the pan-democratic camp and "0" otherwise. The coefficients on this variable of interest are statistically significant at 1 % across the four specifications. The negative signs suggest that the powerful effect of the District Councils is not confined to the pro-establishment camp; the pan-democratic camp is also able to lower Beijing-sponsored parties' support in LegCo elections by capturing District Council Constituencies. The effect size is somewhat smaller, however. For instance, as indicated by the cubic polynomial specification, Beijing-sponsored parties' LegCo vote share would shrink by 3.657 % points in District Council Constituencies that the pan-democrats control, falling short of what the pro-establishment camp can do to the pan-democrats in reverse.

These twelve specifications in Table 6.2 together paint an interesting picture of the electoral dynamics between the two elected tiers. In particular, the Beijing-sponsored parties' occupation of a District Council Constituency poses no *direct* threat to pan-democratic parties' voter support in LegCo elections in that DCC. But the *indirect* effect is very much potent. For Beijing-sponsored parties, if they do not crowd out the pan-democrats in the District Councils, their pan-democratic rivals will then be able to make use of the District Council offices to undermine the LegCo support of Beijing-sponsored parties. Another important implication we read from Table 6.2 is that non-Beijing-sponsored, pro-establishment parties matter. From Beijing's perspective, it should not rely solely on Beijing-sponsored parties to weaken the pan-democrats, because it is the pro-establishment camp as a whole, rather than Beijing-sponsored parties alone, which can deliver Beijing's desired outcome. And why would the pro-establishment camp achieve a better short-term result than Beijing-sponsored parties alone? My conjecture is that the ideological position of Beijing-sponsored parties is too salient, which prevents their District Councillors from neutralizing moderate voters in LegCo elections. By contrast, non-Beijing-sponsored pro-establishment parties or those candidates who are pro-Beijing and "independent" are less ideologically discernible, so that the District Councillors with this background are able to disguise their political leaning and, thus, take away moderate votes from the pan-democrats.

The regression discontinuity design is known as a quasi-experimental design because cases in the neighborhood of the discontinuity are very similar to each other, and the only systematic difference between them is that some happen to receive the "treatment" by chance, while others do not. In other words, the treatment assignment is "as good as randomized." In randomized experiments where the treatment and control groups are balanced, there is no need to control for other effects. But to ensure that the empirical results are not biased due to the omission of other variables, I rerun the first eight specifications in Table 6.2 by adding control variables pertaining to District Council Constituencies, including, but not limited to, population, voter turnout in the last District Council election, the pan-democrats' vote share in the last LegCo election, and the population share of males, college graduates, and the elderly. Table 6.3 shows that the statistical results of Table 6.2 carry over to these regression specifications, despite the inclusion of a variety of control variables. In particular, the pro-establishment camp as a whole fares better than Beijing-sponsored parties alone in the use of District Council offices to undermine the pan-democratic camp.

To Beijing-sponsored parties, one important function of weaving a big network of District Councillors is to facilitate vote coordination in LegCo elections. Effective vote coordination would reduce the amount of "waste votes" generated under the proportional representation rule. With their dominant position in the District Councils, do Beijing-sponsored parties perform better than the pan-democrats in vote coordination? We can find out the answer by examining how efficiently each political camp translates its votes into seats. One way to measure this is to divide its seat share by its vote share in a given election. If the number is smaller than one, this implies that achieving a given level of seat share requires a higher level of vote share. In other words, some votes would be "wasted."

Figure 6.1 shows the respective seat share to vote share ratio by political camp. The pan-democratic camp achieved its most efficient allocation in 1998. Since then, its seat-to-vote ratio has never surpassed 1.09. Its ratio even drops below 1 in 2004 and 2012. In contrast, the performance of the pro-establishment camp has improved over time. Its seat-to-vote ratio has never dropped below its 1998 level. As already discussed, within the pro-establishment camp, Beijing-sponsored parties are the most successful in terms of grassroots penetration. Not surprisingly, their efficiency in vote allocation is also the most impressive. As may be seen from Fig. 6.1, their seat-to-vote ratio has been consistently greater than 1 since 1998. Even in 1998, the figure was very close to 1. Remarkably, in 2012, its ratio reached 1.26. The result reflects its success in coordinating votes among the District Council Constituencies it controls.

6.3 Conclusion

In Chinese, the term for political brokers is *zhuangjiao*. Literally, it means piles. The term is a vivid characterization of the undertaking of voter mobilization; it is analogous to the construction of a house, which entails driving piles into the ground to support the vertical structure. Beijing-sponsored parties have attempted to

Table 6.3 Effect of controlling a District Council on the rival camp's vote shares of Legislative Council election: adding controls

Dep. var.	Pan-democratic camp's vote share in LegCo election							
Definition of pro-establishment	Beijing-sponsored parties only				Pro-establishment parties and individuals			
Polynomial function	Linear	Quadratic	Cubic	Quartic	Linear	Quadratic	Cubic	Quartic
D	−2.319**	1.475	0.134	2.445	−4.246***	−4.152***	−5.050***	−5.030***
	(1.078)	(1.582)	(2.029)	(2.341)	(0.720)	(0.920)	(0.960)	(1.008)
Pan-Democrat Vote Share$_{t-1}$	0.262***	0.238***	0.237***	0.240***	0.232***	0.229***	0.216***	0.217***
	(0.038)	(0.038)	(0.038)	(0.038)	(0.037)	(0.037)	(0.037)	(0.037)
DC Turnout	−0.052	−0.059	−0.060	−0.063	−0.044	−0.049	−0.053	−0.051
	(0.054)	(0.054)	(0.054)	(0.054)	(0.052)	(0.052)	(0.052)	(0.052)
DC Total Voters ('0000)	2.026	2.295	2.234	1.966	2.409	2.25	2.221	2.065
	(2.315)	(2.303)	(2.306)	(2.308)	(2.234)	(2.248)	(2.228)	(2.241)
Pan-Democrat Margin$_{t-1}$	0.001	−0.004	−0.004	−0.004	−0.003	−0.004	−0.003	−0.002
	(0.012)	(0.012)	(0.012)	(0.012)	(0.012)	(0.012)	(0.012)	(0.012)
Post-secondary	0.305***	0.298***	0.298***	0.282**	0.309***	0.317***	0.320***	0.312***
	(0.111)	(0.110)	(0.110)	(0.111)	(0.107)	(0.108)	(0.107)	(0.107)
Income < 10K	0.030	0.024	0.019	0.022	0.054	0.060	0.049	0.049
	(0.084)	(0.084)	(0.084)	(0.084)	(0.081)	(0.082)	(0.081)	(0.081)
Income 20K to 40K	−0.064	−0.065	−0.070	−0.065	−0.052	−0.050	−0.062	−0.058
	(0.087)	(0.086)	(0.086)	(0.086)	(0.083)	(0.084)	(0.083)	(0.083)
Population ('0000)	1.627	1.34	1.272	1.315	1.628	1.673	1.444	1.492
	(1.084)	(1.08)	(1.085)	(1.083)	(1.046)	(1.055)	(1.049)	(1.053)
15 < age < 24	0.145	0.136	0.138	0.126	0.175*	0.173*	0.165	0.165
	(0.106)	(0.105)	(0.105)	(0.105)	(0.102)	(0.103)	(0.102)	(0.102)
Age > 65	0.275***	0.282***	0.290***	0.282***	0.246**	0.243**	0.262***	0.262***
	(0.104)	(0.103)	(0.104)	(0.104)	(0.101)	(0.101)	(0.101)	(0.101)

Male	0.932***	0.833***	0.851***	0.876***	0.809***	0.800***	0.781***	0.793***
	(0.245)	(0.244)	(0.245)	(0.245)	(0.237)	(0.238)	(0.236)	(0.238)
Born in Hong Kong	0.179***	0.169***	0.170***	0.171***	0.169***	0.171***	0.175***	0.176***
	(0.057)	(0.057)	(0.057)	(0.057)	(0.055)	(0.056)	(0.055)	(0.055)
Employees	0.236*	0.252**	0.247*	0.244*	0.200	0.216*	0.216*	0.211*
	(0.126)	(0.126)	(0.127)	(0.126)	(0.122)	(0.123)	(0.122)	(0.122)
Elementary workers	−0.053	−0.060	−0.059	−0.044	−0.076	−0.072	−0.071	−0.064
	(0.105)	(0.104)	(0.104)	(0.104)	(0.101)	(0.101)	(0.100)	(0.101)
Professionals	0.129	0.143	0.138	0.175	0.162	0.153	0.141	0.159
	(0.227)	(0.225)	(0.226)	(0.227)	(0.219)	(0.220)	(0.218)	(0.220)
Constant	−52.016***	−47.717***	−45.022***	−46.576***	−40.980**	−41.510**	−37.599**	−37.374**
	(17.457)	(17.370)	(17.257)	(17.237)	(16.929)	(17.008)	(16.726)	(16.784)
N	422	422	422	422	422	422	422	422
R^2	0.58	0.59	0.59	0.59	0.61	0.61	0.62	0.62
AIC	2,727.5	2,720.3	2,723	2,722.4	2,697.1	2,700.1	2,694.4	2,697.6

Notes: D is the treatment status, with the value "1" denoting the District Council controlled by the pro-establishment camp and "0" otherwise. "Pro-establishment" is defined either as "Beijing-sponsored parties only," or as "pro-establishment parties and individuals," depending on the specification. Unless specified otherwise, the units of all socioeconomic variables are a share of the population. "DC Turnout" is the voter turnout of District Council elections. All regressions control for year and LegCo constituency fixed effects, and the incumbent District Councillor's margin of victory in a District Council election held at time t. Standard errors are in parentheses

* <0.10; ** <0.05; *** <0.01

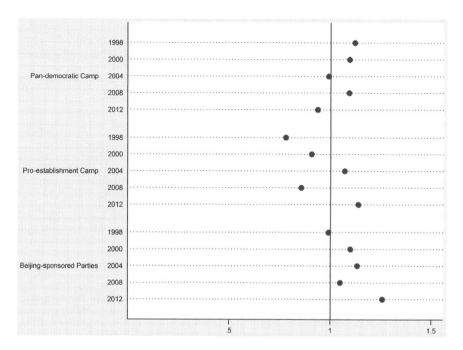

Fig. 6.1 Seat-to-vote ratio by political camp and by LegCo election (Source: Author's calculation based on election data from the HKSAR Electoral Affairs Commission)

erect a large political structure in postcolonial Hong Kong's legislature, in hopes of marginalizing the popular opposition force. To lay the groundwork for their edifice, they need to plant a lot of "piles" into the ground. This is the origin of their District Council strategy; they aggressively expand into this lowest elected tier, with a view to have their District Councillors act as political brokers in order to strengthen the parties' position in LegCo elections and, thus, undermine their pan-democratic rivals' electoral support from the ground up.

The empirical results presented in this chapter show that the District Council strategy of Beijing-sponsored parties has paid off handsomely. By occupying more District Council seats, the pro-establishment camp can erode the pan-democrats' grassroots support, which in turn undermines the latter's performance in LegCo elections. Beijing-sponsored parties also benefit from their dominant position in the District Councils by preventing the pan-democrats, especially the moderate prodemocracy parties who have an elaborate grassroots support base, from playing out exactly the same bottom-up strategy. In addition, controlling the District Councils allows Beijing-sponsored parties to improve their vote-coordination strategies during LegCo elections. An efficient allocation of votes would benefit the entire political camp as a whole.

It is worth noting that the empirical analysis of this chapter covers only the short-term effect of controlling the District Councils. Its long-term effect is no less important. For one thing, failing to control at least some District Council seats is likely to hinder a party's long-term development because the party will be deprived of an effective mechanism to groom and cherry-pick new candidates for higher elected offices. Given the Beijing-sponsored parties' inexorable rise in the District Councils, the harmful long-term effect on opposition parties will gradually emerge in the coming elections.

An important policy implication for pan-democratic parties is that they should devise an appropriate District Council strategy in response to Beijing-sponsored parties' encroachment. Failing to do so would hurt not only the opposition camp as a whole but also individual opposition parties. As clearly shown in Table 6.1, controlling a District Council Constituency can increase an opposition party's LegCo vote share by as many as 30% points. The cost of abandoning the District Councils is simply too high for any opposition party serious about getting a LegCo seat.

Appendix: Details on the Regression Discontinuity Design

In a laboratory experiment, a researcher randomly assigns subjects to the treatment and control groups. Because randomization tends to produce relatively balanced control and treatment groups, the researcher can significantly minimize the risk of omitted variable bias. As such, the identified effect is more likely due to the treatment effect rather than the effects of other confounding factors. In the current context, an ideal research design would be to randomly assign District Council seats to political parties. For instance, some pro-establishment parties would land on districts that are ideologically predisposed to the pro-establishment camp, and some would land on districts in favor of the pan-democrats. In other words, we can avoid the situation where only districts that are ideologically inclined to Beijing-sponsored parties would self-select to be led by pro-establishment parties. We can then examine the effect of occupying a District Council seat on LegCo elections by comparing the vote shares obtained by Beijing-sponsored parties and those obtained by the pan-democrats.

In reality, I cannot affect the data-generating process of the District Council elections, but if I can apply regression discontinuity, a quasi-experimental research design, I would be able to find out the causal effect. The idea of regression discontinuity is simple.[13] If occupying a District Council Constituency has some effect on the outcome of the legislative elections, the relationship between the pan-democrats' LegCo vote shares and the Beijing-sponsored parties' District Council vote shares, for example, should be best characterized by a function discontinuous

---

[13]There is a growing number of applied election studies using the regression discontinuity design. Notable examples include Fujiwara (2011), Gerber et al. (2011), Eggers and Hainmueller (2010), and Hainmueller and Kern (2008).

at a certain threshold (such as 50 % in a two-party vote of the District Council elections). The discontinuous jump is the causal effect of capturing a District Council seat on the outcome of the LegCo elections. The reason is that no matter how close a pro-establishment's District Council vote share gets to the threshold, the party would not get elected and hence cannot occupy the District Council office until its vote share just surpasses the threshold. The validity of regression discontinuity hinges upon the assumption that districts are very similar to each other in the neighborhood of the discontinuity. The only difference that sets them apart is whether or not they happen to receive the "treatment" by chance; that is, whether the Beijing-sponsored party obtains, due to random uncontrollable factors, barely sufficient votes to carry the districts. In other words, we have balanced treatment and control groups in the neighborhood of the discontinuity as if in a randomized experiment, so that the causal effect that is identified is more likely due to the effect of the treatment rather than the effect of other factors such as the district's ideological predisposition. This argument is formalized in the study by Lee (2008).

To estimate the electoral effect of the District Council office, I examine the relationship between the pan-democratic camp's LegCo vote share in each District Council Constituency (the dependent variable) and a Beijing-sponsored party's (or a pro-establishment District Councillor's) margin of victory in the same District Council Constituency (the independent variable or the forcing variable).

More formally, we can express the regression discontinuity design in the following way:

$$D_i = \begin{cases} 1 & \text{if } x_i > 0 \\ 0 & \text{if } x_i \leq 0 \end{cases}$$

where D_i is the treatment status of District Council Constituency i, with the value "1" denoting the constituency controlled by a Beijing-sponsored party (or a pro-establishment District Councillor) and "0" otherwise, while x_i is the pan-democratic camp's margin of victory in the District Council Constituency i.

This leads to the main regression specification:

$$y_i = f(x_i) + \delta D_i + \mu_i \tag{6.1}$$

where y_i is the pan-democratic camp's LegCo vote share in constituency i, $f(x_i)$ is a polynomial function, δ is the causal effect of interest, and μ_i is an error term assumed to be independent and identically distributed. The polynomial function is intended to provide a flexible functional form to model the relationship between y_i and x_i, which is not necessarily linear, in order to avoid mistaking nonlinearity for discontinuity.[14]

---

[14] Angrist and Pischke (2009) provide a detailed discussion on this point.

Chapter 7
Elephants Versus Termites: Lessons from Hong Kong

In the early stage of the "Anti-Patriotic Education Movement," a high-ranking government official answered a reporter's query about a condition under which the government would shelve the controversial national education curriculum. "When the elephant reveals itself to the government," said he half-jokingly. The government official used "elephant" as a metaphor for public discontent, suggesting that the government would drop the curriculum when a sufficient number of people voice their opposition to it. Since then, the organizers of the movement have made the elephant as the movement's mascot, in hopes of bringing out more protesters to humble the government. Eva Chan, one of the movement's organizers, draws an analogy between the parent activists and elephants: peaceful and moderate, but when they unleash their power, no one is able to stop them.[1]

The elephant metaphor is relevant not only to the "Anti-Patriotic Education Movement" but also to the prodemocracy movement of postcolonial Hong Kong, which is characterized by a panoply of demonstrations and protest activities. Occasionally, the protests are able to unleash great political power to force the government to back down on a certain policy. This Hong Kong-style prodemocracy movement is made possible by the high degree of civil liberties provided by the Basic Law, the mini-constitution of Hong Kong. Liberal-minded social activists and prodemocracy parties can freely air their discontent with the HKSAR government and Beijing. They can also take advantage of the freedom of assembly to organize mass protests against government authorities. One of the most remarkable examples is the July 1, 2003 protest, in which half a million people took to the streets to call for the resignation of the then Chief Executive, Tung Chee-hwa, and the suspension of the controversial legislation of national security laws. The protest was successful, for it did halt the legislation. Later Tung also stepped down before finishing his second term.

---

[1] See Eva Chan's speech delivered in a mass protest on September 1, 2012. Retrieved May 22, 2014, from http://www.youtube.com/watch?v=gbkbvyK9thk

© Springer Science+Business Media Singapore 2015
S.H.-W. Wong, *Electoral Politics in Post-1997 Hong Kong*,
DOI 10.1007/978-981-287-387-3_7

The success of the July 1, 2003 protest has left a far-reaching impact on Hong Kong's prodemocracy movement, for it showed that public protests are able to bring about immediate political changes, as long as the turnout is large enough. Many come to see protests as a viable means in the struggle for democracy. Consequently, since 2003, Hong Kong has witnessed a proliferation of mass demonstrations as liberal social activists and politicians alike attempt to use street protests to draw support and to advance their causes. Behind their effort is a hope that, at some point, they can call out enlightened masses to demonstrate the people's power once again and shock the government in the same way as the July 1, 2003 protest did, so that they can effect immediate policy change or even tear down the authoritarian edifice in one fell swoop.

Against this background, civil society in Hong Kong has grown vibrantly. In addition to the ritualistic annual July 1 protest, various large-scale social movements have appeared since 2003. Liberal social activists have also become increasingly receptive to the use of a confrontation approach in pressing for changes. In politics, radical opposition parties have emerged and become significant political players. Riding the wave of contentious politics, the elected members of these parties have constantly updated their "repertoires of contention," including filibuster and object throwing, that aim to disrupt legislative sessions. Some opposition parties also made use of mass mobilization to drum up political support, as evidenced by the occurrence of the 2010 quasi-referendum movement.

All these protest activities and political brawls have created noise, as they have dominated media coverage. While media exposure of this kind may have served the individual groups involved well, it has serious repercussions for the entire prodemocracy movement for two reasons. First, dependence on this noisemaking strategy has intensified the internal strife between opposition parties. This is not only because the media are more interested in exploiting the internal conflicts among the prodemocracy elite but also because radical parties find it more effective to shore up political support by assailing their allies' ideological stance, rather than the establishment's. The internal strife has prevented the pan-democrats from coalescing into a unifying force to fight for democratization against Beijing and hence has undermined their collective bargaining power.

The second reason why the prodemocracy movement fails to benefit from the noisemaking tactics is that these political confrontations have alienated moderate voters, who also represent a large segment, if not the majority, of the supporters for the movement. On the one hand, the moderate voters cannot identify themselves with the antagonistic approach of the radical wing of the prodemocracy movement. On the other hand, they have been bombarded with inflammatory ideological criticisms of the moderate opposition parties, who have been often depicted as a conspirator for Beijing or as its running dog. Even if moderate voters still have trust in these parties' political integrity, they may lose faith in these parties' ability to lead, or even represent, the movement. Feeling demoralized and frustrated, some moderate voters lose passion for the cause, while others may be attracted instead to moderate pro-establishment parties. Ironically, this kind of parochial political disputes over ideological purity is all too familiar to Hong Kong's "leftists." They have a name for it: left-leaning adventurism, which is considered by the CCP as a serious strategic mistake because the outcome of such disputes is inevitable alienation of supporters of the cause. It was the very mistake for which the "leftist" elite in Hong Kong paid a dear price in the 1967 Leftist Riots.

If the prodemocracy movement in postcolonial Hong Kong can be symbolically represented by an elephant, the living organism that would best characterize Beijing-sponsored parties is termites. The image of termites is the polar opposite of that of elephants just as the strategic differences are between the two political camps. While loud, bulky, and conspicuous street protests have epitomized the struggle of the pan-democrats, the strategies of Beijing-sponsored parties have been much more quiet, subtle, and barely visible.[2] They have focused on enlarging their social support base by building a united front at the grassroots level. They have invested a great deal of resources in training an army of political brokers, whose main duty is to deliver labor-intensive constituency services. Mundane as they are, these constituency services have helped Beijing-sponsored parties penetrate into local communities and forge a close relationship with the residents. This kind of community engagement is also less controversial and hence less likely to be challenged by the opposition on ideological grounds.

The July 1, 2003 protest did not derail Beijing-sponsored parties' long-term strategic plan. On the contrary, the historic protest has only entrenched it. In one interview, a DAB party official makes a sobering analogy, "We have been building a dam. After 2003, we redoubled our efforts to consolidate it. Now our dam is at least twice as high as before."[3] Their efforts have paid off handsomely, as Beijing-sponsored parties, or the pro-establishment camp in general, have nibbled away at the pan-democrats' local support networks, culminating into its current domination of the District Councils, the lowest elected tier of Hong Kong. Beijing-sponsored parties' ambition, of course, goes beyond the District Councils. The ultimate goal for them is to marginalize the pan-democrats in the legislature, if not also in society. Or, at the very least, the dam that they have built should be able to protect them from another political tsunami akin to the July 1, 2003 protest.

A test came in 2012. The "Anti-Patriotic Education Movement" was the largest social mobilization since the July 1, 2003 protest. The organizers did bring out the "elephant," that is, public opposition, to humble the government. The movement grew in the summer of 2012 and reached its zenith in early September, when the activists decided to camp out in the government headquarters, a move that attracted massive public support in the form of continual solidarity rallies. The timing coincided with the LegCo Election, which was scheduled to take place on

---

[2]Interestingly, the CCP had used the "termite" analogy in relation to its Hong Kong policy. For example, in 1955, Liao Chengzhi, the person-in-charge of Hong Kong Affairs in Beijing, gave advice to his fellow cadres who were stationed in Hong Kong: "[You] should make friends with all walks of life. Never say anything like 'you are a reactionary, centrist, and I am a leftist, communist.' Instead, you should never let your enemy know who you are and where you come from. We should do our work in the same way as termites" (Wang 2006, p. 537).

[3]Personal interview with a District Councillor on January 4, 2014 (Code: 12).

September 9. Bowing to public pressure, and possibly to electoral pressure as well, the government announced on the eve of the 2012 LegCo Election an indefinite suspension of the controversial curriculum. The government's acquiescence signaled the triumph of the movement. Prodemocracy supporters hoped that the momentum of the movement would carry over to the election to wipe out the pro-establishment camp. To their surprise, what happened on the next day was one of the opposition camp's worst electoral defeats.

"Our dam stood the test," so the DAB official says assuredly. Worried that I could not grapple with the precarious situation they were in, he added, "Do not forget that there were two additional tidal waves in 2012: the Li Wangyang Incident and the political rise of Leung Chun-ying. Our dam survived all these tsunamis." Indeed, the two incidents he mentioned had sparked off mass demonstrations in that year. For the first one, Li Wangyang was a Chinese human rights defender, who had served more than 20 years in prison for his participation in the 1989 student-led prodemocracy movement. Li was found dead in a hospital, shortly after he had an interview with a Hong Kong television station, during which he called for a vindication of the prodemocracy movement. The Chinese local authorities claimed that Li committed suicide, while many in Hong Kong believed it was a political homicide. Tens of thousands of people joined a public rally to call for an open and transparent investigation of his death. As for Leung Chun-ying, he was elected as Hong Kong's Chief Executive in 2012. Members of liberal civil society groups have a deep distrust of Leung because he is widely suspected to be an underground CCP member. On the day of his inauguration, hundreds of thousands of people took to the streets to protest against his rule.

The Beijing-sponsored parties' grassroots strategy reflects their pragmatic approach to dealing with the pan-democrats. Their goal is crystal clear: to marginalize the prodemocracy opposition force. In order to achieve this goal, they are willing to put ideology aside. Their pragmatism has an ancestral root in the CCP's conception of realpolitik. In particular, the idea of the united front, which is considered by the CCP as one of the three keys to its political success (Mao 1952b, p. 7), underpins much of the Beijing-sponsored parties' strategic thinking. The essence of the united front tactic is to enlarge one's support base by co-opting even those with dissimilar ideologies in order to isolate and conquer one's enemy. Even if one cannot obtain the support of a co-optation target, one should seek to neutralize it, so that it would not become the enemy's ally.[4]

In the context of Hong Kong's situation, the "enemy" of Beijing-sponsored parties is the prodemocracy opposition elite, while the co-optation target is the swing voters, who are ideologically committed to neither the pan-democrats nor the Beijing-sponsored camp. Deng Xiaoping had long set the tone for the formation of the ruling coalition to govern Hong Kong: a few leftists, a few rightists, and better

---

[4]The united front tactic is succinctly summarized by Mao (1976) in a famous party motto: Unite the majority, attack the minority, exploit the enemies' contradictions, and conquer them one by one (tuanjie duoshu, daji shaoshu, liyong maodun, gege jipo).

with more centrists (Deng 2003, p. 74). His comment, which suggested that co-opting the centrists is key to consolidating Beijing's control of Hong Kong, offers an important working guideline for Beijing-sponsored parties after 1997.

How is Deng's guideline carried out in practice? Li Xiaohui (2010) provides by far the most detailed open discussion of the actual implementation of this guideline in Hong Kong. Li, who is the deputy editor-in-chief of *Wen Wei Po*, a Beijing-sponsored Hong Kong newspaper, argues that while only 30 % of the Hong Kong population fulfill the narrow criterion of "being patriotic to China and Hong Kong" (*aiguo aigang*),[5] centrist voters in Hong Kong, who constitute the majority of the populace, should not be excluded from the patriotic camp. These centrist voters, he explains, "have only moderate political demands, no obvious political leaning, and only care about the economy and livelihood" (Li 2010, p. 94). For this reason, Li argues that the pro-establishment camp should adopt a pragmatic and strategic approach to dealing with the centrist voters, namely, to actively seek their political support (Li 2010, pp. 97–98). He further points out that the centrist voters are the key to break the "60-40 rule," which is the general perception of the vote share ratio of opposition parties to pro-establishment parties in LegCo elections. If the middle 10 % desert the opposition, "the 60-40 rule will vanish once and for all" (Li 2010, p. 102).

The aforementioned strategic calculus has structured the grassroots strategy of Beijing-sponsored parties. In particular, their aggressive expansion at the District Council level aims to extend their support base to include those who "only care about the economy and livelihood." As discussed in the previous chapter, their major *tour de force* is to reach out their target constituents with diligent constituency services.

Two caveats are in order. First, although Li's account of the role of centrist voters seems highly instrumental, political shenanigans alone may not be able to completely explain the motives of pro-Beijing District Councillors when it comes to the actual delivery of constituency services. My interviews with many Beijing-sponsored District Councillors suggest that some of them do have a genuine concern for the well-being of their community, and over the years they have developed a deep bonding with the constituents they serve. One should not dismiss their effort as pure skullduggery. For some elderly people who live alone, for example, they have been visited more frequently by their District Councillors than by their own children. In this respect, the District Councillors' service is creating important social value, although their political parties may be driven primarily by ulterior political motives.

---

[5]Deng Xiaoping suggests that Hong Kong must be ruled by those who are "patriotic to China and Hong Kong." The definition of what it means to be patriotic has been a bone of contention in Hong Kong. Members of the prodemocracy opposition elite emphasize that they, too, fulfill this criterion, because they are patriotic to the country, though not to the CCP. To Beijing, however, "patriotic to China and Hong Kong" implies supporting the single-party regime in Beijing.

The second caveat is that although Beijing has enormous influences on Beijing-sponsored parties, obeying the instruction of Beijing alone may not be able to explain the success of Beijing-sponsored parties' grassroots strategy. Without these local parties' dutiful cooperation and the availability of ample resources, the grassroots strategy would never have achieved its intended effect. There are two reasons for their dutiful cooperation. The first is that many senior leaders of these parties had first-hand experience with the 1967 Leftist Riots. Fully aware of the devastating power of "left-leaning adventurism," they have become skeptical about political radicalism and hence receptive to a pragmatic grassroots approach. But the most important reason is that such a strategy makes eminently good sense with respect to party development. As predicted by my model presented in Chap. 2, in the presence of a liberal media environment, an authoritarian regime can still undermine opposition parties by building an effective spoil system. In the case of Hong Kong, Beijing has been constrained by the economic status of Hong Kong, which makes it costly to impose heavy media controls. Under such circumstances, a rational move is to develop an elaborate spoil system to strengthen Beijing's political support, while helping these parties veer away from confronting the opposition's attack on ideological grounds.

How can Hong Kong's protracted democratization experience as analyzed in the previous chapters contribute to our understanding of democratization? Extant studies argue that media freedom is conducive to democratic transitions for various reasons such as keeping citizens informed (Dahl 1971), making collective actions feasible (Roscigno and Danaher 2001), and exposing corrupt officials (Brunetti and Weder 2003). Given its exceptionally high degree of media freedom, which is an exogenous factor inherited from the late British colonial period, postcolonial Hong Kong provides a valuable case to test these previous theories. It turns out, however, that the effect of free media has fallen short of the theoretical expectations. No doubt the freedom of expression, of the press, and of publication as prescribed by the Basic Law has allowed Hong Kong citizens to effectively monitor the government. The freedom of assembly also enables the citizens to stage large-scale public demonstrations without fear of persecution. Simply put, the high degree of civil liberties has nurtured a vibrant civil society in postcolonial Hong Kong. But all these favorable factors do not seem to benefit the central pillar of the entire prodemocracy movement – the opposition parties. Not only do they fail to resolve internal conflicts and present a unified coalition to bargain with Beijing, they also have great difficulty sustaining their camp's electoral performance, as the pro-establishment camp has continued to gnaw away at the opposition's vote share and seat share in LegCo elections. So how come these opposition parties have failed to grow stronger in the presence of a liberal media environment?

The experience of pan-democratic parties in postcolonial Hong Kong suggests that media freedom is unlikely a sufficient condition for democratization. Whether media freedom is a necessary condition is still too early to judge, given that democratic transition is still under way. What is clear from the Hong Kong case is that media freedom may actually bring negative impacts on opposition parties, if not also on the prodemocracy movement. The reason is fourfold:

1. Reduce Opposition Parties' Incentive to Develop Grassroots Organization
   When the media are free, they can serve as an effective mobilizing agent. The variety of social movements that have occurred in postcolonial Hong Kong attests this point. Newspapers, radio broadcasts, and social media have played an important role in promoting political participation. Traditionally, political parties reach out to supporters through grassroots party organizations. When political parties discover the media as an effective tool to rally support, their incentive to invest in such organizations would be weakened because the construction and maintenance of grassroots organizations are costly. However, the media are not able to completely replace the function of party organizations. For one thing, the media cannot build a close bond between political parties and potential supporters. Parties with weak grassroots organizations may not be able to sustain supporters' loyalty for long.

2. Marginalize Moderate Opposition Parties
   Even if the media are free from political censorship, they may not be free from market competition. Under keen competition, the media are pressured to report stories that are eye catching. Radical parties and activists have a comparative advantage in capturing media attention because they are prone to adopt an unconventional, if not controversial, approach to fight for their causes. As the experience of postcolonial Hong Kong shows, radical parties have gradually crowded out moderate parties with respect to media exposure, and the coverage of political news has been overwhelmed by confrontational street protests and inflammatory political bickering, especially those within the pan-democratic camp. In short, the media have helped the radical wing promote its interests, leaving the moderate opposition elite sidelined.

3. Demoralize the Prodemocracy Movement by Exposing Internal Strife within the Opposition Elite
   The media are inherently interested in exposing conflicts, because conflicts are dramatic and sensational. Conflicts between the prodemocracy elite are no exception. While exposing the internal strife among prodemocracy elite may make best-selling news stories, it does little to help the prodemocracy movement. On the contrary, when voters are bombarded with political mudslinging between the so-called democracy fighters, their support for the movement as a whole is likely to wane. After all, why would people want to replace the ruling elite with those who do not seem to be any more upright? Moderate prodemocracy voters are particularly susceptible to this kind of political cynicism because they are relatively less committed to the cause. However, it is precisely the moderate vote, which constitutes a large segment of the electorate that is necessary for the ouster of the authoritarian regime in the voting booth.

   The corrosive effect of the exposure to elite dissension is evident in the pan-democratic voters' waning trust in political parties and in the legislature. As may

be seen from Fig. 7.1, which is based on public opinion survey data provided
by the Asian Barometer Survey, the percentage of pan-democratic voters who
trust political parties fluctuate around 40 %. The figure reaches 36 %, its lowest
point, in Wave 3, which was conducted in 2012. In contrast, the percentage of
pro-establishment voters who trust political parties has consistently increased
over time. Note also that pan-democratic voters used to be more likely to trust
both political parties and the legislature than the pro-establishment voters. But in
the latest survey, pro-establishment voters have overtaken their pan-democratic
counterpart on both scores. In particular, the percentage of pan-democratic voters
who trust the legislature has experienced a significant drop.

The problem of political distrust is sobering when we put Hong Kong in
comparative perspective with other countries. Figure 7.2 displays similar trust
data of selected countries from the Asian Barometer Survey, and what is striking
is that public trust in political parties and in legislature is significantly lower in

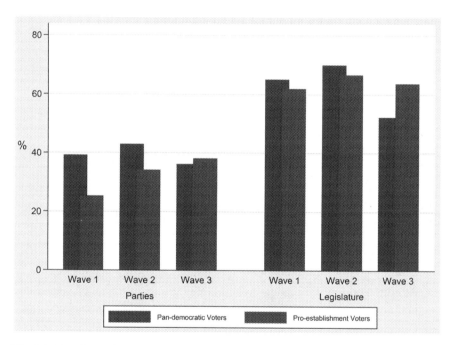

Fig. 7.1 Voters' trust in political parties and legislature by political camp. Notes: The Asian
Barometer Survey provides data on public opinions about political values and governance. Three
waves of survey have been conducted in about thirteen countries (including Hong Kong) since
2001. The "trust" data are constructed from a survey question that asks respondents to rate their
trust in political parties (legislature): (1) none at all, (2) not very much trust, (3) quite a lot of trust,
and (4) a great deal of trust. The *bars* in the figure indicate the percentage of people answering
(3) and (4). The data on respondents' political affiliation are based on another survey question that
asks respondents to identify a political party that they feel closest to (Source: Asian Barometer
Survey, various waves)

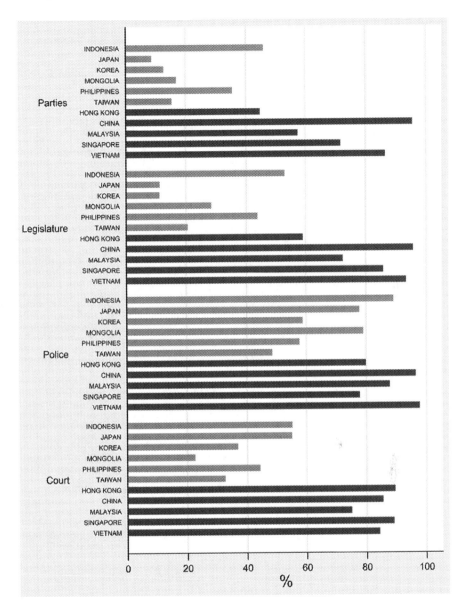

Fig. 7.2 Voters' trust in various political institutions by regime. Notes: The Asian Barometer Survey Wave 3 provides data on public opinions about political values and governance. The "trust" data are constructed from a survey question that asks respondents to rate their trust in the related institution: (1) none at all, (2) not very much trust, (3) quite a lot of trust, and (4) a great deal of trust. The *bars* in the figure indicate the percentage of people answering (3) and (4). Democracies are indicated by *orange bars*. The data on Hong Kong are pooled across political camps (Source: Asian Barometer Survey Wave 3)

established democracies than in authoritarian regimes. We cannot rule out the possibility that the survey respondents of authoritarian regimes are lying due to political pressure. However, the key question here is not so much about why authoritarian regimes have high political trust, but why political trust is so low in established democracies, where respondents would not be punished by telling the truth. A plausible explanation, as proposed by Norris (1999), is that political institutions in established democracies fail to live up to democratic ideals, which renders citizens increasingly critical of their representative government. If this is the case, then Hong Kong as a non-democracy presents an interesting anomaly. As shown in the figure, although political distrust in Hong Kong is not as serious as in countries such as Japan and Korea, its trust level with respect to political parties and the legislature is lower than that of all the authoritarian regimes. Also, Hong Kong people find the police and the court more trustworthy than parties and the legislature. In short, Hong Kong people may have caught a mild "critical citizen" syndrome, even before they have attained democracy. For the sake of democratization, the premature exposure to the "critical citizen" syndrome may not be a welcoming sign. This is because in established democracies, whether voters approve of the performance of political parties is unlikely to change the fundamental political system. In non-democracies, however, opposition parties play an important role in negotiating democratization with the authoritarian incumbent. If these parties fail to obtain the people's basic trust, their bargaining position would become weaker, making democratic transition much harder to achieve.

4. Increase Tensions between Civil Society and Opposition Parties

If political parties are able to take advantage of media freedom to mobilize support, so, too, can social activists. This would reduce social activists' incentive to seek cooperation with, or organizational assistance from, political parties, especially when the media prove to be an effective mobilizing agent. To the extent that the separation between civil society and opposition parties is beneficial to the prodemocracy movement, this is not a problem. But in reality, this may not always be the case. The reason is that civil society groups differ from political parties with respect to both constituencies and objectives. While many civil society groups work on a narrow issue area, opposition parties seek to change the fundamental political order. For this reason, opposition parties are based on a broader coalition of support in society, whereas civil society organizations often draw support from a small group of concerned individuals. Such differences have two important implications.

First, it would be relatively easier for civil society groups to extract concessions from the ruling elite, who may find the groups' demands less threatening to its vested interests. On the contrary, opposition parties who fight for a wholesale change of the political order may be unable to make any progress despite protracted negotiations with the regime. Second, the media may often find civil society organizations more newsworthy than political parties. This is not only because their causes are simpler and easier to understand (e.g., opposing the construction of a chemical plant versus designing a democratic electoral system) but also because the actions of social activists are more colorful. Consequently, civil society groups may crowd out political parties in the media. If social activists manage to extract regime concessions from time to time, their success, together with the glory and media attention they constantly obtain, would embarrass political parties and entrench their ineffectual image. As the current study shows, many liberal social activists in Hong Kong consciously distance their movements from opposition parties for fear of "guilt by association"; the farther away from opposition parties they are, the more virtuous they appear. In this sense, their success brings little positive complementarity effect to the strengthening of opposition parties. Instead, it feeds on the opposition parties' failure. The simultaneous occurrence of a vibrant civil society and a depressed coalition of opposition parties in postcolonial Hong Kong is therefore no coincidence. Rather, the two events are causally linked.

This is not to say that civil society will always benefit from the media's mobilization power. The experience of liberal civil society groups in postcolonial Hong Kong suggests a possible, albeit subtle, side effect. Like political parties, if social activists can easily rally support through the media, they would have little incentive to invest in the organizational capacity of their groups. This will hinder the development of civil society organizations in the long run. Take the "Anti-High Speed Rail Movement" as an example. One of the activists, Bobo Yip, feels regretful that the movement failed to harvest a large number of followers because of its emphasis on "de-organization."[6]

In addition, without a solid organizational network, members' loyalty would be relatively weak. This makes the organizers of a movement reluctant to show solidarity with other civil society organizations, in order to avoid antagonizing some of their members. The result is compartmentalization of civil society, preventing social activists from forming a unifying alliance against the authoritarian regime. The "Anti-Patriotic Education Movement" is a case in point. One of the organizers in the "National Education Parents Concern Group" told me of recurrent internal disputes about whether and how they should voice out views on other thorny social issues, including political reforms.[7] But they have chosen to remain silent most of the time either because they lacked the time and manpower to investigate into the rising issues or because they failed to reach a consensus on how to respond. For example, on one occasion, the members ran into a debate on whether they should support the annual commemoration of the June 4 Incident. The group ended up deciding to steer clear of it, for fear of losing some members who are not sympathetic about the prodemocracy movement in the mainland.

This reaction of the "National Education Parents Concern Group" stands in stark contrast to that of the Hong Kong Professional Teachers' Union (PTU). As discussed in Chap. 4, the PTU is one of the largest and most organized liberal civil society groups in Hong Kong, with a membership of 80,000 strong.

---

[6] Personal interview with Bobo Yip on March 27, 2014 (Code: 30).

[7] Personal interview with a group member on May 16, 2014 (Code: 33).

For many years, the PTU has been a staunch supporter of the prodemocracy movement in both Hong Kong and the mainland. Not only does it make statements to show its concern over various issues, it also helps disseminate information to its members to raise public awareness and provides logistic support to social activists on occasion. Apparently, the PTU cannot offer such practical support to other civil society groups without a strong organizational capacity.

As Beijing has agreed that the earliest time for Hong Kong to implement universal suffrage would be in the city's election for Chief Executive in 2017, Hong Kong's civil society is unlikely to remain quiescent until then. In fact, at the time of this writing, Hong Kong is mired in a serious governing crisis, which was instigated by an unprecedented social movement known as the *Occupy Central with Love and Peace.* The organizers of this movement had threatened to mobilize concerned citizens to occupy Hong Kong's central business district in case Beijing refuses to give Hong Kong people a genuine democratic election. The occupy movement came into being in the late September of 2014,[8] soon after Beijing announced a very conservative framework for the Chief Executive Election in 2017, stating that candidates are required to obtain the majority approval of a pro-Beijing nomination committee and that the number of candidates is limited to two or three. Under this framework, it is unlikely that the pan-democrats would have a chance to get the nomination.

Whether this conservative framework would become the reality is unclear. After all, the pan-democratic camp, given its critical minority position, still has the power to veto any political reform proposal. What is certain, though, is that if Hong Kong's civil liberties remain largely intact, the media will continue to play a crucial role in molding the city's prodemocracy movement in years to come. In particular, they will demonstrate great mobilization power to facilitate large-scale, spontaneous, albeit short-lived social movements. They will also empower Hong Kong's civil society by allowing concerned citizens to build horizontal linkages among themselves. Nevertheless, a successful democratic transition cannot depend on civil society alone, however strong it is. As the experience of postcolonial Hong Kong shows, the horizontal networks forged by liberal civil society groups are instrumental in triggering momentary public outcries but not very useful for resisting the inexorable rise of Beijing-sponsored parties that employ a grassroots strategy based on vertical networks of a patron-client relationship. The termites seem to have outflanked the elephants.

All this suggests the importance of political institutionalization. Diamond (1994, p. 15) has long argued that "the single most important and urgent factor in the consolidation of democracy is not civil society but political institutionalization." A stable and institutionalized organization allows opposition parties to form close

---

[8]At the time of this writing, the occupy movement has already lasted for more than forty days. Part of the downtown area, including Admiralty, Mongkok, and Causeway Bay, has been occupied.

and enduring ties with their supporters. Such supporters, who are recruited by party organization rather than because of ideological incentives, are essential to opposition parties in the struggle for democracy. Without them, opposition parties would need to draw political support predominantly from ideological voters. Consequently, they would not dare to make political compromises with the incumbent for fear of antagonizing their core followers (DeNardo 1985, pp. 84–86). However, if the opposition wants to persuade the ruling elite to relinquish power for good, it cannot avoid taking some expedient measures during the lengthy negotiation with the authoritarian regime.

The grassroots strategy of Beijing-sponsored parties offers different glimpses of the Chinese authoritarian state. Far too often the Beijing government is seen as ruthless and repressive. But as many scholars of authoritarian politics point out, few autocracies can survive on repression alone. In most cases, co-optation – or in the CCP's language, the "united front work" – plays a decidedly more important role in consolidating authoritarian rule. Postcolonial Hong Kong provides an interesting quasi-experimental setup to study the power and limitations of authoritarian co-optation. Because of Hong Kong's unique history and economic significance, Beijing has refrained from imposing heavy-handed political controls, for fear of jeopardizing the city's capitalist system. Co-optation became Beijing's major tool to establish its control over this former British colony. This tool, which manifests itself in the Beijing-sponsored parties' grassroots strategy, has turned out to be a great success, as evidenced by the ever-improving electoral performance of these parties at all levels of elections.

The electoral advances of Beijing-sponsored parties provide little sign of hope for the pan-democrats. If the former parties' grassroots encroachment continues unabated, pan-democratic parties may soon lose a critical minority in the LegCo, which implies that they will not be able to veto a conservative political reform bill that Beijing favors. From the perspective of prodemocracy voters, this may be a discouraging scenario. Nevertheless, it is important to note that the pan-democratic parties' failure to secure a critical minority in the legislature is also indicative of their declining popularity among voters. Should this really happen, the pan-democrats would not fare much better even if Beijing were willing to give Hong Kong full democracy.

While the electoral prospect of Beijing-sponsored parties may look rosy, there still exist several factors which may derail their success. First, internal strife among the pro-Beijing elite exists, albeit less visible. Thus far the success of Beijing-sponsored parties hinges upon their adherence to their grassroots co-optation strategy, which de-emphasizes ideology. However, their grassroots co-optation strategy is useful only because they have developed extensive patronage networks. Not all members of the pro-Beijing elite have access to such networks. If these members want to vie for political power, they are likely to adopt a different strategy in order to draw political support. In fact, Hong Kong has witnessed a rising tide of mass mobilization from the pro-Beijing camp since 2012. The organizers of these mobilization events are mostly new faces. Their strategies are also markedly different from those adopted by Beijing-sponsored parties. For instance, they are prone to the use of loud and ideological tactics. Their controversial tactics may help them draw media attention as well as political support from radical pro-Beijing voters, but their presence may also cause a backlash against the pro-establishment camp as a whole in the coming elections – exactly the same problem that has plagued the pan-democrats. If the internal power competition among the pro-Beijing elite escalates, such ideological and media-driven political campaigns will multiply, which may eventually undermine the success of the Beijing-sponsored parties' low-key grassroots strategy.

Second, the fact that Hong Kong can still preserve much of its civil liberties is predicated on Beijing's self-restraint. But this self-restraint is not inevitable. In fact, since the inception of the *Occupy Central* movement, Hong Kong's civil liberties, media freedom in particular, have been under threat. For example, there were reported cases where Chinese state-owned banks stopped placing ads in newspapers that are considered neutral (BBC News 2014). Several outspoken journalists, radio hosts, and columnists were abruptly dismissed from their jobs. The Independent Commission Against Corruption raided the home of Jimmy Lai, the owner of the *Apple Daily*, over political donations. When the *Occupy Central* movement organized an unofficial referendum in June 2014, its online voting system endured a massive state-sponsored cyberattack. Although there have been no evidence to link these incidents to Chinese authorities, their occurrence within such a short period of time has already caused a chilling effect in Hong Kong. If Beijing loses its tolerance of Hong Kong's vocal civil society or if Beijing no longer considers the city as economically important as before, it may well take back the freedoms that Hong Kong people are currently enjoying and impose more heavy-handed controls over Hong Kong's society. The decline of civil liberties may result in a backlash against Beijing-sponsored parties in the voting booth. But of course, if Beijing decides to govern Hong Kong more forcefully, this would indicate a fundamental departure from its long-standing policy toward Hong Kong. In other words, co-optation will no longer be Beijing's only option and its dependence on Beijing-sponsored parties, its central co-optation machine, would therefore decrease. Under such circumstances, Beijing will likely overhaul the rules of electoral contestation.

Finally, the success of Beijing-sponsored parties hinges upon the enormous investment which they have injected into an elaborate local patron-client network. If their resources dry up, for whatever reasons, their seemingly invincible grassroots edifice may just well crumble.

Appendix A
Interviews Conducted

Code	Date of interview	Affiliated political camp/movement involved	Independent candidate	Number of District Council elections participated	LegCo election experience	Party management level
Politicians						
1	12-Jun-12	Pan-democratic	Y	>5 times	N	N
2	14-Jun-12	Pan-democratic	Y	>5 times	N	N
3	15-Jun-12	Pan-democratic	Y	3–5 times	Y	N
4	12-Oct-12	Pan-democratic		<3 times	Y	Y
5	18-Dec-12	Pro-establishment		<3 times	N	N
6	18-Dec-12	Pro-establishment		<3 times	Y	N
7	2-Jan-13	Pro-establishment		<3 times	N	N
8	2-Jan-13	Pro-establishment		<3 times	N	N
9	2-Jan-13	Pro-establishment		3–5 times	N	N
10	3-Jan-13	Pro-establishment		>5 times	Y	Y
11	3-Jan-13	Pro-establishment		3–5 times	N	N
12	4-Jan-13	Pro-establishment		<3 times	Y	Y
13	9-Jan-13	Pro-establishment		3–5 times	Y	N
14	9-Jan-13	Pro-establishment		3–5 times	Y	Y
15	11-Jan-13	Pro-establishment		<3 times	Y	N
16	11-Jan-13	Pro-establishment		<3 times	Y	Y
17	23-Jan-13	Pan-democratic		3–5 times	N	N
18	23-Jan-13	Pan-democratic		<3 times	Y	N
19	23-Jan-13	Pan-democratic		3–5 times	Y	N
20	31-Jan-13	Pan-democratic		<3 times	Y	Y
21	31-Jan-13	Pan-democratic		3–5 times	Y	N
22	31-Jan-13	Pan-democratic		<3 times	N	N

(continued)

© Springer Science+Business Media Singapore 2015
S.H.-W. Wong, *Electoral Politics in Post-1997 Hong Kong*,
DOI 10.1007/978-981-287-387-3

Code	Date of interview	Affiliated political camp/movement involved	Independent candidate	Number of District Council elections participated	LegCo election experience	Party management level
23	7-Mar-13	Pan-democratic		3–5 times	Y	Y
24	21-Sep-12	Pan-democratic		<3 times	Y	Y
25	21-Sep-12	Pan-democratic		<3 times	Y	Y
26	28-Sep-12	Pan-democratic		<3 times	Y	Y
27	28-Sep-12	Pan-democratic		<3 times	Y	Y
28	3-Oct-12	Pan-democratic		3–5 times	Y	Y
29	11-Apr-14	Pan-democratic		>5 times	Y	Y

Social activists

Code	Date of interview	Affiliated political camp/movement involved	Independent candidate	Number of District Council elections participated	LegCo election experience	Party management level
30	27-Mar-14	Anti-Patriotic Education Movement, Anti-High Speed Rail Movement				
31	12-May-14	Anti-Patriotic Education Movement				
32	15-May-14	Anti-High Speed Rail Movement, Queen's Pier Preservation Campaign				
33	16-May-14	Anti-Patriotic Education Movement				
34	5-Jun-14	Anti-Patriotic Education Movement				
47	11-Aug-14	Annual July 1 protest and 2010 quasi-referendum				

Voters

Code	Date of interview	Affiliated political camp/movement involved	Independent candidate	Number of District Council elections participated	LegCo election experience	Party management level
35	4-Jan-14					
36	4-Jan-14					
37	4-Jan-14					
38	4-Jan-14					
39	4-Jan-14					
40	4-Jan-14					
41	7-Jan-14					
42	7-Jan-14					
43	7-Jan-14					
44	15-Jan-14					
45	15-Jan-14					
46	15-Jan-14					

Bibliography

Adsera, A., Boix, C., & Payne, M. (2003). Are you being served? Political accountability and quality of government. *Journal of Law, Economics, and organization, 19*(2), 445–490.

Aldrich, J. H. (1995). *Why parties? The origin and transformation of party politics in America* (Vol. 15). Chicago: University of Chicago Press.

Alvarez, M., Cheibub, J. A., Limongi, F., & Przeworski, A. (1996). Classifying political regimes. *Studies in Comparative International Development, 31*(2), 3–36.

Angrist, J. D., & Pischke, J. S. (2009). *Mostly harmless econometrics: An empiricist's companion.* Princeton: Princeton University Press.

Apple Daily. (2003). New political group civic act-up achieved election rate 60 percent, 25 Nov 2003.

Apple Daily. (2010a). Organize movement online and seek no political advantage, 16 Jan 2010.

Apple Daily. (2010b). Pro-Beijing figure threatens allies not to participate in the by-election. chen yongqi: Participating by-election considered against the central government [qinjingpai xia zhijiyou wu canxuan chen yongqi: canjia buxuan yutong zhongyang guowuqu], 23 Jan 2010.

Apple Daily. (2012a). Pro-establishment parties mobilized elderly in legco elections [zhiji jiezaidao piaozhan tiezhi xietou 9/804 zuopai chu zhangxinlei baibu changzhe], 10 Sept 2012.

Apple Daily. (2012b). Wearing Mask to Protect Government, Fake Independents Make Greater Damage and Steal Pan-democrats' Votes [daizhao mianju baohuang shashangli geng lihai jia duli houxuanren qiangjie fanmin piao], 4 Sept 2012.

Au, N.-h. (2015). Democratic regression under electoral authoritarianism: Regime consolidation and elite co-optation in post-1997 Hong Kong. MA Thesis, Chinese University of Hong Kong.

BBC News. (2014) Is Hong Kong's Media under Attack?, 11 Mar 2014.

Bennett, W. L. (2012). *News: The politics of illusion* (12th ed.). Boston: Longman.

Bickers, R., & Yep, R. (2009). *May days in Hong Kong: Riot and emergency in 1967* (Vol. 1). Hong Kong: Hong Kong University Press.

Black, D. (1958). *The theory of committees and elections.* Cambridge: Cambridge University Press.

Blaydes, L. (2010). *Elections and distributive politics in Mubarak's Egypt.* Chicago: Cambridge University Press.

Boix, C., & Svolik, M. W. (2013). The foundations of limited authoritarian government: Institutions, commitment, and power-sharing in dictatorships. *The Journal of Politics, 75*(02), 300–316.

Bratton, M., & Van de Walle, N. (1997). *Democratic experiments in Africa: Regime transitions in comparative perspective.* Cambridge: Cambridge University Press.

Brownlee, J. (2007). *Authoritarianism in an age of democratization.* Cambridge: Cambridge University Press.

© Springer Science+Business Media Singapore 2015
S.H.-W. Wong, *Electoral Politics in Post-1997 Hong Kong,*
DOI 10.1007/978-981-287-387-3

Brunetti, A., & Weder, B. (2003). A free press is bad news for corruption. *Journal of Public economics, 87*(7), 1801–1824.

Bueno de Mesquita, B., Smith, A., Siverson, R. M., & Morrow, J. D. (2003). *The logic of political survival*. Cambridge, MA: MIT.

Bunce, V. J., & Wolchik, S. L. (2006). Favorable conditions and electoral revolutions. *Journal of Democracy, 17*(4), 5.

Carroll, J. M. (2007). *A concise history of Hong Kong*. Lanham: Rowman & Littlefield.

Census and Statistics Department of Hong Kong. (2012). Hong Kong monthly digest of statistics, 4 2012.

Central Committee of the Communist Party of China Party Literature Research Office. (1998). *Liu Shaoqi's manuscripts after the founding of the state [jianguo yilai Liu Shaoqi wengao]* (Vol. 1). Zhongyang wenxian chubanshe.

Cha, L. Y. (1984). *On Hong Kong's future*. Hong Kong: Ming Pao Daily News.

Chan, K.-M. (2005). Civil society and the democracy movement in Hong Kong: Mass mobilization with limited organizational capacity. *Korea Observer, 36*(1), 167–182.

Chan, J. M., & Chung, R. (2003). Who could mobilize half a million to take to the street?, 15–16 July 2003.

Chan, J. M.-M., Fu, H., & Ghai, Y. (2000). *Hong Kong's constitutional debate: Conflict over interpretation* (Vol. 1). Hong Kong: Hong Kong University Press.

Cheibub, J. A., Gandhi, J., & Vreeland, J. R. (2010). Democracy and dictatorship revisited. *Public Choice, 143*(1), 67–101. ISSN 0048-5829.

Cheng, J. Y.-S. (1984). *Hong Kong: In search of a future*. Hong Kong: Oxford University Press.

Cheng, J. Y.-S. (2004). The 2003 district council elections in Hong Kong. *Asian Survey, 44*(5), 734–754.

Cheung, A. B. L. (2000). New interventionism in the making: Interpreting state interventions in Hong Kong after the change of sovereignty. *Journal of Contemporary China, 9*(24), 291–308.

Cho, Y. N. (2010). *Local people's congresses in China: Development and transition*. New York: Cambridge University Press.

Chung, R., & Chan, J. M. (2003). July 1 protest's revelation: Internet mobilization triggers new democratic power, 24–25 July 2003.

Chwe, M. S. Y. (2003). *Rational ritual: Culture, coordination, and common knowledge*. Princeton: Princeton University Press. ISBN 0691114714.

DAB. (2013a). Local branches [zhibu]. http://www.dab.org.hk/?t=10&mmode=c. Retrieved 31 Mar 2013.

DAB. (2013b). Our manifesto. http://www.dab.org.hk/?t=247&mmode=ada.

Dahl, R. A. (1971). *Polyarchy: Participation and opposition* (Vol. 254). New Haven: Yale University Press.

DeGolyer, M. E. (2004). How the stunning outbreak of disease led to a stunning outbreak of dissent. In C. Loh (Ed.), *At the epicentre: Hong Kong and the SARS outbreak*. Hong Kong: Hong Kong University Press.

DeGolyer, M. E., & Scott, J. L. (1996). The myth of political apathy in Hong Kong. *The Annals of the American Academy of Political and Social Science, 547*, 68–78.

Deibert, R. (2010). *Access controlled: The shaping of power, rights, and rule in cyberspace*. Cambridge, MA: MIT.

DeNardo, J. (1985). *Power in numbers: The political strategy of protest and rebellion*. Princeton: Princeton University Press.

Deng, X. (2003). *Selected works of Deng Xiaoping* (Vol. 3). Beijing: Renmin Chubanshe.

Deng, X. (2004). *Deng Xiaoping lun 'Yiguo Liangzhi' [Deng Xiaoping Discusses 'One Country Two Systems']*. Hong Kong: Joint Publishing.

Diamond, L. J. (1994). Toward democratic consolidation. *Journal of democracy, 5*(3), 4–17.

Diaz-Cayeros, A., Magaloni, B., & Weingast, B. R. (2003). Tragic brilliance: Equilibrium hegemony and democratization in Mexico. Manuscrito. Disponível em: http://papers.ssrn.com/sol3/papers.cfm.

Dimitrov, M. K. (2013). *Why communism did not collapse: Understanding authoritarian regime resilience in Asia and Europe*. Cambridge: Cambridge University Press.

Downs, A. (1957). *An economic theory of democracy*. New York: Harper.

Edmond, C. (2013). Information manipulation, coordination, and regime change. *The Review of Economic Studies, 80*(4), 1422–1458.

Eggers, A. C., & Hainmueller, J. (2010). MPs for sale? Returns to office in postwar British politics. *American Political Science Review, 103*(4), 513.

Egorov, G., Guriev, S., & Sonin, K. (2009). Why resource-poor dictators allow freer media: A theory and evidence from panel data. *American Political Science Review, 103*(4), 645.

Electoral Affairs Commission. (2011). Report on the Recommended Constituency Boundaries for the 2011 District Council Election. http://www.eac.gov.hk/en/distco/2011dc_boundary_v1_report.htm.

Feng, B. Y. (1997). *Xianggang Huazi Caituan: 1841–1997 [Hong Kong Chinese Conglomerates]*. Hong Kong: Joint Publishing.

Fenno, R. F. (1978). *Home style: House members in their districts*. Boston: Little, Brown.

Fewsmith, J. (2013). *The logic and limits of political reform in China*. Cambridge: Cambridge University Press.

Fong, P. K. W., & Yeh, A. G. O. (1987). Hong Kong. In Ha, K.-S. (Ed.), *Housing policy and practice in Asia*. New York: Croom Helm.

Fox, J., & Hernández, L. (1995). Lessons from the Mexican elections. *Dissent, 42*(1), 29–33.

Friedman, M. (2009). *Capitalism and freedom*. Chicago: University of Chicago Press.

FTU. (2002). The FTU eager for international year of volunteers [gonglianhui jiji canyu guoji yigongnian gexiang fuwu huodong wusi fengxian wei shequn yuqian yigong huo jiaxu]. http://www.ftu.org.hk/zh-hant/about?id=17&nid=97. Retrieved 9 Aug 2012.

Fujiwara, T. (2011). A regression discontinuity test of strategic voting and Duvergers law. *Quarterly Journal of Political Science, 6*(3–4), 197–233.

Gandhi, J. (2008). *Political institutions under dictatorship*. New York: Cambridge University Press.

Gandhi, J., & Lust-Okar, E. (2009). Elections under authoritarianism. *Annual Review of Political Science, 12*, 403–422.

Gandhi, J., & Przeworski, A. (2006). Cooperation, cooptation, and rebellion under dictatorships. *Economics & Politics, 18*(1), 1–26.

Gandhi, J., & Przeworski, A. (2007). Authoritarian institutions and the survival of autocrats. *Comparative Political Studies, 40*(11), 1279.

Geddes, B. (1999). What do we know about democratization after twenty years? *Annual Review of Political Science, 2*(1), 115–144.

Geddes, B. (2005). Why parties and elections in authoritarian regimes? In *Annual meeting of the American political science association* (pp. 456–471). Washington, D.C.

Geddes, B., & Zaller, J. (1989). Sources of popular support for authoritarian regimes. *American Journal of Political Science, 33*(2), 319–347.

Gehlbach, S., & Keefer, P. (2011). Investment without democracy: Ruling-party institutionalization and credible commitment in autocracies. *Journal of Comparative Economics, 39*(2), 123–139.

Gelman, A., & King, G. (1994). Enhancing democracy through legislative redistricting. *American Political Science Review, 88*(3), 541–559.

Gerber, A. S., Kessler, D. P., & Meredith, M. (2011). The persuasive effects of direct mail: A regression discontinuity based approach. *Journal of Politics, 73*(1), 140–155.

Ghai, Y. P. (1999). *Hong Kong's new constitutional order: The resumption of Chinese sovereignty and the Basic Law*. Hong Kong: Hong Kong University Press.

Gilley, B. (2010). Democratic enclaves in authoritarian regimes. *Democratization, 17*(3), 389–415.

Ginsburg, T., & Moustafa, T. (2008). *Rule by law: The politics of courts in authoritarian regimes*. Cambridge: Cambridge University Press.

Goodstadt, L. F. (2005). *Uneasy partners: The conflict between public interest and private profit in Hong Kong*. Hong Kong: Hong Kong University Press.

Gramsci, A. (1971). *Selections from the prison notebooks* (Q. Hoare & G. N. Smith (Eds. and Trans.)). New York: International Publishers Company.

Hainmueller, J., & Kern, H. L. (2008). Incumbency as a source of spillover effects in mixed electoral systems: Evidence from a regression-discontinuity design. *Electoral Studies, 27*(2), 213–227.

Hamilton, A., Madison, J., & Jay, J. (2008). *The federalist papers.* Oxford/New York: Oxford University Press.

Handley, L., & Grofman, B. (2008). *Redistricting in comparative perspective.* Oxford/New York: Oxford University Press.

Hayek, F. A. (1945). The use of knowledge in society. *The American Economic Review, 35*(4), 519–530.

Hayek, F. A. (1960). *The constitution of liberty.* Chicago: University of Chicago Press.

HKSAR. (2006). Second report of the Hong Kong Special Administrative Region of the People's Republic of China in the Light of the International Covenant on Civil and Political Rights. http://www.legco.gov.hk/yr05-06/english/panels/ha/papers/ha0310cb2-iccpr-e.pdf.

HKSAR. (2012). Combined third and fourth reports of the People's Republic of China under the Convention on the Rights of the Child – Part Two: Hong Kong Special Administrative Region. http://www.legco.gov.hk/yr11-12/english/panels/ca/papers/ca0618-rpt20120525-e.pdf. 25 May 2012.

HKSAR. (2013). Legislative Council Question: Registration of Organizations. http://www.info.gov.hk/gia/general/201307/10/P201307100420.htm. 10 July 2013.

Home Affairs Department. (2012a). Community involvement activities [shequ canyu jihua] (in Chinese). http://www.had.gov.hk/file_manager/tc/documents/home/activities.pdf. Retrieved 9 Aug 2012.

Home Affairs Department. (2012b). Public services – Minor works programmes. http://www.had.gov.hk/en/public_services/minor_works_programmes/minor_work.htm. Retrieved 9 Aug 2012.

Hong Kong Commercial Daily. (2010). Difficult for Audrey Eu to Avoid Defeat [Yu ruowei baibu nanhuo], 25 May 2010.

Hong Kong Economic Journal. (2006). Wong yuk-man claims LSD extreme leftist, 2 Oct 2006.

Hong Kong Economic Journal. (2010a). Audrey Eu: Automatically elected tantamount to winning without fighting [Yu ruowei: zidong dangxuan dengyu gongtou buzhan ersheng], 18 Feb 2010.

Hong Kong Economic Journal. (2010b). Wong yuk-man: Benefited from quasi-referendum LSD aims for 5 seats in the next election, 19 May 2010.

Hong Kong Economic Journal. (2012). Tsang Yok-sing: Central Government Has Reservations about Party Politics [Tsang Yok-sing chang: zhongyang dui zhengdang zhengzhi rengyou baoliu], 29 Feb 2012.

Hong Kong Economic Times. 2010. Two parties quit, pro-establishment camp eyes on three constituencies, scholar says "uprising" slogan alienates moderate voters [liangdang qingci jianzhipai zhugong xanqu qiyi zuo kouhao xuezhe zhi liushi wenhe xuanmin], 22 Jan 2010.

Hong Kong Federation of Trade Unions. (2013). *FTU walking with you: 65th anniversary historical essays.* Hong Kong: Chung Hwa Book Company.

Hong Kong Government. (2012). Basic law full text. http://www.basiclaw.gov.hk/en/basiclawtext/chapter_4.html#section_2. Retrieved 9 Aug 2012.

Hong Kong Housing Authority. (2012). Housing in figures 2012. http://www.housingauthority.gov.hk/en/about-us/publications-and-statistics/index.html#p2.

Hong Kong Special Administrative Region Government. (2013). Electoral Affairs Commission Ordinance.

Huffington Post. (2011). Egypt's Facebook Revolution: Wael Ghonim Thanks the Social Network, 11 Feb 2011.

Hughes, R. (1968). *Hong Kong: Borrowed place, borrowed time.* London: Deutsch.

Hung, T.-W., Lai, A., Leung, C.-K., Ng, S., Pong, Y.-Y., Taylor, R., & Zimmerman, P. (2010). Hong Kong interchange option: A cheaper, faster, and better express rail link. Technical report, Professional Commons.

Information Services Department. (2013). Political assistants appointed. http://www.info.gov.hk/gia/general/201303/15/P201303150252.htm. Retrieved 31 Mar 2013.

Ip, C.-I. (2009). New political power: The development of Hong Kong independent media [xinzhengzhi liliang: xianggang duli meiti de fazhan]. *Mass Communication Research [Xinwenxue yanjiu]*, 99, 221–239.

Kamo, T., & Takeuchi, H. (2013). Representation and local people's congresses in China: A case study of the yangzhou municipal people's congress. *Journal of Chinese Political Science, 18*(1), 41–60.

Kiang, S.-K. (2011). *The Chinese Communist Party in Hong Kong* (Vol. 1). Hong Kong: Cosmos Books.

Kiang, S.-K. (2012). *The Chinese Communist Party in Hong Kong* (Vol. 2). Hong Kong: Cosmos Books.

King, A. Y.-C. (1975). Administrative absorption of politics in Hong Kong: Emphasis on the grass roots level. *Asian Survey, 15*(5), 422–439.

King, G., Pan, J., & Roberts, M. E. (2013). How censorship in China allows government criticism but silences collective expression. *American Political Science Review, 107*(2), 326–343.

Ku, S.-M. A. (2007). Constructing and contesting the "order" imagery in media discourse: Implications for civil society in Hong Kong. *Asian Journal of Communication, 17*(2), 186–200.

Kuan, C.-H., Lau, K.-S., Louie, S.-K., & Wong, Y.-K. (Eds.). (1999). *Power transfer and electoral politics: The first legislative election in the Hong Kong special administrative region*. Hong Kong: Chinese University Press.

Kwong, B. K.-K. (2010). *Patron-client politics and elections in Hong Kong*. London/New York: Routledge.

Lai, C. P. (2007). *Media in Hong Kong: Press freedom and political change, 1967–2005*. London/New York: Routledge.

Lam, C.-H. (1984). *Thoughts and facts about the problems of Hong Kong's future*. Hong Kong: Hong Kong Economic Journal.

Lam, C.-H. (1989). Emigrants left with money drains funds for infrastructure, 28 Nov 1989.

Lam, M.-W. (2004). *Understanding the political culture of Hong Kong: The paradox of activism and depoliticization*. Armonk: ME Sharpe.

Lam, M.-W. (2012). Political identity, culture, and participation. In: W.-W. Wilson, L.-L. Percy, & L. Wai-man (Eds.), *Contemporary Hong Kong government and politics* (2nd ed.). Hong Kong: Hong Kong University Press.

Lau, K.-S. (1981). The government, intermediate organizations, and grass-roots politics in Hong Kong. *Asian Survey, 21*(8), 865–884.

Lau, K.-S. (1984). *Society and politics in Hong Kong*. Hong Kong: Chinese University Press.

Lau, K.-S., & Kuan, H.-C. (1988). *The ethos of the Hong Kong Chinese*. Hong Kong: Chinese University Press.

Lau, K.-S., & Kuan, H.-C. (2000). Partial democratization, "foundation moment" and political parties in Hong Kong. *The China Quarterly, 163*, 705–720.

Lau, K.-S., & Kuan, H.-C. (2002). Hong Kong's stunted political party system. *China Quarterly, 172*, 1010–1028.

Lee, E. W. Y. (1999). Governing post-colonial Hong Kong: Institutional incongruity, governance crisis, and authoritarianism. *Asian Survey, 39*(6), 940–959.

Lee, D. S. (2008). Randomized experiments from non-random selection in US House elections. *Journal of Econometrics, 142*(2), 675–697.

Lee, F. L. F. (2011). Taking message-attitude congruence as media effects: Examining perceived influence of political talk radio in Hong Kong. *Journal of Radio & Audio Media, 18*(2), 176–195.

Lee, F. L. F., & Chan, J. M. (2011). *Media, social mobilisation and mass protests in post-colonial Hong Kong: The power of a critical event*. New York: Routledge.

Legislative Council. (2012). Remuneration package for district council members. http://www.info.gov.hk/gia/general/201211/14/P201211140405.htm. Retrieved 31 Mar 2013.

Leung, S.-W. (1991). The "China factor" in the 1991 legislative council election: The june 4th incident and anti-Communist China syndrome. In S.-K. Lau & H.-C. Kuan (Eds.), *The Hong

Kong tried democracy: The 1991 elections in Hong Kong (pp. 187–235). Hong Kong: Hong Kong Institute of Asia-Pacific Studies.

Leung, S.-W. (1996). The "China factor" and voters' choice in the 1995 legislative council election. In H.-C. Kuan, et al. (Eds.), *The 1995 legislative council elections in Hong Kong* (pp. 201–44). Hong Kong: Hong Kong Institute of Asia-Pacific Studies.

Levi, M. (1989). *Of rule and revenue*. Berkeley: University of California Press.

Levitsky, S., & Way, L. A. (2002). The rise of competitive authoritarianism. *Journal of Democracy, 13*(2), 51–65.

Levitsky, S., & Way, L. A. (2010). *Competitive authoritarianism: Hybrid regimes after the cold war*. New York: Cambridge University Press.

Li, H. (1997). *The course of reunification [Huigui de Licheng]*. Hong Kong: Joint Publishing.

Li, X. (2010). *Impasses and Breakthroughs: Case study on Hong Kong's critical issues*. Hong Kong: Cosmos Books.

Li, P.-K. (2012). The executive. In W.-M. Lam, L.-T. L. Percy, & W. Wong (Eds.), *Contemporary Hong Kong Government and Politics* (pp. 27–43). Hong Kong: Hong Kong University Press.

Lieberthal, K. (1992). The future of Hong Kong. *Asian Survey, 32*(7), 666–682.

Lindberg, S. I. (2006). *Democracy and elections in Africa*. Baltimore: Johns Hopkins University Press.

Lo, S.-H. (1994). An analysis of Sino-British negotiations over Hong Kong's political reform. *Contemporary Southeast Asia, 16*(2), 178–209.

Lo, S. S.-H. (2007). One formula, two experiences: Political divergence of Hong Kong and macao since retrocession. *Journal of Contemporary China, 16*(52), 359–387.

Lo, S.-H., Yu, W.-Y., & Wan, K.-F. (2002). The 1999 district councils elections. In M. K. Chan & A. Y. So (Eds.), *Crisis and transformation in China's Hong Kong* (pp. 139–165). Armonk: M.E. Sharpe.

Lu, P. (2009). *Lu Ping's oral history of Hong Kong's reunification [Lu Ping Koushu Xianggang Huigui]*. Hong Kong: Joint Publishing.

Lui, T.-L., Kuan, H.-C., Chan, K.-M., & Chan, S. C.-W. (2005). Friends and critics of the state: The case of Hong Kong. In R. P. Weller (Ed.), *Civil life, globalization, and political change in Asia* (pp. 58–75). London/New York: Routledge.

Lust-Okar, E. (2005). *Structuring conflict in the Arab world: Incumbents, opponents, and institutions*. Cambridge/New York: Cambridge University Press.

Lust-Okar, E. (2006). Elections under authoritarianism: Preliminary lessons from Jordan. *Democratization, 13*(3), 456–471.

Lust-Okar, E. (2009). Legislative elections in hegemonic authoritarian regimes: Competitive clientelism and resistance to democratization. In: I.-L. Staffan (Ed.), *Democratization by elections: A new mode of transition* (Vol. 2009, pp. 226–45). Baltimore: Johns Hopkins University Press, c2009.

Ma, N. (2005). Civil society in self-defense: The struggle against national security legislation in Hong Kong. *Journal of Contemporary China, 14*(44), 465–482.

Ma, N. (2007a). *Political development in Hong Kong: State, political society, and civil society*. Hong Kong: Hong Kong University Press.

Ma, N. (2007b). State-press relationship in post 1997 Hong Kong: Constant negotiation amidst self restraint. *The China Quarterly, 192*, 949–970.

Ma, N. (2008). Civil society and democratization in Hong Kong paradox and duality. *Taiwan Journal of Democracy 4*(2), 155–175.

Ma, N. (2012). *An oral history of democratic movement of Hong Kong in the 1980s [Xianggang 80 niandai minzhu yundong koushu lishi]*. Hong Kong: City University of Hong Kong.

Ma, E. K.-W., & Chan, J. M. (2007). Global connectivity and local politics: SARS, talk radio, and public opinion apparatus in Hong Kong. In Davis, D., & Siu, H. (Eds.), *SARS: Reception and interpretation in three Chinese cities*. London: Routledge.

Ma, N., & Choy, I. (1999). The evolution of the electoral system and party politics in Hong Kong. *Issues & Studies, 35*(1), 167–194.

Ma, N., & Choy, I. (2003). *Political consequences of electoral systems: The Hong Kong proportional representation system.* Hong Kong: City University of Hong Kong Press.

Magaloni, B. (2006). *Voting for autocracy: Hegemonic party survival and its demise in Mexico.* Cambridge: Cambridge University Press.

Magaloni, B. (2008). Credible power-sharing and the longevity of authoritarian rule. *Comparative Political Studies, 41*(4/5), 715.

Manion, M. (2008). When Communist party candidates can lose, who wins? Assessing the role of local people's congresses in the selection of leaders in China. *The China Quarterly, 195,* 607–630.

Manion, M. (2014). "good types" in authoritarian elections the selectoral connection in Chinese local congresses. *Comparative Political Studies,* 0010414014537027.

Mao, Z. (1952a). *Chinese revolution and Chinese Communist Party [Zhongguo Geming he Zhongguo Gongchandang].* Renmin Chubanshe.

Mao, Z. (1952b). *Communists: Foreword ["Gong chan dang ren" fa kan ci].* Beijing: Renmin Chubanshe.

Mao, Z. (1952c). *War and strategic problems [Zhanzheng he Zhanlue Wenti].* Beijing: Renmin Chubanshe.

Mao, Z. (1976). *On policy [lun zhengce].* Beijing: Renmin Chubanshe.

Mathews, G., Ma, E., & Lui, T.-L. (2007). *Hong Kong, China: Learning to belong to a nation* (Vol. 10). London: Routledge.

McCarthy, J. D., & Zald, M. N. (1977). Resource mobilization and social movements: A partial theory. *American Journal of Sociology, 82*(6), 1212–1241.

Miners, N. (1995). *The government and politics of Hong Kong.* Hong Kong: Oxford University Press.

Ming Pao Daily News. (2003). Shouting "down with tung" under burning sun, 2 July 2003.

Ming Pao Daily News. (2004a). Alan leong denies champerty [liang jiajie fouren baolan susong], 29 July 2004.

Ming Pao Daily News. (2004b). Lam Yuk Wah quits, and Ivan Choy loses morale [Lin xuhua gongtong jintui cai ziqiang yixing lanshan], 29 July 2004.

Ming Pao Daily News. (2007). Secrets of the pro-Beijing camp in district council elections: An insider's observation [shenmeren fangwen shenmeren: ouxuan wujiandao], 25 Nov 2007.

Ming Pao Daily News. (2010a). Audrey Eu: 50% Victory Benchmark Unchanged [Yu ruowei: wucheng toupiaolv chenggong mubiao bubian], 18 Feb 2010.

Ming Pao Daily News. (2010b). The dab grooms new generation in local elections [haoliangnian shijian ziyuan minjianlian dazao diqu xinxing], Aug 18 2010.

Ming Pao Daily News. (2010c). Kam nai wai sold his property to raise hk$2 million for 2008 legco election [gannaiwei sanxuan quecai zengmailou taoxian erbaiwan], 31 Oct 2010.

Ming Pao Daily News. (2010d). The LSD promises "three nos" and boycotts district councils' super-seats [sheminlian sanbu beige quhui yixi], 22 June 2010.

Ming Pao Daily News. (2011a). Liberal party implicates civic party as the "black hand" [ziyoudang anpi gongmindang heishou], 29 Sept 2011.

Ming Pao Daily News. (2011b). Investment tips from chan hak kan [chenkeqin maiche mailou zai maipu], 4 Feb 2011.

Ming Pao Daily News. (2012a). Government regulations on the community halls abused for profit-making [mianzu tuanti she lanyong shequ huitang mouli minzhengshu zeng guiguan changyin koufenzhi], 4 June 2012.

Ming Pao Daily News. (2012b). Pong Oi Lan Implicated as Goddaughter of Liaison Office Denies Meeting Liaison Office While Rejecting Position-Labelling [Pang ailan beifeng zhonglianban qinv fouren wu zhonglian guanyuan chen wuxu biaoqian lichang], 26 Aug 2012.

Ming Pao Daily News. (2013a). Dab's lawmakers failed to declare for employing their party fellows by government subvention [pindangyou renzhuli minjianlian meishenbao], 16 Mar 2013.

Ming Pao Daily News. (2013b). New territories associations of societies aims to recruit 20,000 members [xinshelian ji nianzeng liangwan huiyuan], 16 Feb 2013.

Ming Pao Daily News. (2013c). Preparing 2016 LegCo Election DB Provides Subsidies and DAB Introduces A Point System, 22 June 2013.

Ng, H.-M. (2011). *Ng Hong Man oral history: Hong Kong's political and patriotic education (1947-2011)*. Hong Kong: Joint Publishing.

Ngo, T.-W. (2002). Industrial history and the artifice of laissez-faire colonialism. In T.-W. Ngo (Ed.), *Hong Kong's history: State and society under colonial rule*. London/New York: Routledge.

Nie, R. (2005). *The Memoir of Marshal Nie Rongzhen [Nie Rongzhen yuanshuai huiyilu]*. Beijing: Jiefangjun Chubanshe.

Norris, P. (1999). *Critical citizens: Global support for democratic government*. Oxford: Oxford University Press.

O'Brien, K. J. & Li, L. (1999). Selective policy implementation in rural China. *Comparative Politics, 31*(2), 167–86.

O'Brien, K. J. & Li, L. (2006). *Rightful resistance in rural China*. Cambridge: Cambridge University Press.

Offe, C. (1985). New social movements: Challenging the boundaries of institutional politics. *Social Research, 52*(4), 817–868.

Olson, M. (2008). *The rise and decline of nations: Economic growth, stagflation, and social rigidities*. New Haven: Yale University Press.

Oriental Daily. (2010). Video of longhair cursing szeto wah goes viral online [changmao zhou situa hua wangshang rebo], 27 June 2010.

Oriental Daily News. (2011). Welfare and recreational activities determine local elections, to kwan hang lamented [atao hong shezhaibingzong zhudao diqu], 14 Sept 2011.

Ortmann, S. (2011). Singapore: Authoritarian but newly competitive. *Journal of Democracy, 22*(4), 153–164.

Paletz, D. L., & Entman, R. M. (1981). *Media power politics*. New York: Free Press.

Petersen, C. J. (2005). Hong Kong's spring of discontent: The rise and fall of the national security bill in 2003. In H. Fu, C. J. Petersen, & S. N. M. Young (Eds.), *National security and fundamental freedoms: Hong Kong's article 23 under scrutiny*. Hong Kong: Hong Kong University Press.

Pichardo, N. A. (1997). New social movements: A critical review. *Annual Review of Sociology, 23*(1), 411–430.

Przeworski, A. (2000). *Democracy and development: Political institutions and well-being in the world, 1950–1990*. Cambridge: Cambridge University Press.

Qian, Q. (2004). *Ten diplomatic anecdotes [waijiao shiji]*. Hong Kong: Joint Publishing.

Qiang, S. (2008). *Zhongguo Xianggang: Wenhua yu Zhengzhi Shiye [Chinese Hong Kong: Cultural and Political Perspectives]*. Hong Kong: Oxford University Press.

Registration and Electoral Office. (2011). 2011 district councils election – District councils brief. http://www.elections.gov.hk/dc2011/eng/dcbriefs.html. Retrieved 9 Aug 2012.

Roscigno, V. J., & Danaher, W. F. (2001). Media and mobilization: The case of radio and southern textile worker insurgency, 1929 to 1934. *American Sociological Review, 66*(1), 21–48.

Schaffer, F. C. (2007). *Elections for sale: The causes and consequences of vote buying*. Boulder: Lynne Rienner Publishers.

Schedler, A. (2002). The nested game of democratization by elections. *International Political Science Review, 23*(1), 103–122.

Schiffer, J. R. (1991). State policy and economic growth: A note on the Hong Kong model. *International Journal of Urban and Regional Research, 15*(2), 180–196.

Scott, I. (1989). *Political change and the crisis of legitimacy in Hong Kong*. Honolulu: University of Hawaii Press.

Scott, I. (2000). The disarticulation of Hong Kong's post-handover political system. *The China Journal, 43*, 29–53.

Sing, M. (2004). *Hong Kong's tortuous democratization: A comparative analysis* (Vol. 2). London/New York: RoutledgeCurzon.

Sing, M. (2010). Explaining mass support for democracy in Hong Kong. *Democratization, 17*(1), 175–205.

Sing, M., & Tang, Y.-S. (2012). Mobilization and conflicts over Hong Kong's democratic reform. In: W.-W. Wilson, L.-L. Percy, & L. Wai-man (Eds.), *Contemporary Hong Kong government and politics* (2nd ed.). Hong Kong: Hong Kong University Press.

Sing Pao. (2009). DP's Veto on Quasi-referendum Causes LSD Worries [Minzhudang foujue zongci sheminlian hong pohuai gongtou], 15 Dec 2009.

Sing Pao. (2010a). CP and LSD Refuse to Support "Universal Suffrage Detour" [Gongshe liangdang ju zhichi "puxuan douhao yuanlu"], 19 June 2010.

Sing Pao. (2010b). Wong Yuk-man Criticizes DP for Breaking Promises [Yumin hong minzhudang beixinqiyi], 25 June 2010.

Sing Tao Daily. (2005). On his mythical resignation, wong yuk man: Because of blaming commercial radio for helping donald tsang putting on an act [huiying shangtai chaoyou zhimi huangyumin henpi wei baotai zuosao rehuo], 05 July 2005.

Sing Tao Daily. (2010). Alan Leong Says DP Saves Donald Tsang [Liang jiajie zhi minzhudang jiu baotai], 19 July 2010.

So, A. Y. (2008). Social Conflict in Hong Kong after 1997: The emergence of a post-modern mode of social movements. In M. K. Chan (Ed.), *China's Hong Kong transformed: Retrospect and prospects beyond the first decade.* Hong Kong: City University of Hong Kong Press.

So, A. Y. (2011). "One country, two systems" and Hong Kong-China national integration: A crisis-transformation perspective. *Journal of Contemporary Asia, 41*(1), 99–116.

So, C. (2003a). How Hong Kong newspapers report news about legislation of article 23. *Media Digest*, January 2003.

So, C. (2003b). Look again how Hong Kong newspapers report news about legislation of article 23. *Media Digest*, February 2003.

South China Morning Post. (2010). Quitters denied a parting shot by walkout, 28 Jan 2010.

South China Morning Post. (2013). Give pan-democrats home return permit, 14 Feb 2013.

State Statistical Bureau, the People's Republic of China. (1987). China- trade and price statistics in 1987.

Stockmann, D. (2012). *Media commercialization and authoritarian rule in China.* Cambridge: Cambridge University Press.

Stokes, S. C. (2005). Perverse accountability: A formal model of machine politics with evidence from Argentina. *American Political Science Review, 99*(3), 315.

Stokes, S. C., Dunning, T., Nazareno, M., & Brusco, V. (2013). *Brokers, voters, and clientelism.* Cambridge: Cambridge University Press.

Stone, W. J., Maisel, L. S., & Maestas, C. D. (2004). Quality counts: Extending the strategic politician model of incumbent deterrence. *American Journal of Political Science, 48*(3), 479–495.

Svolik, M. W. (2012). *The politics of authoritarian rule.* New York: Cambridge University Press.

Szeto, W. (2011). *In the endless river eastward flows: A memoir of Szeto Wah [Dajiang Dongqu: Situ Hua Huiyilu].* Hong Kong: Oxford University Press.

Ta Kung Pao. (2009). Longhair expelled for throwing paper-made microwave oven [changmao zhi zhiza weibolu beizhu], 19 Nov 2009.

Ta Kung Pao. (2011). Civic party creates trouble for Hong Kong's future [gongmindong weixian luangang huohai wuqiong], 11 Oct 2011.

Ta Kung Pao. (2012). James Tien Mocks Ronny Tong: Should Leave Civic Party [Tianshao zhao Tang jiahua ying tuidang], 26 Aug 2012.

Ta Kung Pao. (2013). Tsang Yok-sing suggests chief executive should have party background [Tsang Yok-sing chang teshou ju zhengdang Beijing], 29 May 2013.

Takeuchi, H. (2013). Vote buying, village elections, and authoritarian rule in rural China: A game-theoretic analysis. *Journal of East Asian Studies, 13*(1), 69–105.

Takungpao. (2010). CP and LSD promote Hong Kong independence [gongshe liangdang yunniang gangdu], 5 May 2010.

The Sun. (2010). David chu: Losing orderliness [feitianzhu kantianxia: yulai yuwu guiju], 28 Jan 2010.

Towngas. (2010). Towngas 230,000 mooncakes for the less fortunate. http://www.hkcg.com/txteng/corp/mediacentre/spotlights/mooncakes_2010.aspx. Retrieved 31 Mar 2013.

Treisman, D. (2007). What have we learned about the causes of corruption from ten years of cross-national empirical research? *Annual Review of Political Science, 10,* 211–244.

Tsang, S. Y.-S. (2001). *Judicial independence and the rule of law in Hong Kong.* Hong Kong: Hong Kong University Press.

Ufen, A. (2009). The transformation of political party opposition in Malaysia and its implications for the electoral authoritarian regime. *Democratization, 16*(3), 604–627.

Vogel, E. F. (2011). *Deng Xiaoping and the transformation of China.* Cambridge: Harvard University Press.

Wang, C.-S., & Kurzman, C. (2007). The logistics: How to buy votes. In F. C. Schaffer (Ed.), *Elections for sale: The causes and consequences of vote buying* (pp. 61–78). Boulder, CO: Lynne Rienner Publishers.

Wang, J. (2006). *Laio Chengzhi: A Biography [Laio Chengzhi zhuan].* Beijing: Renmin chubanshe.

Washington Post. (2000). Discontent Afflicts Hong Kong; Protest Epidemic Reflects Rising Anxiety of Midle Class, 28 June 2000.

Washington Post. (2011). New Pages in Egypt's Facebook Revolution, 23 Mar 2011.

Wen Wei Po. (2009). The dab helps professionals start their businesses in pearl river delta [minjianlian zhu zhuanyerenshi tuo zhusanjiao shichang], 18 Aug 2009.

Wen Wei Po. (2010a). Alan leong's "three routes plan" shows evil intentions [liang jiajie santiao luxian baocang huoxin], 17 Nov 2010.

Wen Wei Po. (2010b). Blaming ADPL and NWSC, LSD Says No Coordination in District Councils Election Next Year [Ze minxie jiegong chen mingnian quxuan buxietiao], 7 Feb 2010.

Wen Wei Po. (2010c). Changing Victory Benchmark Shows CP and LSD are Sore Losers [Qiekan gongshe lian gongtou shengfu biaozhun de bianhua shudayingyao mociweishen], 18 May 2010.

Wen Wei Po. (2011a). Civic party's "black hand" unveiled in the bridge lawsuit: Madam zhu's goddaughter zheng li er says in magazine interview the party approached zhu again for re-appeal [daqiao guansi xiehua gongmindang heishou xianxing zhupopo qinu zhenglier jieshou zhoukan fangwen bao yuzhao popo zai shangsu], 6 Nov 2011.

Wen Wei Po. (2011b). Secretary for justice: At least 200,000 new applicants for comprehensive social security assistance should foreign domestic helpers receive right of abode [lu zhengsi: waiyong tanghuo juquan zhixhao ershiwanren shen zengyuan], 2 Aug 2011.

Wen Wei Po. (2012a). Chan ka lok can't distance himself from the three big lawsuits damaging Hong Kong by sophism [sanda haigang guansi chen jialuo qineng kao guibian pieqing], 23 Aug 2012.

Wen Wei Po. (2012b). Court ruling as the best method to correct wrong judgment [fating jiuzheng cuopan shi zuihao banfa], 29 Mar 2012.

Wen Wei Po. (2012c). The dab raised 20 million dollars in a fundraising dinner [minjianlian choukuan wanhui jinzhang erqian wan], 6 Nov 2012.

Wen Wei Po. (2012d). Audacious Electioneering by "National Education Concern Group" ["guojiao guanzhu zu" minghuo zhizhang gao xuanju caozuo], 27 Aug 2012.

Wen Wei Po. (2012e). DAB Youth Branch Enlisting New Members at 10th Anniversary: Eye on 2,000 Members, 2 Dec 2012.

Wen Wei Po. (2013). Anticipating Universal Suffrage, DAB Re-open Training Program for Grooming Political Talents, 3 Dec 2013.

Wen Wei Po. (2014a). The dab broke record, raising 68.38 million dollars in fundraising dinner [minjianlian wanhui choukuan pojilu liuqian babai sanshiba wan], 16 Apr 2014.

Wen Wei Po. (2014b). Occupy central's and quasi-referendum's hidden agenda: Hong Kong independence [zhanzhong gongtou de gangdu depai], 1 Jan 2014.

Weng, B. (1998). The first year of the HKSAR: Changes in the political institutions. *CSIS Hong Kong Update,* 1–4.

Wong, S. H.-W. (2012). Authoritarian co-optation in the age of globalisation: Evidence from Hong Kong. *Journal of Contemporary Asia, 42*(2), 182–209.

Xia, M. (2007). *The People's congresses and governance in China: Toward a network mode of governance*. Abingdon/New York: Routledge.

Xiao, Y. (1990). *"One country, two systems" and Hong Kong basic legal system [Yiguo liangzhi yu xianggang jiben falu zhidu]*. Beijing: Peking University Press.

Xu, J. (1993). Xu jiatun xianggang huiyilu [xu jiatun's Hong Kong memoir]. *United Daily News*.

Xu, J. (1998). *Memoirs and thoughts of Xu Jiatun*. New York: Mirror Books Limited.

Xu, Z. (2013). *Resisters [Kangzhengzhe]*. New Taipei City: Gusa Publishing.

Yep, R. (2009). 'One country, two systems' and special administrative regions: The case of Hong Kong. In J. H. Chung & T.-C. Lam (Eds.), *China's local administration: Traditions and changes in the sub-national hierarchy* (pp. 86–110). London/New York: Routledge.

You, Z., Shu, B., & Shan, L. (2011). *Interviews with Zhang Junsheng [Zhang Junsheng Fangtan Lu]*. Hong Kong: Chunghwa Book and Zhejiang University Press.

Young, S. N. M., & Cullen, R. (2010). *Electing Hong Kong's chief executive*. Hong Kong: Hong Kong University Press.

Young, S. N. M., Law, A., & Exchange, C. (2004). *A Critical Introduction to Hong Kong's Functional Constituencies*. Hong Kong: Civic Exchange.

Youngson, A. J. (1982). *Hong Kong, economic growth and policy*. Hong Kong: Oxford University Press.

Yuen, K.-W. (2011). *The soul journey of building Hong Kong: The fate with the DAB [Jiangang Xinlu: Yu Minjianlian De Yuanyufen]*. Hong Kong: Chung Hwa Book.

Zaller, J. (1999). A theory of media politics. Manuscript, 24 Oct 1999.

Zhao, Y. (2000). From commercialization to conglomeration: The transformation of the Chinese press within the orbit of the party state. *Journal of Communication, 50*(2), 3–26.

Zhonggong Zhongyang Wenxian Yanjiushi. (1991). *Since the 13th Party Congress: A Collection of Important Documents [Shisanda Yilai: Zhongyao Wenxian Xuanbian]*. Beijing: Renmin Chubanshe.

Zi, D. (2004). *The biography of Li Qiang [Li Qiang Zhuan]*. Beijing: Renmin Chubanshe.

Zong, D. (2007). *Oral history of Zhou Nan [Zhou Nan Koushu: Yaoxiang Dangnian Yushan Lunjin]*. Jinan: Qilu Shushe.

Index

© Springer Science+Business Media Singapore 2015
S.H.-W. Wong, *Electoral Politics in Post-1997 Hong Kong*,
DOI 10.1007/978-981-287-387-3